MIMESIS
INTERNATIONAL

ATMOSPHERIC SPACES
n. 12

What is an "Atmosphere"?

According to an aesthetic, phenomenological and ontological view, such a notion can be understood as a sensorial and affective quality widespread in space. It is the particular tone that determines the way one experiences her surroundings.

Air, ambiance, aura, climate, environment, genius loci, milieu, mood, numinous, lived space, Stimmung, but also Umwelt, ki, aida, Zwischen, in-between – all these words are names hiding, in fact, the founding idea of atmospheres: a vague ens or power, without visible and discrete boundaries, which we find around us and, resonating in our lived body, even involves us.

Studying atmospheres means, thus, a parte subjecti, to analyse (above all) the range of unintentional or involuntary experiences and, in particular, those experiences which emotionally "tonalise" our everyday life. A parte objecti, it means however to learn how atmospheres are intentionally (e.g. artistically, politically, socially, etc.) produced and how we can critically evaluate them, thus avoiding being easily manipulated by such feelings.

Atmospheric Spaces is a new book series whose aim is to become a point of reference for a community that works together on this philosophical and transdisciplinary subject and for all those whose research, more broadly, is involved in the so-called "affective turn" of the Social Sciences and Humanities.

ELENA MANCIOPPI

OSMOSPHERES

Smell, Atmosphere, Food

MIMESIS
INTERNATIONAL

This volume is published with the support of the University of Gastronomic Sciences of Pollenzo (Italy).

Book series: *Atmospheric Spaces*, n. 12

Isbn: 9788869774317

CONTENTS

ACKNOWLEDGMENTS

I especially want to thank Tonino Griffero for giving me the opportunity to publish this book.[1] All my gratitude to my closest friends, to my family, to my father, to my beloved Arturo and Mnemosine. I express my appreciation to Maddalena. Heartfelt thanks to my wonderful mother. I am infinitely grateful to my mentor Nicola Perullo, to whom this book is dedicated.

---

1   *Osmospheres* is the result of a profound reworking of my first monograph, *L'olfattivo*, which is an elaboration of my doctoral thesis.

PREFACE

If the weather is fine, I write outside.
I light one end of the spiral of insect repellent, although it is
hardly needed. But I burn it anyway, as I quite like the smell.
It is a sign that I am thinking.

Tim Ingold

A thought by Gaston Bachelard, in his *Water and Dreams*, always resonates with me. The passage reads:

> the odor of water mint calls forth in me a sort of ontological correspondence which makes me believe that life is simply an aroma, that it emanates from a being as an odor emanates from a substance, that a plant growing in a stream must express the soul of water (Bachelard 1983, 7).

This memory answers the author's purpose to argue that "being is before all else an awakening, and it awakens in the awareness of an extraordinary impression" (ibid). The *I* is the subjective pole emerging from the encounter with *this* smell as a spark of a primitive form of consciousness. The I exists *with* and *in so far as* this smell is present, in a self-manifestation implying that the I has been affected. A few lines later, the French philosopher confides that the *rêverie* disclosed itself as "an ever-emanating universe, a fragrant breath that issues from things through the dreamer" (ibid). Close to water and its flowers, Bachelard seized the *rêverie* as the unfolding of daydreaming through the material world.

It recalls Gernot Böhme's relational theory of atmospheres as the *in-between* subjects and environment. Atmospheric perception is the result of the ambient irradiating its ecstatic qualities, and the state of the perceiver who has attuned accordingly. Atmospheric perception is the feeling of a presence which endows a space with an affective character. Although atmospheres have to do with all the senses, Böhme (2019, 262) is but one of many scholars who have insisted on the atmospheric nature of odours, stating that "smells as factors have an extraordinary position".[1] The same was brought forth in the late 1960s by Hubertus Tellenbach, who achieved such a correlation by observing the simultaneousness between people's scent and their atmosphere, which is "tasted" like a food. Indeed, "more than any other sensory experience our sense of smell reveals that, beyond the mere fact of sensory reception, something enters into perception and tells us about the inherent nature of the thing, thus received" (Tellenbach 1981, 227). In various respects, food is emblematic of such an affective and material interplay, transcending the nutritive sphere and becoming the symbol of intimate exchanges. Today, many align with this stance, in the wake of counterbalancing a long-lasting philosophical disinterest for odours and food, which may occasionally result into the overturning of traditional hierarchies.

As for me, my intent is neither to celebrate smell as *the* sense of atmospheres, nor to prove that smells are the most atmospheric stimuli. Instead, this book wants to probe the hypothesis that atmospheric perception is a mode of sensing and feeling which is comparable to "olfactive" modality. To put it differently, I suggest that atmospheres entail an olfactive way of perceiving, since they display relationships, affective processes and resonances rather than objects. This perspective encourages to insist on the cross-sensory and multi-modal nature of perception, thus fostering an inquiry on smell as framed within the all-encompassing perceptual experience in which all the senses are interwoven along the unified plane of the ecological horizon. Just as olfactory silence can constitute an atmospheric massive presence, auditory silence[2] can turn into an olfactory quality — the "odour of silence is so old", according to the poet Oscar Vladislas de Lubicz Milosz (1960, 187).[3]

Despite a performative contradiction might be lamented — how can smell be even distinguished from the other senses? and an odour from its absence? —, this shift provides many possibilities for investigation, with a definitive inclination to capturing the phenomenological occurring of

---

1   See also Böhme 1998, 50; 2017b, 125. For an analytical introduction to Böhme's theory, Griffero 2010.

2   Silence includes countless atmospheric textures depending on the overall circumstance: "[E]xpansive and dense in the case of festive silence, even more expansive and dense as oppressive silence, expansive and gentle as the silence of a pristine morning" (Schmitz 2019b, 65).

3   From here onwards and unless otherwise indicated, translations from non-English sources are by the author.

what I call *osmospheres*. From □σμή, "smell, odour", and σφα□ρ□, "sphere, globe", *osmospheres* are the irradiances which give persons, commodities, situations and places a vague but unique *flavour*. In a nutshell, an osmosphere manifests when the *how* coincides with the *what*, in the way in which the mode of perceiving corresponds with its content.

Through the perspective of relational and ecological aesthetics, I investigate the many atmospheric expressions of smell and food. The aim is to put forth an aesthetics of the osmospheres as an affective and perceptual field, fitting into the current debate that hinges on the mutual bond between human beings and the environment they are immersed in. Food along with its affective aura is the means by which the topic is unravelled. Indeed, food and smell epitomise the porous boundaries between subjects and objects, identity and alterity, knowing and feeling. They also demonstrate that aesthetic qualities are relational and contextual. Moreover, food does not merely represent the prevailing source of smell, but it exemplifies the inescapable mingling, physical no less than affective, among the entities inhabiting the world. By intersecting the edible with the non-edible, olfactory perception seems inherently rooted in food and in the idea of eating, as it implies the intimate ingestion of an alterity. More than other senses, smell blurs the lines between the I and the non-I: "I am, first of all, the odor of mint, the odor of mint water" states Bachelard (1983, 7) while rephrasing Condillac's myth of the animated statue.

Before outlining the chapters, a terminological note and a premiss on the theoretical framework are in order. Firstly, from a rigorous perspective, the noun "smell" is synonymous with odour, aroma, scent, whiff and the like, pertaining the sensory data obtained only through olfaction. Differently, "flavour" indicates the result of the combination of smells, tastes, textures, etc., involving the superposition of multiple stimuli processed by the sense organs which work as perceptual systems. Nonetheless, I sometimes use the two interchangeably on purpose. On the one hand, because, though not properly tasted in the mouth, food scents are often perceived as being savoured, that is as a cross-sensory complex where the gustatory sphere is eminent, giving rise to immediate judgements and hedonic reactions. On the other hand, because English figurative language seems to privilege the term "flavour" over olfactory word clusters, providing the former with emotional nuances that are normally associated to the latter in other languages. After all, as poets well know, every word has its peculiar atmosphere: at times, "flavour" is more incisive than olfactory equivalents.

Secondly, this research is marked by interdisciplinarity, referring, beside philosophy and aesthetics, to literature, anthropology, sociology, psychology, geography, sensory history and consumer sciences. Since "purely" aesthetic studies on the topic are mostly fragmented, such an approach is almost unavoidable. Nonetheless, it allows a wide-scope inquiry.

My effort consists of transferring the acquisitions proposed by scholars who have philosophically thematised on atmospheres and smell (notably Hubertus Tellenbach and Gernot Böhme) to the theoretical coordinates of the ecological theory of perception and relational aesthetics. For the overall orientation, Gaston Bachelard's imaginative materialism and James J. Gibson's ecological theory constitute my central points of reference, while the position in favour of a relational, less hierarchical and more inclusive aesthetics is borrowed from aestheticians like Arnold Berleant. In addition, I resort to several thinkers who have proven useful to unravel the idea of osmosphere: among others, Peter Sloterdijk, Michel Serres and Georg Simmel. Italo Calvino is also a very recurrent author, which needs some rationale. The works by the Italian writer are helpful to outline, in a negative way, the ineffable, relational, affective and indivisible nature of osmosphere. As a rationalist in method but an imaginative dreamer in attitude, Calvino clashes against the impossibility of an objective adherence to the world but through transfiguration, showing the limits of an oculocentric perspective to grasp life as it unfolds. Indeed, as Bachelard (1983, 7) teaches, *life is simply an aroma*, and daydreaming *an ever-emanating universe, a fragrant breath that issues from things through the dreamer*.

Chapter 1 outlines some ontological, moral and epistemological similarities shared by atmospheres and smells. After offering a general overview, I focus on the role of affectivity by paying attention to the way both are felt and experienced in the lived body. In order to do so, I largely draw on new phenomenological insights and literature; I also comment on testimonies of people suffering from olfactory disorders as they reveal the commutability between atmospheric feelings and smells. As a conclusion, I set forth the multifaceted notion of contagion through odours. I then scrutinise the human "being-in-the-air" as the precondition for life, highlighting its repercussions on smell as the most aerial and pneumatic of the senses. Weather, climate, air and breathing are viewed in their olfactory and atmospheric dimension. Furthermore, I discuss a peculiar and auratic way of knowing through the nose which goes under the name of sagacity, running through some idioms and foregrounding temporal dynamics of odours. Finally, I elucidate the relationship between smell and memory, interpreting the latter as an eminently osmospheric modality of perceiving, as suggested by manifold philosophers and authors.

Chapter 2 implements what introduced above to the context of food. Firstly, food flavours are meant as the affective grounds through which the personality is shaped in the relation with the others. The affective value of food osmospheres plays a pivotal role in the experience of space and time, hence I deal with the scent of places as identitarian whiffs which model atmospheric and gastronomic geographies, and with the food scent a season is imbued with. The investigation on food osmospheres progresses by drawing inspiration from Italo Calvino's works: through fictional episodes where smells and cuisine convey atmospheric values, the analysis unfolds through the different ways food osmospheres can be perceived, and their significance in emotional terms. A last case portrays gendered values implied in food; the sources are eclectic, spanning from gender and food studies to cultural history. Market trends and scented commodities are taken into account to remark such a sexualisation of food scents, and through it I formulate the hypothesis of different oriented intimacies linked to osmopheric perception.

Chapter 3 aims at showing the extent to which flavours partake in socio-political dynamics, and how social identities are forged and negotiated through food smells. Starting from the olfactory issues of evolution and civilisation, the main topics revolve around food, smell and identity. Resorting to some morphological metaphors as proposed by Sloterdijk's *spherology*, I analyse the aesthetic and social significance of aromas by pondering ethnic and class tensions embodied or caused by food smells, which may ignite frictions but also promote a sense of community. A brief excursus on truffle and social status denotes how food osmospheres take up economic and moral values, as well. The chapter closes with a section devoted to the thorny problem of smells when dealing with law and regulations; reflections mainly take their cues from the historical case of U.S. Prohibition, pointing out the consequences of olfactory discriminations which follow contextual and politically-oriented osmospheric narratives and constructions.

Chapter 4 is concerned with the technological developments of chemical industry and the subsequent creation of an unquantifiable spectrum of flavourings available to food industry and brands. In this respect, I devote an excursus to the aroma of truffle, addressing the way its affective values have changed with the increasing use of synthetic flavourings associated with it. Thereafter, particular attention is paid to contemporary practices where food osmospheres are designed and staged to convey emotions and to affect consumer behaviour. The notion of air design in relation to smell marketing and environmental scenting is the core issue of the following pages, to which a further excursus is attached. It describes the dystopian artistic project *The Ghost Food Truck*, which sheds light on flavourings as the ultimate bastions which condense the emotional value of ingredients on the verge of extinction due to the ecological crisis. All this leads to the idea of *osmospheric foodification* which seems to capture the essence of today's urban and domestic dwelling, even in connection to non-edible items and spaces. Lastly, I speculate on its psychological and socio-political aesthetic implications.

Chapter 5 addresses the olfactory question in aesthetics and the arts. After displaying the most common philosophical arguments causing the exclusion of smell as a non-aesthetic sense, the inquiry takes into consideration how smells have been infiltrating the arts, and the academic attempts to include them within the aesthetic realm. A reference to odours and food scents in Futurism is instrumental in introducing the potentialities of smells in gastronomy, art and performances, all of which leads to pondering on some contemporary gastronomic paradigms using food odours to replace the materiality of the edible matter and the side-effects which follow its ingestion. I conclude by propounding the state of the art of food osmospheres, by offering an overview of artistic cases grouped under the two thematic areas of decay and identity, where olfactory stimuli related to food convey the very sense of the work of art.

1
OSMOSPHERES

Smell is a strange way of seeing.
It evokes sentimental scenes,
sketched all of a sudden
by the subconscious.
Fernando Pessoa

1.1 *Atmosphere And Smell: An Overview*

Smell is the atmosphere endowed with
its fundamental quality.
Eugène Minkowski

Atmosphaera is a Latin neologism coined at the beginning of the 17th century in mathematical and astronomical works to designate the gaseous layers surrounding the Earth where meteorological phenomena occur.[1] Translated into several European languages, its meaning gradually underwent different shifts as a result of scientific findings and the cosmological understanding of the nature of the air.[2] Starting from the 18th century, the term "atmosphere" has also been adopted in medicine, specifying the humoral, and *mostly olfactory*, emanations of a body through which the doctor could diagnose its pathological condition.[3] At the same time, it has acquired further semantic nuances, epitomising the mood by which a space or situation is pervaded. Atmosphere has become, in many respects, a synonymic expression for *Stimmung, aura* and *ambiance*.[4]

---

1   From □τμ□ς, "vapour, steam, emanation, odour", and σφα□ρα, "sphere, globe". See Tedeschini 2019.
2   Martin 2015.
3   Corbin 1986, 35-43; Riedel 2019a, 86-87; 2019b, 299-301; Robinson 2020.
4   Carnevali 2006.

The two main acceptations of atmosphere coexist to this day: in natural sciences, from a chemical and physical perspective, it specifies the aerial region where the weather takes place; in philosophy and the humanities, it reveals the existence of diffused aesthetic feelings. Both meanings overlap in the idea of *climate*, which denotes the temperamental character of events, beings and places.[5]

As the point of convergence between the geopsychic tradition of the *genius loci* and the phenomenological idea of *Leib* (Griffero 2008, 76), atmosphere can be roughly defined as a widespread sentimental tonality, or as the "comprehensive occupation of a surfaceless space in the range of that which is experienced as present", to use Hermann Schmitz's (2019b, 68) words. From a specifically aesthesic standpoint, atmospheres are synesthetic.[6] They constitute the ways one is affected by inter- and cross-sensory values intersecting not only the distinctions between the senses, but also the difference between physical and emotional level. "Is the bitterness of feeling really less bitter for us than the bitterness of quinine?" Eugène Minkowski (1999, 81) rhetorically wonders while investigating polymodality as it occurs in self-perceiving. Although theories on atmospheres are all but univocal,[7] philosophers are by and large inclined to consider it a promising tool to rethink traditional ontology and the dichotomy between mind and body, or emotion and cognition. In this sense, the notion of atmosphere has increasingly been integrated into various disciplines with a view to interpreting human experiences as affective engagements with the world.[8]

Understood as an all-embracing and pervasive *flavour*, the atmosphere consists in the vague affective quality perceived "in the air".[9] Given the aerial supremacy in different terms correlated to the idea of atmosphere — air, aura, *ki*[10] —, this would suggest that, even in a metaphorical sense, it "might be something which is primarily somehow inhaled and smelled" (Diaconu 2006a, 136). As such, several scholars have underlined a sort

---

5   Griffero 2014, 55-60; McCormack 2008, 2018; Ingold 2015, 69-83.
6   Böhme 2017b, 66-75; Schmitz 2019a; Plessner 1980.
7   Griffero 2014, Tedeschini 2019.
8   Among others, sociology, anthropology, literature, media and cultural studies. Providing an exhaustive bibliography on all these subjects would be challenging to say the least; I will only mention some works that also consider smell throughout the book.
9   Griffero 2021a, 14; 2022b.
10   On *ki*, Tellenbach 1968, 57-58; Ogawa 2018; Marinucci 2019.

of "atmospheric primacy" of smell,[11] establishing a direct relationship between odours and atmospheres.

The correlation between smell and atmosphere finds its specific depiction in *Geschmack und Atmosphäre*, published in 1968 by German psychiatrist Hubertus Tellenbach. It constitutes the first, pioneering aesthetic and psychopathological investigation on atmospheres *as* smells, which has been widely addressed by scholars.[12] By resorting to the notion of *oral sense*,[13] but mostly focusing on olfaction, Tellenbach strategically ties it to the occurrences of atmospheres. Psychotic episodes or psychic disorders reveal the contextuality of smell and atmosphere; such an overlapping is taken as an advantage to prompt the development of investigation methods suitable for their understanding, since both are castaways of Western thought, "ineffable entities, therefore dysfunctional, marginal theoretical objects, outside the domain of rationality" (Mazzeo 2013, 7).[14] Tellenbach (1981, 229) compares the family aura the child is plunged into to the "smell of the nest [that] clings to the baby-bird", hinting at the vague but distinctive and all-encompassing *whiff* that radiates the most intimate tonalities outwards, inwardly condensing a peculiar way of opening up to the world. In his view, this flavour determines the person's future psychic destiny. This is why Tellenbach devotes much attention to the baby-mother relationship, whose nucleus resides in the former while *tasting* the fragrance of the latter, a flavour that is concurrently coloured by *something-more*. In his terms, it is a *surplus* that "lies beyond the actual fact of the experience, but which we sense as belonging to it" (ibid, 227).

A more physiological understanding of atmospheres is propounded by Australian philosopher Teresa Brennan who, in her *The Transmission of Affects*, probes the thesis that smell, in particular when below the threshold of sensory consciousness, "is critical in how we 'feel the atmosphere' or how we pick up on or react to another's depression when there is no conversation or visual signal through which that information might be

---

11   Hauskeller 1995, 94-101; Bischoff 2006; Griffero 2014, 63-69; 2022a.
12   Costa *et al.* 2014; Griffero 2019, especially 25-26; Tedeschini 2019. In general, on psychopathology and atmospheres, Francesetti, Griffero 2019.
13   The *Oralsinne* theorised by Ludwig Edinger at the beginning of the 20th century, namely the complex apparatus (or *perceptual system*, as J.J. Gibson would call it) olfactory, gustatory, epidermic and kinetic perceptions are to be imputed to.
14   Numerous works have been written on the problematic status of smell with respect to philosophy and science. To name a few: Jaquet 2010, 15-86; Shiner 2020, 19-34; Mancioppi 2022a, 17-84. Although a comprehensive review would be beyond the scope of this book, some pivotal points will be addressed when deemed useful (esp. in ch. 5).

conveyed" (Brennan 2004, 9). Sympathetic to the still-debated hypothesis of an extended inter- and intra-specific chemosensory communication through which we *do* smell other people's mood,[15] Brennan understands atmospheres as energetic or pheromonal fields that have to do with emotions but are not limited to the private sphere of the individual, being transmissible between subjects through the environment.[16]

Despite the traditional prominence of visual aspects, architects have addressed not only atmospheres, with the explicit purpose of comprehending the way the lived body engages with the environment,[17] but also smells. Juhani Pallasmaa (2014, 24) puts it plainly, writing that ambience itself is understandable as "an invisible fragrance or smell that fuses and heightens the sensory experience". The same applies to geographers. Many agree that "[s]cents capture the aesthetic-emotional quality of place" (Tuan 1995, 69), or that smell "perceives the quality of an interior" (Illich 1985, 52). Actually, the way odours *spread* hints at the atmosphere as a peculiar voluminous dimension,[18] as stressed by Minkowski (1999, 115): "smell does not spread either on or in any object, but by mixing with the ambient atmosphere in a particularly intimate way, provides it with a primary quality and thus reveals its existence to us". Indeed, odours do not fit the criteria of geometrical space, having no sides, being neither measurable nor separable. Not incidentally, smell is paramount for a *poetics of space*, in that a "whiff of perfume or even the slightest odor", Bachelard (2014, 191) maintains, "can create an entire environment in the world of the imagination".

Beyond etymology — *atmos* is mainly related to olfactory qualities[19] —, smells *act* by revealing the very aesthetic and moral quality of the atmosphere. It is enough to read the pages that Minkowski devotes to *l'olfactif* to grasp this structural link. As a matter of fact, an odour is able "to penetrate the others, to directly influence them, or to model them in its likeness" (Minkowski 1999, 119). As many have noticed, one's scent constitutes the peculiar radiation or "olfactory fingerprint", that is, one's

---

15 Copious olfactory artworks are based on this idea. Just to give one example of many, scent artist Sissel Tolaas has worked on fear. *21/21: The FEAR of Smell — the Smell of FEAR* (2006) consists in walls painted with a special substance added with underarm sweat samples collected from men suffering from severe phobia.
16 Gandy 2017, 360-361.
17 References are manifold. Just to mention a few: Bressani 2019, Alison 2020, Robinson 2021, De Matteis 2022a, Canepa 2022.
18 Ólafur Elíasson writes that "[f]og makes space explicit; so does smell" (Studio Ólafur Elíasson 2016, 31).
19 Beekes 2010, 164.

tenacious *essence*: the *spirit* or *signature* of a body, as Jean-Luc Nancy (2008, 155) puts it.[20] Personality as an active force — that is, "ethical" in how it behaves, participating in collective life — is at the same time supported and enveloped by an olfactory aura that *creates* the environment that surrounds it. Since the volatile ineffability of smell discloses itself as an overall quality which is neither fragmentable nor distinguishable into discrete elements, this also means that the entire personality manifests itself atmospherically as a global condensation. Therefore, the atmosphere as the volatile emanation of a personality has always to do, in a sense, with a performing spirituality.

A quick glance at hagiographies, religious texts or rituals shows the persistence of such an aesthetical-moral correspondence: the smell of decay often reveals spiritual corruption. Many scholars have highlighted the role of smell in conveying moral stigma,[21] whereas odour consists of a "moral marker" as well as a "marker of the atmosphere".[22] Indeed, mephitic atmospheres are diabolic and spread evil;[23] conversely, the "odour of sanctity" is a mystical redolent emanation that reveals the purity of a holy soul after the death of its body, enveloping the devoted people in a sensual as well as ethical atmosphere.[24] What can appear as discrepancies between the most diverse cults fades once we consider the omnipresence of the olfactory dimension on which rituals are usually based. Aromas help put people in an emphatic or even mystical state.[25] In general, as bridges between the terrestrial and the celestial, fragrances unveil or summon divine presences,[26] whence the custom of olfactory offerings to gods and the almost universal use of incense in churches, aimed "to delight us and arouse and purify our senses to make us more fit for contemplation" (Montaigne 1948, 229).

---

20   See also Diaconu 2003.
21   Le Guérer 1994, 27-34.
22   Le Breton 2017, 136, 156-158.
23   Tuzin 2006. In the Christian tradition, sulphurous vapours announce the Devil, and the offensive stink of Hell inflicts on the damned a punishment no less severe than the others. On the contrary, Mary, Christ and Paradise are associated with pleasing scents.
24   Roch 2009; Classen, Howes, Synnott 1994, 51-54. In Dostoyevsky (1950), the doubt about the real sanctity of the Father Zossima is precisely instilled by an olfactory contradiction; for an analysis, Tellenbach 1968, 77-83. I will resume the issue of hate and mistrust later, especially when dealing with socio-aesthetics.
25   Böhme (2019, 264) talks about *profane mystic* when dealing with odours.
26   McHugh 2012; Reinarz 2014, 25-51; Clements 2015; Ponzo 2021.

By removing the distance that may exist between people who are immersed in it, smell takes on opposite sentimental meanings. It can be experienced either as a glue for a stronger emotional closeness, or as an invasion to the detriment of one's own vital space, thus giving rise to an ever more marked emotional distance. The understanding of these dynamics is all the more urgent in an increasingly globalised and interconnected world, where distance or closeness between individuals, rather than topological, is inherently affective, political and aesthetic. Through the notion of *osmosphere*, I try to do so by emphasising the spherical nature of the olfactory "aura" enveloping individuals and social groups. Like Tellenbach's *Dunstkreis* — "sphere of influence", where *Dunst* means "mist, smoke, emission" —, an osmosphere is always perceived from within, being both a protection and an exposition. Since every being is embraced by their own osmospheric "bubble", osmospheres are relational, ecological, situated and self-reflexive, in a steady and mutual play of negotiation with substantial sociological implications. Indeed, every osmosphere is immersed in its very breath; on the other, its existence implies that of an external breath circumscribing its otherness. The parting membrane is subjected to the endogenous and exogenous forces of tension, expansion or reduction. Every mutual irruption can only occur through the partial collapse of such an osmospheric membrane, as it occurs in breathing and eating. Although quite successful and useful to thematise olfactory dimensions,[27] I do not resort to the idea of *smellscape* (Porteous 1985) because, among other things, it is still marred by an ocular, bi-dimensional and geometrical comprehension of space.[28]

By elucidating the affinities between smells and atmospheres, the ensuing pages attempt to better delineate what osmospheres are or, rather, *how they occur*. The inquiry is built around four pivotal keynotes: affectivity, beings-in-the-air, sagacity and memory.

---

27 The fortune of the term is evident, being nowadays quite pervasive in many disciplines, from computer science to sensory history: Henshaw 2014, Henshaw *et al.* 2018, Zhou 2022.

28 Philippopoulos-Mihalopoulos 2021, 97-98. By collecting olfactory data (through interviews, measurements *in loco*, "smell walks", or social media and digital interfaces), recent studies have been creating "smell maps", *visual* renderings of the olfactory tangle which envelops environments and cities (see Kate McLean's works: https://sensorymaps.com/). On the suffix -scape and its connection to sight, Ingold 2011, 126.

1.2 *Affectivity*

> So, in smell lies something consubstantial with all the
> affections the I can be engaged with, and the messages it brings
> us from the surrounding air spread as far as the intimacy of our
> individual existence.
>
> Jean Nogué

In the wake of the so-called "affective turn",[29] there has been an atmospheric turn in the humanities;[30] unsurprisingly, philosophical studies on smell have been booming.[31] Atmospheres, as well as smells, are felt in the lived body through an attunement in which the cognitive, aesthetic and ethical realms are tightly interwoven; moreover, both are "affective powers of feeling, spatial bearers of moods" (Böhme 2017a, 16). As Diaconu (2021, 60) observes, a causal link seems to bind the current reappraisal of the sense of smell to "the tendency of some subject theories to move away from an intentional subject to an affectable subject, or 'patheur'".

In Latin, *affectus* (or *adfectus*, the Augustinian translation for the Greek πάθος) comes from the verb *afficere*, which means "to handle, have an effect on, move", whence "affected" as something or someone that has passively undergone an influence, a modifying action or an impression, in physical as well as psychic terms. "To be affected" is a *vox media* that can take on either a positive or a negative connotation: one can be affected by strength, love, or by diseases, envy. As a noun, affect corresponds to affection, understood as the effect of being affected, and to the disposition towards something or someone: *affectio est inclinatio animi ad aliquid*,[32] according to the definition proposed by St. Thomas Aquinas in *Summa Contra Gentiles,* which sums up most of the long Christian tradition attached to the term. Therefore, affectivity includes the passive faculty of

---

29   Clough, Halley 2007; Thompson, Hogget 2012; Anderson 2014; Slaby, von Scheve 2019; De Matteis 2021.

30   Griffero 2019; for an interdisciplinary account on atmospheres, see the different contributions in Griffero, Moretti 2018.

31   However, this trend in philosophical and cultural accounts was preceded by a flourishing of scientifically oriented studies, especially after an important discovery, namely the identification of olfactory receptors in 1991 by Linda Buck and Richard Axel, who won the Nobel Prize for Medicine in 2004 (Barwich 2020, 54-59, 70-76).

32   "[A]ffection is a certain inclination of the soul towards something" (*SCG*, LXVIII, 6, 226).

being affected, the middle voice of being sensitive to affects, and the active capacity of triggering and expressing them. Schmitz, who formulated the theory of atmospheres and of emotions as "half-things",[33] sketches an overview of the affective paradigms which is worth summarising. Broadly speaking, the largely predominant idea that the psychical and emotional functions are internal to the subjects and housed in their inner souls is the result of a *psychologistic-reductionist-introjectionist objectification* (Schmitz 2019a, 55)[34] that was established in the second half of the 5th century BC. In the pre-classic period, humans understood emotions and even ideas as residing outside, something they were taken by and filled with, so much so that moods and inspirations were attributed to worldly and external forces (often personified by deities) which, once absorbed, acted on, or through, the subject. The sharp dichotomy between the latter and the world, inside and outside, flesh and spirit, anchored its roots to the idea of psyche. The body ended up being seen as the material and corruptible shell that holds the immaterial soul, as notoriously claimed by Plato. Thus, humans provided themselves with an internal dimension thanks to which they could distinguish themselves not only from the world, but also from their own bodies. While gaining the possibility of mastering themselves and partially controlling external powers, they also took on the responsibility for their spiritual and emotional life.[35] Such a shift was not without epistemological consequences. According to the modern scientific paradigm, to achieve "real" and universal knowledge of objects, the subject's affections are to be sealed off, hence the importance in Western thought of sight as *the* distal, neutral and reliable sense, at the expense of taste and especially smell — the *affective* one *par excellence*, as emblematically shown in the Kantian system.

Indeed, Immanuel Kant (2006, §21, 50) considers smell not just the least free and rational, but also the more subjective and affective of the

---

33   This philosophical project, also called "New Phenomenology", has been developed in his work *System der Philosophie*, composed of ten volumes published between 1964 and 1980. Schmitz posits that emotional atmospheres possess a precise authority that can differ in degree and be inferred investigating what he calls "social emotional contrast" (Schmitz 2019a, 96). As an example, when a joyful person bumps into a sad one, the former moderates their cheery radiation, never the other way around. According to Schmitz, this has nothing to do with education, respect or conventions; rather, it pertains to the space of felt presence that each atmosphere claims. In a nutshell, when atmospheres collide, the one with more authority takes over the other.

34   See also Griffero 2020a, 21-28.

35   Schmitz 2011.

senses, in that "taking something in through smell (in the lungs) is even more intimate than taking something in through the absorptive vessels of the mouth or throat". If the convivial dimension of a meal allows diners to freely decide what and how much they taste, smell can neither be dosed nor avoided, since it is triggered only after inhaling the molecules (ibid, §22, 50-52). Smells are therefore pervasive and indiscreet.[36] Disregarding for now the social and political repercussions stemming from this, such an authority also unveils the power of smell, which is the focal point in the world-renowned novel *Perfume* by Patrick Süskind (1986, 161):[37]

> For people could close their eyes to greatness, to horrors, to beauty, and their ears to melodies or deceiving words. But they could not escape scent. For scent was brother of breath. Together with breath it entered human beings, who could not defend themselves against it, not if they wanted to live. And scent entered into their very core, went directly to their hearts, and decided for good and all between affection and contempt, disgust and lust, love and hate. He who ruled scent ruled the hearts of men.

Smells and atmospheres share an all-encompassing and enveloping character that makes them indistinguishable. In other words, both are experienced as comprehensive and overwhelming wholes engendering homogeneity between the subject and the world. Indeed, the smeller is deluged by odours, which are "perceptible bonds. There is a continuity in their very bodies. There are no discontinuous odors" (Bachelard 1988a, 137). *What* we smell and *how* we feel coincide thanks to a kind of metonymic relationship:

> Precisely because smell fills a (pre-dimensional, lived) space, it is the perfect vehicle of the more general felt-bodily communication between the perceiver and the whole world. And precisely because of the way smell emotionally permeates the space we could find in its spatial diffusiveness one of the main reasons of its alleged atmospheric primacy (Griffero 2022a, 84).

---

36   "The odor", Bachelard notices (1964, 103), "is a primitive quality which imperiously compels recognition either by its most insidious or by its most importunate presence. It truly violates our privacy".

37   Albeit in a less direct way, also the movie *Little Joe* (2019, directed by Jessica Hausner) plays on the theme of perfume as an inducer of love. The story is about a flower designed by plant breeders to make people happy. "Scent engineering" is at the basis of some artistic works by Peter de Cupere (2016, 78-81).

The forcefulness of odours in tuning affective dispositions could be proved through countless literary examples.[38] As the famous incipit of Gabriel García Márquez's *Love in the Time of Cholera* reads, the fate of unrequited love has the scent of bitter almonds. The similar but sweeter fragrance of hawthorn saturates Marcel Proust's pages, evoking a mystic and childlike affection rather than erotic love.[39] Were one asked to support the assumption that "a beloved odor is the center of an intimacy" (Bachelard 1969, 136), it would suffice to recall a passage from *Swann's Way* which clarifies the interchange between an atmosphere and the smells pervading it, where Proust (1998, 66-67) describes the olfactory nuances of the universe condensed in the two adjoining rooms of the house his aunt was practically confined to. It is worth reporting in full:

> They were rooms of that country order which — just as in certain climes whole tracts of air or ocean are illuminated or scented by myriads of protozoa which we cannot see — enchants us with the countless odours emanating from the virtues, wisdom, habits, a whole secret system of life, invisible, superabundant and profoundly moral, which their atmosphere holds in solution; smells natural enough indeed, and weather-tinted like those of the neighbouring countryside, but already humanised, domesticated, snug, an exquisite, limpid jelly skilfully blended from all the fruits of the year which have left the orchard for the store-room, smell changing with the season, but plenishing and homely, offsetting the sharpness of hoarfrost with the sweetness of warm bread, smells lazy and punctual as a village clock, roving and settled, heedless and provident, linen smells, morning smells, pious smells, rejoicing in a peace which brings only additional anxiety, and in a prosaicness which serves as a deep reservoir of poetry to the stranger who passes through their midst without having lived among them. The air of those rooms was saturated with the fine bouquet of a silence so nourishing, so succulent, that I never went into them without a sort of greedy anticipation [...].

These "states of feeling" are pivotal, according to Tellenbach (1968, 17), to grasp aromatic experiences *qua* atmospheric, which immediately meld, producing a syntony between the subject and the world. In this sense, Böhme (2019, 263) goes even further, claiming that the emotional values of smells are "intrinsically given with their sensual quality". This is a pivotal aspect that would contradict a thesis supported by several philosophers including Frank Sibley (2006, 249), who maintains that odours are aesthetically limited; "unlike the major arts, they have no expressive connections with

---

38   A systematic study is Rindisbacher 1993; see also Hsu 2019.
39   Jaquet 2010, 127 ff.

emotions, love or hate, grief, joy, terror, suffering, yearning, pity, or sorrow — or with plot or character development".[40] If Böhme is correct when he argues that the emotional value of smells is *congenital* to their sensual quality, odours, rather than *expressing* emotions, *are* emotions.

While comparing different emotions, Schmitz puts forward the idea that each one has precise embodied stirrings and suggestions of motion. Affective space calls for the comprehension of the phenomenological experience of expansion or contraction, folding or unfolding, which is felt at different stages that are not just of intensity but also of quality. For instance, sadness and joy are respectively characterised by fatigue and freshness, where one is the reverse of the other in terms of bodily stirrings: the former weighs on the subject and is oriented downward (to be in *low* spirits); the latter lightens and is oriented upward (to cheer *up*).[41] Since his theory is not interested in the five senses and in the perceptual body schema, he does not resort to odours except parenthetically. Nevertheless, such a variability in spatial impositions on the oral sense is pointed out by William James (1981, 808, n. 29), who notices that some tastes and smells are more spacious than others; for instance, that of vinegar appears "less spatially extended than heavy, suffocating odors, like musk" (ibid). If, basing on the James-Lange theory, "the bodily changes follow directly the *perception* of the exciting fact, and [...] our feeling of the same changes as they occur *is* the emotion" (James 1884, 189-190), the fact that scents like vinegar "inhibit inspiration by their sharpness" (James 1981, 808 n. 29) whereas musky ones "are drawn into the lungs, and thus excite an objectively larger surface" (ibid), can also be translated in phenomenological terms by sketching some hypotheses on osmospheres.

According to Burke (1998, 78), neither tastes nor smells can be sublime, with the partial exceptions of "excessive bitters, and intolerable stenches" that *can* produce a grand sensation.[42] Böhme (2001, 79) would probably disagree since, to exemplify the oceanic feeling (*das ozeanischen Gefühl*), he precisely resorts to the case in which one dissolves in the atmosphere by sniffing a dizzyingly inebriating smell. Intoxication is an osmospheric category that deserves attention, from the more feminine excitement caused by flowers to the virile sexual and warlike exaltation triggered by chemical and electrifying scents among which that of petrol takes pride

---

40 See also Sibley 1965; for a critique, Brady 2012, 70-71.
41 Expressions such as "to jump for joy" or "to have a heavy heart" are common to several languages, and express emotional states through their respective bodily stirrings; see also Julmi 2017, 15-49.
42 Korsmeyer 1999, 59.

of place. A symbol of "leaping forward, power" (Proust 2003, 381) and similar to the military signal of the bugle call, it comes as no surprise that Futurists loved it so much that they raised it to the dignity of a perfume. How not to mention the famous line "I love the smell of napalm in the morning" uttered by Lieutenant Colonel Bill Kilgore in *Apocalypse Now*, referring to a 12-hour bombardment that wiped out an entire hill, and ended up smelling like, as he concludes, *victory*. In all these examples, scent as a euphoric atmosphere demands to fully adhere to its tendencies, which are characterised by a syncopated expansion, mainly upward and forward.

Given the close relationship smell has with all the different forms sadness can take due to its link to memory (nostalgia, melancholy and the like), let's try to sketch how sadness — typically sweet in orosensory terms — can be experienced osmospherically. A verse by Jules Supervielle, where he states he knows a kind of sadness that smells of pineapple, gives Bachelard (2014, 218) the opportunity to comment that "I myself feel less sad, I feel gently sad". Differently from Jean-Paul Sartre's (1956, 61) heavy sadness as the "listlessness in my whole body", and also from "the heavy, sweet, sweet odour of existence" (Sartre 1964, 101), this osmospheric sadness does not possess sweetness as a haptically steaky and nauseating quality.[43] The sadness that smells of pineapple seems to be, rather, a sadness tempered by one of its contraries, a pinch of joyful and fresh sourness, which lifts the otherwise descending, dull gravity counterbalancing it with a rising, warbling tartness. Something similar is detectable in Eugenio Montale's (2012, 5) poem on lemon trees, where their smell is "inseparable from earth,/that rains its restless sweetness in the heart". By recollecting his childhood blackberry picking whose bountiful harvest used to turn rotten and bad-smelling, Irish poet Seamus Heaney (1980, 10) plays precisely on the combination between sadness, sweetness and sourness:

> We hoarded the fresh berries in the byre.
> But when the bath was filled we found a fur,
> A rat-grey fungus, glutting on our cache.

---

43   For the aesthetic polymodality of sweetness as an affective quality that exceeds gustatory taste: Borsato 2023, esp. ch. 1. Indeed, sweetness has manifold nuances. Osmospheric sweetness can either be the delicate touch of melancholy conveyed by the "sweet smells that linger in the empty rooms" (Bachelard 2014, 81) of the house of memory, or the relaxing calm elicited by sweet fragrances, as Burke (1998, 139) maintains, distinguishing them from the floral smell that "disposes people to drowsiness". Incidentally, the same osmosphere of drowsiness lingers in the Baudelairean reliving of De Quincey's cottage, embedded in the "insipid odor of opium" (Bachelard 2014, 61).

The juice was stinking too. Once off the bush
The fruit fermented, the sweet flesh would turn sour.
I always felt like crying. It wasn't fair
That all the lovely canfuls smelt of rot.
Each year I hoped they'd keep, knew they would not.

The relationship between a sweetish-acidic scent and an atmosphere of decay is extremely recurrent. The "sour smell of old age" is the "smell of human fermentation", as García Márquez (1989, 335) puts it in a page rich in olfactory remarks. In this sense, Bachelard reminds us of some lines of *Aurora* by Michel Leiris, where the writer experiences the deterioration and death of things caused by "an acid dispersed in the air like animal suint, acrid and melancholy, with the smell of withered old underlinen" (cit. in Bachelard 2011, 91). Before turning to a suffocating pestilential stench, the odour of death has indeed sugary tones. "I can feel myself unfolding in the dark sunshine of death/to something flowery and unfulfilled, and with a strange sweet perfume" writes D.H. Lawrence (1977, 677).[44] This osmospheric connection is even clearer in *The Leopard* by Giuseppe Tomasi di Lampedusa. The cloying and almost putrid smell the garden flowers emit reminds the Prince of "the nausea diffused throughout the entire villa by certain sweetish odors before their cause was traced: the corpse of a young soldier" (Tomasi di Lampedusa 1960, 21). Not by chance, the dead body was lying under a lemon tree. Along these lines, in a kind of sad dream made by a sick child, Milosz's (1959, 33) *Maison du Passé* is in ruins and filled with "a bittersweet smell of spoiled fruits" in the ticking of the clock of death. The bitter nuance can be here related to a sense of regret mingled with the sweetness of melancholy. Even in its severe pathological version, melancholy results in a disgusting osmosphere of putrefaction and decomposition that is perceived as endogenous, having its internal cause in the melancholic person. The "theme of these olfactory and gustatory sensations is the putrid", Tellenbach (1968, 125) maintains. Although the German psychopathologist does not specify further what he means, it may hypothetically be assumed that those fall within the olfactory spectrum of the sweetish, given its firm connection with disgust and decay as also noted by Aurel Kolnai (2004, 34), who identifies the latter as a "weak, sweet smell".

The present research does not aspire to scrutinise all the possible combinations (assuming that this inventory is even feasible), but aims at opening new lines for a further and systematic investigation. Such an

---

44   See Brault-Dreux 2021.

osmospheric variability can be ascribed to the very nature of olfaction and odours. The range of smells and flavours is not only the most subtly nuanced in the perceptual realm, but it is also limitless in quantitative terms. Blends, which increase drastically in parallel to the creation of new materials and the development of chemical synthesis, are not the sheer sum of their addends, but completely new stimuli.[45] Moreover, a single odour can be felt as a cross-sensory quality: for instance, "by itself, the odor of mint is a complex of warmth and freshness" notes Bachelard (1969, 138). In this sense, when Böhme (2019, 263) posits that it is legitimate to "talk about a cold blueness or a warm redness, but this is not possible with smells", one might raise the objection that thermic and chromatic timbres do make sense when associated to smells to determine their moods; think of green odours, olfactory white, or the difference between fresh and warm fragrances.

If, as Pessoa (2003, 233) suggests, "[s]mell is a strange way of seeing. It evokes sentimental scenes, sketched all of a sudden by the subconscious", olfactory disorders are useful negatives to see to what extent smell moulds our affective engagement with the world. A deep sense of detachment from existence is conveyed by the following lines by Kierkegaard (1946, 114):

> My life has been brought to an *impasse,* I loathe existence, it is without savor, lacking salt and sense. If I were hungrier than Pierrot, I should not be inclined to eat the explanation people offer. One sticks one's finger into the soil to tell by the smell in what land one is: I stick my finger into existence — it smells of nothing. Where am I? Who am I?

The role of olfaction in navigating the environment[46] has also a sentimental nuance, given that everything — people, food, seasons, places, etc. — has its distinctive flavour. We usually "let perfumes veer, and they make us veer toward or away from them" (Morton 2019, 98) but, once we miss the perception of scents, the nose cannot act as an affective compass that connects us with a densely expressive and redolent environment. "Smell blindness", technically called *anosmia*, causes, at least, apathy: the relationships with the world get loose and life sheds "a good deal of its savour [...] as a rich unconscious background to everything else" (Sacks

---

45   Condillac (1982, 187) claims that it is indeed "a knowledge of odorous objects [...] that has taught us to recognize two smells in a third [...], [and] if the mixture is done with enough skill that no particular smell prevails, [...] not one of them remains unchanged; and several result in just a single one".
46   Porter *et al.* 2005, Jacobs *et al.* 2015, Wu *et al.* 2020.

1987, 159). Smell loss is not seldom followed by more or less severe types of depression that can even lead to suicide.[47]

The covid-19 pandemic has noticeably revealed the atmospheric effects of olfactory malfunctioning, fuelling new research on smell. As is well known, the most common symptoms of such a disease concern olfactory dysfunctions that usually recover in a few days; anosmia is present in more than 50% of the people who get infected (Wu *et al.* 2022). Approximately 10% of them suffer from a post-covid condition, which includes long-lasting olfactory impairment (Burges Watson *et al.* 2021, 2); almost 8% of these cases never recover (McWilliams *et al.* 2022). These sensory disruptions often coincide with a feeling of disinterest for and disengagement from the world, which appears "very blank. Or if not blank, shades of decay" (Burges Watson *et al.* 2021, 10). Olfactory inability breaks off the vital links one has with people and the surroundings, triggering an affective disorientation that overshadows the "I" as the core, the *here*, from which every experience unfolds. Some people precisely complain of a sense of alienation from themselves, together with a lingering sensation of loneliness. Besides causing many psychological disorders including paranoia (I cannot smell myself, so I am in the constant fear of stinking), smell dullness can even make one feel claustrophobic in their own body.[48] Walled in a grey area that has no access to the resonances of the world, we might say that the anosmic person seems discombobulated by being trapped in a weightless dimension deprived of affective gravity and cardinal points. The philosopher Marta Tafalla (2013b, 1295), who lacks the sense of smell, argues that the spatial and temporal horizons are limited for the anosmic person, who cannot have access to many of the affective qualities the world is pervaded by.

Pandemics also provide the pretext to discuss the relationship between smells and contagion as affection. Considering the first social effects of the spreading of coronavirus, Phillip Vannini (2020, 269) distinguishes between disease and *dis-ease*: the former coincides with sickness and disorder; the latter, with "a social malaise infecting the public body via atmospheric contagion" (ibid). Especially during lockdown or social distancing measures, smelling others entails the risk of viral transmission. Hence, the very "smell-print of other humans takes on new significance during the pandemic" (Allen 2022, 272), usually corresponding to anxiety.

---

47 Engen 1991, ch. 9; Herz 2008, 1-11; Yom-Tom, Lekkas, Jacobson 2021.
48 I have found these observations in *AbScent Covid-19 Smell and Taste Loss*, a Facebook discussion group created for research purposes. Being private, I will only provide the general website: https://www.facebook.com/groups/AbScentCovid19.

Interestingly, the olfactory artist Peter de Cupere has created or resumed manifold contagion-related handiworks. In addition to gas masks or mouth masks made of different materials (chocolate, cress, earth, shaving foam), he also designed a surgical mask with the words *Distance. I smell you!*, and a perfume called *Distance. Eau de malodor*, a stinky fragrance that aims at helping people keep a safe distance. Half-jokingly, the artist adds that this could also be useful in identifying infected people, namely those that, even if getting too close, are not bothered by the reek because they lack their sense of smell.

The contagious nature of smell has been acknowledged since antiquity. Indeed, the nexus between odours and plagues has always been pivotal. Pre-modern medical theories, dismissed in the 19th century thanks to the development of microbiology, offer the clearest evidence of the affective nature ascribed to smells. Given the historiographical complexity of this topic, I will limit myself to pointing out what is more interesting for us. Semeiotically, odours were understood as symptoms of the patient's condition (hence the "olfactory diagnoses"), while, aetiologically, they were concurrently treated as causes. In turn, opposite smells could constitute the very remedy: the "centrifugal" smell of the affected person was cured by using "centripetal" exhalations through fumigations, scented baths, suffumigation, balms, or the intake of particular herbs, drinks and food. According to Hippocratic-Galenic medicine,[49] dietetics used to have a predominant role given that food, with its qualities, could balance or unbalance the patient's humoral equilibrium.[50] Still further, there was the suspicion that food aromas contributed to the nourishment of those who smelled them, a thesis that Aristotle tried to disprove testifying to its widespread circulation. This persisted until the 19th century when, according to some, food scents were to be understood as no less nutritious than edible substances. In 1844, Professor H. Booth wrote: "From inhaling the odour of beef the butcher's wife obtains her obesity" (cit. in Halliday 2001, 1469).

---

49   The "four temperament theory" developed by Galen expanded on the Hippocratic humoral theory, which was based on the Empedoclean theory of four elements. Medicine assumed that everything consisted of earth, fire, air and water, each characterised by a pair of attributes (cold/hot, wet/dry). In humans, elements corresponded to four types of humours, which in turn were responsible for the four temperaments that shaped the general physical as well as psychological personality.

50   Gentilcore 2016, Grieco 2019.

According to the long-lived miasma theory, air was a vehicle of disease *when* foetid. Infection was caused by breathing *miasmas*,[51] foul-smelling exhalations that were the results of the corruption and death of the air, hence the term *malaria*, literally "bad air" in Italian. The chronicles of plagues in European history from the Hellenistic era to modernity display the deadly role ascribed to the air, the medium of odours that qualified it as a fatal or beneficial vector. Thus, a well-established link between smell and affection has entailed a close intertwining between the aesthetic quality and the affective operativity of effluvia: what smells unpleasant is bad, it corrupts, pollutes and plagues; what smells pleasant is instead good, it heals. Burning balsamic essences met the demand of disinfecting the air by perfuming it. Foucault's (1995, 197) analysis of panopticism, which focuses on a late 17th-century French regulation on measures in the event of a plague, offers various insights about the purification of houses through fragrances. People also used to protect their nose using tissues soaked in perfume, or to wear *pomander*, a ball made of perfume as a shield against contagion.[52] Analogously, the bird-like beak mask of the plague doctor was filled with strong-smelling substances for prophylaxis.

To the same extent that a happy or sorrowful atmosphere "infects" the subject as soon as they feel its presence, so odours contaminate those who smell them. In this sense, the gesture of covering the eyes in front of a disturbing scene is very much akin to holding one's nose in the presence of a stench or a dangerous odour. Unlike the nose, which cannot be sealed without the help of the hands, shutting the eyes is enough not to be upset by overly impactful images. This automatic move, which is completely redundant, seems to have a sort of apotropaic and prophylactic function, as if optic atmospheres became pervasive and contagious like a reek. *When deeply affected, we treat our eyes as if they were a nose.* The affective-contagious nature of smells has political, moral and social consequences as well. From an osmospheric perspective, acclimatising to a different air implies immunising oneself against the new smells by transplanting familiar or disinfectant ones. In the second half of the 19th century, European settlers in South Africa carried out an olfactory colonisation by relocating redolent trees such as eucalypts in order to domesticate the air and improve its quality because it was deemed infected, not only for the

---

51   Parker 1983; Le Guérer 1994, 39-62.
52   Dougan 2015.

physical features of the natural space, but also, socio-geographically, for the aura of their inhabitants.[53]

1.3 *Being-In-The-Air*

> For some material imaginations, the primary
> function of air is to provide a medium for odors.
> An odor has, in the air, an infinity.
> Gaston Bachelard

Luce Irigaray would probably disagree with Sloterdijk (2014, 137) when he states that "the climate, the mood and the atmosphere [...] is the trinity of the encompassing, in whose continuing revelation humans live at all times and in all places". She would argue, and rightly so, for a *quaternity*, including air. In her work on Martin Heidegger's oblivion of air, Irigaray (1999) suggests that "being-in-the-air" is the essential requirement for *being-in-the-world*, as reworded by Sloterdijk (2002, 93). This is of particular interest to us because, thus framed, the above-mentioned attention to air as the medium for smells acquires further significance: "[n] oxious vapors seep into the center of substances, carrying there the germ of death, the very principle of decomposition" (Bachelard 2011, 51). Indeed, as *beings-in-the-air*, we deeply — albeit mostly subconsciously[54] — rely on smells as aesthetic indicators of our *domosphere* (Griffero 2014, 96): not just our homes, but the overall aerial environment we are immersed in.

As already pointed out, the term "atmosphere" was originally used in relation to meteorology, identifying the upper strata of the air surrounding the planet. The scientific meaning and the "metaphorical" one — atmosphere as a feeling hanging in the air — are two twigs budded from a common branch: the weather, which, in turn, is rooted in the aerial realm. The atmospheric polysemy reveals to what extent the two connotations are intertwined in human experience: the weather is always felt affectively (Böhme 2017a, 2). Indeed, whether sunny, rainy, foggy, snowy, stormy,

---

53   Flikke 2016, 2018.
54   For instance, the nostrils normally undergo a spontaneous and alternating congestion which is called "nasal cycle" (see Pendolino *et al.* 2018); this would enable not only a better humidification of the nose, but also the detection of a greater range of smells: the congested cavity perceives compounds which require a lower airflow; the decongested one, on the contrary, chemicals which need less time to bind with the receptors.

etc., the weather is fundamental in determining the general mood, and even the psychological disposition of a population as an organism which exists in symbiosis with its environment.[55] It is often hard to discriminate between one's own state of mind and the current weather conditions. There are even people that, according to Virginia Woolf (1978, 228), "seem to dissolve in a November cloud; depressed, emotional, with no target for emotion".

According to Gibson (1986, 16-19), the *medium* is the atmosphere, whose changes constitute the weather. Meteorological phenomena prevent the air from being completely uniform and static; this entails the adoption of adaptive behaviours by the living beings who dwell in it. From dietary regimes to human clothing or animal furs, from types of shelter to vegetation and biological strategies up to the imaginary, the very biodiversity can be traced back to the atmosphere, which, inscribing itself in the various life forms, determines them. As "elemental spacetimes that are simultaneously affective and meteorological, whose force and variation can be felt [...] in bodies of different kinds" (McCormack 2018, 4),[56] atmospheres exist in what Tim Ingold calls *weather-world*, namely a flux of related substances and materials that *tempers* the entities enveloped in it.[57] Indeed, "a cluster of weather-related words [...] share the root meaning of *temper*" (Ingold 2015, 72), from the Latin word *temperare*, "to mix"; hence the temperaments of human beings as their moods. Similarly to what Serres (2008, 179) means when he maintains that "time does not flow, it percolates; better still, it flows because it percolates" (in French, *temps* indicates time as well as weather, like the Italian *tempo*), Ingold (2015, 72) resorts to this etymological connection to show how weather, affection and air are unified in our experience "as *temperate* (and temperamental) beings".

"Climate" can also designate a lingering mood, being synonymous with atmosphere.[58] The climate of an era or of a situation coincides with the mood one can breathe in the air (in Italian, *l'aria che tira*), something that can be perceived collectively. Air is a mixture of gases *and* a space tinged with feelings: air can be filled with humidity as well as with sadness or hopes; *clearing the air* can mean that pollutants are being removed, but also that somebody is smoothing tensions; *fresh air* is not just the contrary of *hot air* (which is also another way to say "empty boasting"), but refers to the refreshing sensation of positive changes. For Bachelard (1969, 117),

---

55 See Tetsuro 1961.
56 See also McCormack 2008.
57 Ingold 2011, 126-135; 2015, 69-78.
58 See De Matteis 2022c; for a distinction between weather and climate, Hulme 2017.

summer air is fresh not because of the temperature, but because it is an offering, which "always takes on the youth of its symbol". Hence, summer "is a bouquet, an eternal bouquet which could not wilt" (ibid) because, we might say, it brings with it the *winds of change*. Interestingly enough, the German *wittern*, "to sniff", is etymologically related to *Wetter*, "weather", and to *Wind*, the wind as a propulsive and directional force that spreads odours in the air (Tellenbach 1968, 21-22). In this respect, air as a mood has often an olfactory quality: you can get the *flavour* of something by sniffing the air. Indeed, smells are the "most strongly *substantivized* qualities of air" (Bachelard 1988a, 136). Perceiving changing weather is a sensibility which is often ascribed to olfaction, due to its ability to pick up what is not yet manifest. As ethnographic research shows, many traditional weather forecasting techniques are based on sniffing the air, such as *smelling the monsoon* (Garay-Barayazarra, Puri 2011). Helen Keller, American author and activist who lost her sight and hearing when she was 19 months old, used to rely almost exclusively on smell as a way of getting to know the world.[59] In her autobiography, she describes the osmospheric nuances shifting throughout the day according to the weather. When a storm is brewing, air carries its odour, which results in an atmospheric feeling:

> Suddenly a change passed over the tree. All the sun's warmth left the air. I knew the sky was black, because all the heat, which meant light to me, had died out of the atmosphere. A strange odour came up from the earth. I knew it, it was the odour that always precedes a thunderstorm, and a nameless fear clutched at my heart. I felt absolutely alone, cut off from my friends and the firm earth. The immense, the unknown, enfolded me (Keller 2003, 23).

However, air, like smell, has played a marginal role in the Western thought for a long time. Many pages have been written on the centrality of the visible and the solid within the modern scientific and philosophical paradigm. The common destiny they share corroborates their close connection. That smells would be nothing more than the outcomes of substances in the course of their dissolution in the air is what justifies, according to Hegel (1975, 622), their exclusion from aesthetics and philosophy. As we shall see, transience and lack of structure imply the impossibility of contemplation, stability and durability. Indeed, odours "have always presented an ontological problem" (Barwich 2020, 13). Without going into detail,[60] it is worth noting that, with a certain uniformity, smells have often been understood as material

---

59   Keller 1908.
60   Baltussen 2015, Buè 2019.

mixtures during their transitional change of state. Plato considers them to be hybrid entities (*Tim.*, 66d-e); Aristotle (*De Sensu*, v., 443a) sums up some widespread opinions:

> Some people think that smell is a smoky vapour, which is partly earth and partly air. [Indeed all incline to this view about smell.] It is with this idea that Heraclitus has said that, if everything that exists became smoke, the nose would be the organ to perceive it. All tend to regard smell in this way; some as vapour, some as smoke, and some as a mixture of the two.

Like atmospheres, smells seem to be relational processes rather than proper "objects",[61] disclosing a sort of *rarefied ontology* well expressed by Serres (2008, 170):

> Mostly, till now, we moved through air which was changing and carrying ephemeral traces. Nothing resembles circumstance more than this vapour. It mingles with the atmosphere, depending on the time (hour, date and weather), the place (altitude, inside or outside), events, positions, conditions, causes and acts, its occurrence is improbable.

Just as there is no point in wondering where the wind is when it is not blowing (Griffero 2014, 119), in the same way it makes no sense to ask where the smell of winter has gone, when that of spring is lingering in the air: given their intermittency, smells and atmospheres share a queer ontology. If space as atmosphere "is nothing but vibration or *pure conductivity*" (Sloterdijk 2014, 136), or, borrowing some Gibsonian terminology, the medium is what affords the flow of information, air can be understood as a "a *metaxu* or in-between" (Thibaud 2019, 176). This "prompts us to take account of what is happening between things, to look at intervals, spacing, margins, envelopes, membranes and interstices rather than at objects themselves" (ibid). Thus, air is the first and inescapable

---

61　Definitions of atmospheres are manifold. Just to mention the most prominent ones: Schmitz defines them *half-things*, Böhme *quasi-objects*, Griffero *quasi-things*. A quite recent but particularly controversial philosophical issue is whether smells can be considered objects. We can roughly categorise the main views in two macro-positions (leaving aside all the nuances in-between): the first one excludes the possibility of considering them as objects; the second one, the so-called *Olfactory Objects Theory*, questions their alleged non-objectuality. See Millar 2019, Martina 2021; for the premises of such a perspective, together with a critique, Barwich 2019, Cavedon-Taylor 2018; see also Batty 2010a, 2010b, 2014; Young 2016; Keller 2016, 63-90; Bochicchio 2019; Alač 2020. For different analytical contributions, Keller, Young 2023.

connective *and* distinctive tissue between the things in the world. Smells are emblems of such a dynamic, connecting "with different forms of corporeal and material permeability, as well as synesthetic dimensions to time and memory" (Gandy 2017, 358).

The exchanges between humans and the air are at the core of Irigaray's reflection. Stressing the centrality of air in "terrestrial" life, from its basic acts (breathing) to the most refined ones (meditations), olfaction comes into play by metaphorising invisible, hidden and overlooked modes of perception, from "animal olfaction to philosophical scenting" (Irigaray 1999, 161). As she makes clear, it is thanks to air that beings meet, appear, come closer or move apart. We are inescapably rooted in — and mingled with — the aerial element through breathing.[62] Tim Ingold (2015, 67) has extensively remarked how "[b]reathing is the way in which beings can have unmediated access to one another, on the inside, while yet spilling out into the cosmos in which they are equally immersed".[63] Sloterdijk (2002) has instead addressed the repercussions humans undergo when facing the condition of *being-in-the-unbreathable* due to gas warfare. Air hunger and breathlessness embody abrupt isolation from the aerial environment as a precondition of existence; we might say, the fracture between being and breathing.

Air is the discreet yet ubiquitous life-sustaining medium. There are countless cosmologies in which the soul coincides with the breath, as *anemos* or *pneuma*:[64] the living take their last breath as an exhausted flower sheds the last drop of its effluvium. According to Schmitz (2019b, 66), the vital drive, in its purest form, coincides with breathing; breathing is an "irreversible embodied direction" which inscribes itself in a surfaceless volume.[65] Through its depth and rhythm, the way one breathes manifests, in turn, the emotional state of the person. From this point of view, then, the atmospheric primacy of smell, "the one sense grafted on the vital, insuppressible process of breathing" (Marinucci 2019, 113), hinges on its

---

62   Quoting Nogué (1936, 230), "[i]mmersed in the indefiniteness of the aerial environment [...], odours seem first of all a specification of that elementary act which is breathing, that incessantly bond us to the world". According to the Gaia hypothesis, the very homeostasis of the Earth's atmosphere is largely due to the complementary aerobic interplay between the pneumatic dynamics of the living, including that of the Earth itself (Lovelock 1979; see also Boussingault, Dumas 1842).

63   Indeed, "[i]nhalation is wind becoming breath, exhalation is breath becoming wind" (Ingold 2011, 138).

64   Ogawa 2018, 2021; Škof, Berndtson 2018.

65   See also Schmitz 2019a, 92.

adherence to the respiratory system, whose rhythm is not just attuned to but also driven by it. Breathing is indeed the foundation on which olfactory perception unfolds. The concept of *sensomotorischen Verschränkung* ("sensory-motor entanglement") coined by Viktor von Weizsäcker (1940) systematises the discovery that perceiving and acting are interlaced. Action is present in all perceptual systems; indeed, the idea that perceiving is tied to moving is at the basis of the most updated ecological theory of perception.[66] However, the sensory-motor intersection is so evident in the oral sphere that "nowhere else the relationship between perception and movement is and remains so primordial" (Tellenbach 1968, 14). Acting and perceiving cannot be separated in phenomenologically distinguishable moments but, rather, they overlap in a synchronic gap: I smell *while* breathing; or: I smell as I breathe. Since the consciousness of breathing implies perceiving the air, it is hardly necessary to stress that the way I breathe affects *what* and *how* I smell, and the other way round, triggering somatic adaptations aiming at calibrating olfactory stimuli in harmony with their aesthetic values. Gibson (1969, 145) formulates this principle very incisively: "[s]ome odors are 'good' and the individual acts to maximize their intensity. Some odors are 'bad' and the individual acts so as to minimize their intensity".

Air is also the aura that "gives the body a presence beyond the confines of its skin" (Illich 1985, 51), a radiation as the *principium individuationis* that makes a person unmistakable. One can have an air of confidence despite the events, or can give off an air of authority. Like odours, personal air oscillates from being something essential,[67] to being something added to one's personality, designed on purpose. However, no fragrance covers the underlying skin odour but enhances it. As Richard Shusterman (2011a, 153) notices, the mere deodorisation of the body, or the selection of a random perfume, is not enough to make a person desirable; one needs to carefully choose "a fragrance that goes beyond the scent's intrinsic allure but also expresses the particular character, personality, or style that the person in question wants to convey". Simmel devotes many insights on adornments and perfume, which replace and shelter personal atmosphere concurrently making it stand out. In this sense, one can "smell expensive" by wearing a costly fragrance, but if their "air" is vulgar, the perfume will only emphasise such a contradiction. As the saying goes, this person will *smell fishy*. The osmosphere itself is the vehicle for this incongruity.

---

66 See Noë 2004; Sompairac 2021, where the author proposes the term *olf-action*. On ecological aesthetics, Gambaro 2022.
67 It follows the process of the *becoming of the living being* (Fontanille 2004).

Indeed, the ability to smell the "true" air of a person goes under the name of *sagacity*, which is tightly related to smell.

1.4 *Sagacious Is The Nose*

> I was the first to *discover* the truth, by being
> the first to sense — *smell* — the lie as a lie...
> My genius is in my nostrils...
> Friedrich Nietzsche

By a lapidary *aperçu*, Serres (2008, 235) states that, while the *sapiens* knows how to taste, the *sagacious* knows how to smell. From the Latin *sagire*, "sagacity" has precisely to do with olfaction in many respects. *Sagax* means "keen-scented, perceptive" (de Vaan 2016, 534-535), indicating a person who has perspicacity, acumen, shrewdness, that is, someone gifted with a type of intelligence that knows by sniffing in the sense of *getting a whiff of something*. As is well known, *flair* as one of the most reliable ethical instruments runs through Nietzsche's oeuvre, so much so that Bachelard (1988a, 127-160) describes him as the exemplary case of an aerial spirit and ascensional poet. In *Ecce Homo*, Nietzsche (2007, 16) celebrates his sense of smell as *the* means to grasp, to *scent*, the true nature of the human soul and to fathom its depth, stating: "I have an instinct for cleanliness that is utterly uncanny in its sensitivity, which means that I can physiologically detect — *smell* — the proximity or (what am I saying?) the innermost aspect, the 'innards' of every soul...". This proclivity is the result of the ability to detect human filth and their foetid ideas that exhale like a foul odour from an invisible source. In other words, sagacity has to do with smelling the essence as a vapour of ethical-aesthetic nature. Indeed, that smell "is *par excellence* probing" (Kolnai 2004, 101) is an important point for some theories of disgust. Combining an intrusive nature with a preservative function, olfaction can be seen as *the* sense of revulsion. Kant (2006, §21, 50) draws a parallel between smell, filth and nausea, the latter being aroused "not so much through what is repugnant to the eyes and tongue as through the stench that we presume it has".

In the Nietzschean tension towards the enhancement of the animality of humans, the sense of smell is elevated to a bio-psychological sensitivity detecting the very interiority of a body. Thus, olfaction becomes a sort of heuristic extrasensory ability to detect, rooted in the idea of *nosing, smelling* or *sniffing something out*. This prowess is sagacity. However, due to its essential ambivalence, odours are at the same time the least alterable traits and the most manipulable ones. Accordingly, one can *be led by the nose* ("to control" and also "to deceive, to trick", as the Italian *menare per il naso*), as well as be the only one able to unmask a fraud. *Following one's nose* means trusting one's instinct. To quote Nietzsche again (2007, 16): "I have psychological feelers attached to this sensitivity, with which I test every secret by touch and get a grip on it: almost on first contact, I am already conscious of the large amount of *concealed* dirt at the bottom of many a nature, perhaps occasioned by bad blood but whitewashed over by upbringing". This very olfactory skill encourages Nietzsche to move away from the stench of corruption and morality, striving for the crisp and uncontaminated wind blowing over the mountain peaks or on the open sea. As Jaquet (2010) speculates, Bachelard (1988a, 137) is wrong when stating that a "Nietzschean cannot take pleasure in any odor", in that his pneumatic model is based on the subtlest nuances, almost undetectable to normal nostrils. It is an *aesthetics of fine differences* which requires a sensitivity that "covers both sensory and an affective experience" (Diaconu 2006a, 144). We could say that the purest air is never odourless, not so much because it is filled with smells, but because it is lively and fresh. A poem by Edna St. Vincent Millay (1990, 541) expresses it clearly:

> And I rose, half-rose, in bed, and
> Listened to the wind, smelling new snow —
> No smell like that — a smell neither sour nor sweet —
> No fragrance, none at all, nothing to compete with, nothing to interfere
> With the odourless clear passage of the smell of new snow
> Through the nostrils. "Cold," I said [...].

This finds its counterpoint in *stale* air, where the respiratory dynamic responds accordingly: oppression occurs when the "air [is] too scented, it [gives] no breath" (Lawrence 1955, 106). Between the two kinetic and thermic poles of endless movement and stagnation, iciness and sweltering heat, air takes on a variety of osmospheric values.

As it emerges, sagacity cannot be assimilated either to rationality or to analysis. The sense of smell seems to embody the picking up on clues as obscure and approximate as they are certain and peremptory — a *whiff*. Greimas and Fontanille (1991, 12, 21) speak precisely of *le senteur*, insisting on its passional aspects and exemplifying it by using the metaphor of perfume. It is a specific feeling, but never fully graspable in logical and verbal terms, that mostly juxtaposes to the olfactory domain. An atmosphere is assimilated "before we identify its details or understand it intellectually" (Pallasmaa 2014, 232); moreover, "we may be completely unable to say anything meaningful about the features of a situation, yet have a firm image, emotive attitude, and recall of it" (ibid). Without requiring reflection, sagacity is an understanding as immediate as it is inexplicable, atmospheric. Indeed, a connection between smelling and a form of exploratory investigation can be found in many languages,[68] since many idiomatic expressions prove the epistemological weight of smell, contrary to what most philosophers have argued.[69] In English, *to have a nose for something* hints at a kind of perceptual, vague and yet clear intuition without the need to resort to a logic-argumentative reasoning;[70] *to wake up and smell the coffee* (or roses) means becoming aware, reaching the truth of a situation; as a variation on the theme, *to stop and smell the coffee* (or roses) implies taking time to enjoy something. *Smelling a rat* is when something is suspicious and possibly dangerous; indeed, the *smell test* is a way of establishing whether something is credible, trustworthy or acceptable. Furthermore, *throwing someone off the scent* means deliberately misleading or confusing them.

Similarly to Nietzsche, the legend has it that Hilarion of Gaza was gifted with the skill of recognising the demons and vices of people just by smelling "bodies or clothes or other things anyone had touched" (White 1998, 104). Based on these considerations, smell turns out to be a powerful means to sense the atmosphere as "a sort of extension of ourselves thrown into the exterior world" (Nogué 1936, 230). Actually, *I smell you* is another way of saying "I deeply understand you", no need to add anything. The self-externalisation implies the possibility of providing the peripheral volume with an aura that does not adhere to the body, but replenishes it as an atmosphere. However, while allowing one to occupy — or even *claim*, as we shall see later — a space through a presence, this osmospheric exteriorisation also opens up to the risk of losing control over one's most intimate dimension. It is fairly well established that "smell reveals interiority without discussion and declares the mood of the individual, event or place" (Le Breton 2022, 13). Indeed, "to be intrusive" has correspondences with the nose aplenty. *To nose around* is synonym for *to poke/stick the nose into something*, that is, to be *nosy*, but also "to spy, to snoop, to meddle", a parallelism which recurs also, among others, in French and in Italian (*mettre son nez partout* and *ficcare il naso*). This double pun is the basis

---

68   Hoad 1996, 173; de Vaan 2016, 426; Ibarretxe-Antuñano 2021, 93.
69   For a proposal aimed at dismissing the alleged epistemological weakness of smell, Shiner 2021.
70   Le Breton 2022, 7.

of the inaugural meeting narrated by Süskind (1986, 18) between father Terrier and Grenouille as an infant. The latter, who has no odour, reveals nothing about himself, going unnoticed or more often conveying a sense of anguish to others,[71] while using his prodigious olfaction to intrude on them. In the fictional episode, Grenouille is sleeping but his nose is the first that wakes up, starting to move and sniff:

> It seemed to Terrier as if the child saw him with his nostrils, as if it were staring intently at him, scrutinizing him, more piercingly than eyes could ever do, as if it were using its nose to devour something whole, something that came from him, from Terrier, and that he could not hold that something back or hide it [...]. And all at once he felt as if he stank, of sweat and vinegar, of choucroute and unwashed clothes. He felt naked and ugly. [...] His most tender emotions, his filthiest thoughts lay exposed to that greedy little nose [...].

Along these lines, a case recounted by Tellenbach (1968, 150) shows some tragic psychological repercussions. The patient Hallenore Z., diagnosed as schizophrenic, was sure that "*her boss could smell what she was thinking*". Her innermost thoughts had turned into the feeling of emanating a "snake smell". At the total mercy of other people's noses, her thoughts/odours had thus scattered to the wind, shattering the atmospheric veil that defends one's inner self. As any kind of surface, an atmosphere is indeed an interstitial membrane which concurrently exhibits and protects. The patient was in a cruel state of nakedness: her "*thoughts were so spread out that 'one could smell them in the air'*" (ibid, 152). Between *der Geruch* (odour) and *das Gerücht* (rumour) the connection, rather than etymological, lies in their common phenomenology: they spread in the air, condensing and enveloping the targeted subject with an asphyxiating air (ibid, 144).[72] On the other side of the coin, sagacity implies the total exposure of an essence that ought to be protected from the nose of others.

Sagacity discloses two temporal aspects, almost opposite to each other, which is now worth mentioning. The former can be summarised in the idea of *trace*, and has to do, so to speak, with the *felt presence of an absence*

---

71 *Perfume* was one of Kurt Cobain's favourite novels, hence the Nirvana song "Scentless Apprentice" (1993), which revolves around Grenouille as a human being without odour. A parallel can be drawn with *The Nonexistent Knight* by Italo Calvino (1962, 56). The main character Agilulf, when thinking about his condition as a bodiless entity, concludes that, in spite of everything, there are some advantages: he lacks the common defects of carcasses, namely "coarseness, carelessness, incoherence, smell".

72 See also Sloterdijk 2014, 330.

or with the osmospheric persistence of a vestigial event that still lingers in the air after its end, a kind of *aftertaste*. The latter is similar to a *foretaste*, and has to do with what is yet to come: premonition and foreboding as the *felt absence of a pending presentification*. Let us briefly consider them in this order.

"Odor is a trace that dwelling leaves on the environment" (Illich 1985, 51-52);[73] complementarily, sagacity may derive from the hunting lexicon, meaning "to search, to track down", from the Greek □γέομαι.[74] The Sanskrit root *sac-* means "to penetrate", and it is probably related to the Anglosaxon *sêcan*, hence *to seek*. Sagacity bases its meaning on the predator-prey relationship, where "the animal had to resort to the subtle traces its prey leaves behind, allowing it to be followed even when it is absent from all the other sensory domains" (Nogué 1936, 230). Of course, traces are not exclusive to the sense of smell, but in a way characterise its perceptual modality. When dealing with the idea of aspiration understood as the act of "searching", following Minkowski (1999, 65-66), Tellenbach (1968, 49) pays attention to the German word *spüren*, which includes an orientation towards something one seeks to understand, i.e. to perceive or, in the intransitive form, to follow the traces. Jacques Derrida (2008, 55) resorts to the case of scent trails and animal movement when questioning the significance of "being after". Acknowledging the marginality of the olfactive sensibility in philosophy and the arts, he points out that to follow implies to go back "more than once over the same path to pick up the traces, either to sniff the trace of another or to cover its own by adding to it, precisely as though it were that of another, picking up the scent, therefore, of whatever on this track demonstrates to it that the trace is always that of another".

Olfactory traces afford orientation to animals depending on their position in the food chain. Given that carnivores "can follow the air scent carried by airflow, as well as the ground scent from a track" (Gibson 1969, 148), the rule of *oriented locomotion*, as Gibson defines it, is the following: "move in such a way as to keep and maximize the smell of food. [...] This is the rule of the chase. The rule of flight is precisely the opposite: move so as to minimize the scent of the predator" (ibid). This olfactory dynamic explains the large use of odour in animal behaviour. From scent-marking to self-anointing and scent-rubbing, smells leave the trace of a transit in the

---

73 For an overview of the notion of dwelling, De Matteis 2022b; see also Griffero 2022c.
74 Chantraine 1999, 405-406; Beekes 2010, 509; Frisk 1960, 621-622.

environment or, at times, conceal it by adding a different one. This is why the expression "olfactory marks act even in the absence of the occupant of a territory" is inaccurate according to Thomas Kappe (1997, 140): it is *not* absent but, rather, "present on the border through its odours" (ibid). Like a place card, smell performs the functions of the organism who emits it thanks to its persistence. Thus, sagacity seems to be an *ex-post* perception that obeys a displaced temporality. In this sense, as Süskind (1986, 36) maintains, olfactory traces can be even more reliable in *presentifying* what they stand for, in that they afford a much more precise and complete perception precisely as an *afterthought*. Once arrived at the general market square in the evening, Grenouille smells everything that happened there during the day:

> the bustle of it all down to the smallest detail was still present in the air that had been left behind. [...] And he smelled it more precisely than many people could see it, for his perception was perception after the fact and thus of a higher order: an essence, a spirit of what had been, something undisturbed by the everyday accidents of the moment, like noise, glare or the nauseating press of living human beings.

On the contrary, sagacity is also, or perhaps first and foremost, a premonition; namely, a way of perceiving something through a *presentiment*, before its actual experience or evident symptomatology occurs. To feel something in the air and to smell something coming — in Swedish *lukta* (Viberg 2021, 55-56), in Italian *subodorare*[75] — are expressions indicating the ability to detect what has yet to manifest itself, to sniff an approaching phenomenon, which is latent but at the same time pervades the space. *Presage* is indeed synonym for "foreboding, omen", and it entails the same root as *sagire* but preceded by *pre-*, "before". Smell then "contains an important reference to the future; *a fragrance can forecast something*, it can announce a coming event" (Tellenbach 1981, 224). Smell then *perceives beforehand*. The German idiom *das konnte ich ja nicht riechen*, verbatim "I could not smell that", perfectly exemplifies this perceptual-epistemological overlapping, meaning "I could not have foreseen it". Sagacity is therefore largely accountable for the first (and long-lasting) impression that bypasses rational analysis. Even further, if an atmosphere "is the more deeply felt and therefore 'known', the less it is linguistically circumscribable" (Griffero 2014, 73), osmospheres are in

---

75 *Subolfactio*, where the prefix *sub-* means "below", was already used by Latin writers with the same meaning (Strik Lievers 2021, 377-378).

this sense the most emblematic ones, given the problematic relationship between odours and their verbalisation, at least in the Western world.[76] On incomprehensibility, Woolf (2012, 21-22) maintains that "we creep beneath some obscure poem by Mallarmé or Donne, some phrase in Latin or Greek, and the words give out their scent and distil their flavour, and then, if at last we grasp the meaning, it is all the richer for having come to us sensually first, by way of the palate and the nostrils, like some queer odour". In this sense, it is true that smells "evoke an as yet unthought thought" (Studio Ólafur Elíasson 2016, 31).

Being a precursory seeking with respect to other perceptual domains, smell discloses its *pre-judicial* and precautionary character. This issue has not gone unnoticed to philosophers. When Hegel (1975, 729) insists on the essential connection between smell and taste, he nonetheless points out that "smelling itself is still not an actual practical devouring of things, like eating and tasting, but takes up only the result of a process in which things mingle with air and its secret and invisible volatilizing". Sniffing the aromas of food is a sort of *preview* of its consumption. In Jean-Jacques Rousseau's (1979, 156) words, smell "is to taste what sight is to touch. It anticipates taste and informs it about how this or that substance is going to affect it and disposes one to seek it or flee it according to the impression that one has received of it in advance". In this sense, the most incisive definition is proposed by Kant (2006, §22, 51), who delineates smell as a *Vorgeschmack*, a "foretaste". Moreover, despite being the most invasive and affective of the senses, smell anticipates food contact and absorption acting as *ein Geschmack in die Ferne*, a "taste at a distance" (ibid, §21, 50). Poised on the isthmus between proximity and distality,[77]

---

76   According to some research, once we manage to label smells or when we are told their names, their affective impact decreases considerably (Köster *et al.* 2014). The thesis pitting language against olfaction has been supported by scientific findings for a long time; today it is being increasingly questioned; see Savic, Berglund 2004; on anosmia and odour words, Speed *et al.* 2022. Further references are provided in ch. 3.

77   Whether smell has to be considered proximal or distal is a debated question. In the Aristotelian system, smell is placed in an intermediate position (Johnstone 2012). For the majority of thinkers, it is proximal. In this case, odours do not coincide with their source but with the odorous molecules themselves, which are, according to Tellenbach (1968, 27), somehow always *in the nose*: "the perfume of the flower is never over there on the window [...]. There is neither here nor there". According to some, however, it is distal. Hans Jonas (2001, 150), for instance, seems to agree with this interpretation, even if he notes that smell "never gains, always loses by distance". Alternatively, smell has been interpreted as a dual perceptual system (Rozin 1982, Gottfried 2005). Orthonasal and retronasal

prelude and prodrome, smell prefigures the judgement that will follow in case of ingestion, which will actually occur if olfaction does not act as a deterrent. In other words, olfactory experiences are always innervated by premonition and expectation; in this respect, Tellenbach mentions Pavlov's experiments, and the *actual* enjoyment dogs have *before* the food is served. Keller (2003, 43) also confesses that: the "savoury odour of the meat made me hungry long before the tables were set". However, this is not restricted to eating. Troubles can be smelled, as well as success or fame; and when you *smell the barn*, excitement makes you speed up because your destination is around the corner.

Thus, smelling somehow transcends physical contact in a peculiar way: it maintains a separation by concurrently reducing the gap and reversing the very sense of distance. Sagacity is based on a prejudice because it foretells the relationship between the subject and the object through an encompassing affective nuance. Through an oenological example, Serres (2008, 176) maintains that wine, a *quasi-object*, mixes with us and becomes a *quasi-subject*; then, "the subjects become relationship, the relationship becomes subject through the intermediary of the object, of this, the wine". This thoroughly applies to smell and its sagacious predisposition, which is precisely aimed at configuring the *relationship*. This relationship is atmospheric since it is spread out into the space where it hovers; it is felt in the lived body as a peripheral space attuned to the affective unicum which ecologically embraces a perceptual event as a whole. In this sense, it is worth mentioning that the symptoms of some diseases are sometimes heralded by an auratic perception that can be osmospheric. Tellenbach (1968) provides many cases in which the oral sense is the medium conveying the schizophrenic modification occurring in the relationship between the self and the world. Moreover, as specialist literature attests, olfactory hallucinations as a prelude to migraine or epileptic seizures are not uncommon.[78] As a last remark, in the epilogue to Sartre's *Nausea* (1964, 178), the perpetuation of existence is perceived by Antoine Roquentin precisely through an act of sagacity: the "building-yard of the New Station smells strongly of damp wood: tomorrow it will rain in Bouville".

---

perceptions would have dissimilar aims and modalities: whereas the former is environment-oriented, and therefore distal, the latter is proximal since it focuses on edible substances in the mouth (Smith 2015). The duality of smell would explain why olfactory perceptions considerably change according to the pathway the same molecular compounds undertake; it commonly occurs with food.

78   Sacks 1995, 141-142; Carnevali 2006; Grant 2017.

1.5 *Memory, Or The Fragrant Faculty*

> Smell — that is the sense of weight of someone who casts
> his nets into the sea of the *temps perdu*.
> Walter Benjamin

The Mnemogogues is one of the "Natural Histories" Primo Levi published in 1966 under the pseudonym Damiano Malabaila. In this short tale, a young doctor, Dr. Morandi, gets to the small town where he is to practise medicine. The episode deals with his encounter with Dr. Montesanto, the old doctor on the point of retiring, who confides what he considers the most original discovery of his entire career: the creation of a number of olfactory compounds that he calls *mnemogogues*, verbatim "arousers of memory". From the odour of elementary school rooms to that of a religious crisis up to the smell of sun-warmed rock, Dr. Montesanto, as an associate in pharmacology, has developed a large olfactory archive like a scrapbook. "In any event," he argues, "it is a matter of common observation that memories, in order to be suggestive, must have an antique flavor" (Levi 1990, 16). This is just one (rather overlooked) among the countless examples revolving around the tight connection between smell and memory, given that "in fragrance and flavor the enduring element of the past, its atmosphere, is preserved" (Tellenbach 1981, 224).[79] This link is also traceable in memory disorders such as dementia and Alzheimer's disease, where, on the one side, smell loss is a pre-clinical sign of the pathology;[80] on the other side, the use of odours can improve some symptoms.[81]

Smells and atmospheres share an indissolubility that results in a distillate where their extension concentrates, coagulating in a mnestic and affective condensation. An odour evokes an entire atmosphere, taking to the surface "the *essential* of what has been; as this essential has seeped

---

79   A passage taken from the unfinished novel *Jean Santeuil* by Proust (1956, 408) corroborates such relationships: "I cannot say whether I felt this recovered life in the smell, or whether my memory gave it me *accompanied by* the smell, but I should like to think that its place of habitation was somewhere common to, somewhere preserving the essence of, both sense and memory, that what it brought to me was the bred of the sharp assumption by them of identity, as though that identity is necessary before sensation can lose the immediate and particular quality which it has in the perceived present, which memory alone can never take from it".

80   Doty, Tekeli 2012; Nordin 2012.

81   Georgsdorf 2021, 127-128.

into the atmospheric and has converted into it" (Tellenbach 1968, 104). The past, even if only (or *not*) imagined, is resurrected by odour. It follows that "[e]veryone who clings to the past dreams of indestructible odors" (Bachelard 1988a, 137). This peculiarity of the oral sense is well exploited by poets. As Pessoa (2003, 332) notes: "[w]ith what subtle plausibility — taste combined with smell — I recreate the dead stage settings and reinvest them with the colours of a past". As is well known, the author who holds the title of osmospheric poet is Proust, so much so that the resurfacing of involuntary memories triggered by odours is also known as the "Proust Phenomenon".[82] Interestingly, Walter Benjamin draws a parallel between the importance of smell for Proust and asthma he suffered from. In this sense, his condition "became part of his art — if indeed his art did not create it. Proust's syntax rhythmically and step by step reproduces his fear of suffocating. And his ironic, philosophical, didactic reflections invariably are the deep breath with which he shakes off the weight of memories" (ibid). We might say that asthma *generated* his breathing as a constant air hunger; thanks to the consequent bodily stirrings, his osmospheric poetics blossomed. In this case more than in others, every scented breath is a genuine physiological relief. The most famous passage of this poetics is undoubtedly the episode of the madeleine soaked in the decoction of lime-blossom, when Marcel, who is in a foul mood, is offered some tea by his mother. As soon as he drinks the first sip together with a morsel of the sweet, his depressing state of mind vanishes, being invaded by a deep and mysterious pleasure. The pages that follow can be defined as a phenomenological description of his quest to identify the vague recollection that is taking place within him,[83] or the *inarticulate feeling of familiarity* that James (1981, 244) observes in relation to the emotional shock experienced by perceiving a certain tune, odour or flavour. Finally, when the memory reveals itself to Marcel, in *that* moment, "all the flowers in our garden and in M. Swann's park, and the waterlilies on the Vivonne and the good folk of the village and their little dwellings and the parish church and the whole of Combray and its surroundings, taking shape and solidity, sprang into being, town and gardens alike, from my cup of tea" (Proust 1998, 64). Dormant memories re-emerge all of a sudden, recalled by the same aroma to which they adhere.[84] Indeed,

---

82   Chu, Downes 2000, 2002; Herz, Schooler 2002; van Campen 2014.
83   Kluck 2019.
84   For a neuroscientist account, Lehrer 2007, 75-95; on smell, autobiographical memory and emotion in general, Willander, Larsson 2007.

when from a long-distant past nothing subsists, after the people are dead, after the things are broken and scattered, taste and smell alone, more fragile but more enduring, more immaterial, more persistent, more faithful, remain posed a long time, like souls, remembering, waiting, hoping, amid the ruins of all the rest; and bear unflinchingly, in the tiny and almost impalpable drop of their essence, the vast structure of recollection (ibid, 63-64).

Benjamin (1968, 214) points out another pivotal aspect that is worth mentioning for our investigation. Commenting on Proust's poetics, he finds in him the fullest awareness that with "great tenacity memories are preserved by the sense of smell, and smells not at all in memory". This very clarification — smell preserves memories, *not* the other way round — allows us to interpret atmospheric perceiving as an *osmospheric* modality. If the very feeling thinks of its feeling and feels its thinking, it is important to understand, more than the content of perception, the specific dispositional colourings of perceiving.[85] Although memory certainly has cognitive content, the sentimental disposition makes it differ. The eminent olfactive modality is that of remembrance and nostalgia — Sacks (1987, 159) calls it *osmalgia*, Drobnick (2006a, 350-355) *nosealgia*.[86] This is why, after all, "[w]hen memory breathes, all odors are good" (Bachelard 1969, 136): in "days of happiness, the world is edible. And when the great odors which were preparing feasts return to me in memory, it seems to me, Baudelarian that I was, that 'I eat memories'" (ibid, 141). This truth stands out by reading García Márquez (1970, 111), according to whom, sometimes, "over a watercolor of Venice, nostalgia would transform the smell of mud and putrefying shellfish of the canals into the warm aroma of flowers". As Benjamin (1968, 211) points out, the eternity which Proust discloses through smells is *convoluted time* rather than *boundless time*, expressing its passage "in its most real — that is, space-bound — form, and this passage nowhere holds sway more openly than in remembrance within and aging without". The intertwining between time and space through scents is the key feature of the ancient Eastern practice of measuring time by burning incense or even graduated candles. The "incense clock" — *xiāngzhōng*, verbatim "seal of fragrance" (Han 2017a, 55), which appeared for the first time in China during the Song dynasty (960-1279) — is a redolent timekeeper device composed of different kinds of incense,[87] each designed with a

---

85   Griffero 2017a.
86   On food, smell and non-representational memory, Parasecoli 2007.
87   Mentioning this oriental instrument, McLuhan (1964, 146-147) relates smell to memory, corroborating it through the case of some medical experiments.

specific burn rate to measure minutes, hours or days.[88] Byung-Chul Han (2017a, 57) resorts to the example of fragrant clock to argue that, filling the room, the fragrance "even turns time into space; it thus gives it a semblance of duration".[89] Moreover, whereas atomised instants are scentless and meaningless, time "begins to emit a scent when it gains duration; when it is given a narrative or deep tension; when it gains depth and breadth, even *space*" (ibid, 18). Bachelard's (1969, 140) thesis that the "house of one's birth does not smell musty" brings together the osmospheric value of duration and of intimate spaces. In this respect, it comes as no surprise that most of his insights on smell and memory find their specific investigation in relation to childhood (Bachelard 1969, 136-138).

As already seen, osmospheric space is always intertwined with felt time as weather, as seasonal cycle.[90] As Serres (2008, 169-170) argues, smell reveals itself as the realm of *singularity*:

> With our eyes closed, our ears stopped, feet and hands bound, lips sealed, we can still identify, years later and from a thousand other smells, the undergrowth of such and such a place in a particular season at sunset, just before a rain storm, or the room where feed corn was kept, or cooked prunes in September, or a woman.

Here a recurrent aspect is postulated: to properly recollect, sight has to be silenced. Proust underlines the same mechanism, noticing that it is thanks to the flavour of the madeleine while mixed with the tea that a large portion of the past is brought back to life in the form of an osmosphere. On the contrary, the sight of its form — a scallop-shell pastry "so richly sensual under its severe, religious folds" (Proust 1998, 63) — reminded him of nothing. In other words, to say that the "most persistent memory of any space is often smell" (Pallasmaa 2012, 58) is not enough. To dive into the vagueness of memories, odours are unrivalled, but they are best experienced by closing the eyes. "Long ago we closed our eyes to savor them fully", writes Bachelard (1969, 136). Something similar is present in the poetics of Baudelaire who, as many scholars have pointed out, equals Proust in the importance attributed to smells.[91] Commenting on his redolent

---

88   Bedini 1963, 1994.
89   The South-Korean born philosopher devotes further reflection on smell and memory in his *Saving Beauty*, especially when he investigates "Beauty as Reminiscence" (Han 2017b, ch. 13).
90   On the appreciation of garden and smell, see Tafalla 2014, especially part 3, on Transience.
91   See Souriau 1947.

poetics, Sartre (1950, 174) explains his being "fond of scents" not because of his refined olfaction, but because of the very nature of smells, in that Baudelaire seems to have a taste "for those strange objects which resemble the outcropping of being and whose spirituality consists of absence" (ibid). It is worth quoting some verses from *Le Flacon*, where the role of smell in recollection is explicitly combined with the closing of eyes:

> Or poking through a house, in closets shut for years,
> Full of the smell of time — acrid, musty, dank,
> One comes, perhaps, upon a flask of memories
> In whose escaping scent a soul returns to life.
> [...]
> Fluttering to the brain through the unsettled air,
> Rapturous memory pervades the atmosphere;
> *The eyes are forced to close*; Vertigo grasps the soul,
> And thrusts her with his hands into the mists of mind
> (Baudelaire 1993, 97-99 [my italics]).

The various Medieval and Renaissance allegories of the senses seem to confirm such bodily stirring, given the iconographic recurrence of figures with their eyes closed while sniffing.[92] It is especially so with flowers. Their perfume seems to call for specific gestures as the result of bodily stirrings. Eye closed, chin raised, chest wide open, slow and deep breathing. The tension is towards expansion and relaxation, at the same time inwards and onwards. The body becomes the sounding board for the aroma that invades it, concurrently exposing itself to the aerial surroundings. It is worth mentioning an observation by James (1981, 808), who draws a parallel between smell and a sense of *undivided largeness*, since, of "many tastes and flavors, even simultaneously presented, each affects the totality of its respective organ, each appears with the whole vastness given by that organ, and appears interpenetrated by the rest". While smelling, silencing vision seems functional in order to experience the osmospheric space, which is not geometric but volumetric and fluid. This would also underline a sort of unconsciously conscious aesthetic wisdom through which the perceiver creates the conditions for enjoying flavours, by prioritising one perceptual modality to the detriment of others. Hence, there seems to be an *osmospheric* as opposed to an *optic* way of perceiving space.[93] We are in the

---

92   Nordenfalk 1985.
93   Here I draw inspiration from Nicola Perullo's concept of *haptic* as opposed to *optic* perception (Perullo 2018, 2022a, 2022b). This distinction is further discussed later.

osmospheric mode when recollecting our relations with it. The inebriating scent, as the oceanic feeling exemplified by Böhme, calls for an exit from the objectual space to enter in a vectorial one where time as well is not felt as linear.

Indeed, the morphology of olfactory recollection is queer, a sort of shaped amorphism.[94] In smell, "[f]orms reappear, invariant or recurrent, harmonies are transformed, stable across variations, specificity is countersigned by aroma" (Serres 2008, 169). At times, however, the "odor has remained in the *word*" (Bachelard, 1969 137); as flowers exude their fragrance, so do names. A term may exhale an osmosphere; *pension*, according to Léon Daudet (1928, 120), "is already a nasal overview of it" (cit. in Griffero 2014, 65 n. 28). The same is supported by Honoré de Balzac (1951, 31) but, as a realist, he tries to describe the *boarding-house smell* as the "atmosphere has the stuffiness of rooms which are never ventilated, and a mouldy odour of decay. Its dampness chills you as you breathe it, and permeates your clothing. Smells of all the meals that have been eaten in the boarding-house linger in the air. The whole place stinks of the kitchen and the scullery, and it has in addition the reek characteristic of all refuges for the unfortunate". That said, he concludes adding that if "some ways were known to measure the nauseating elements breathed out by every lodger young or old into the air, which is infected by this catarrh or other ailment, *it might then be possible to describe this smell adequately*" (ibid [my italics]). In their linguistic use, however, the poet (not the realist novelist) must be careful not to say too much; otherwise, the readers cannot evoke the uniqueness of *their* childhood smell,[95] which is "the signature of intimacy" (Bachelard 2014, 35) and it is usually "beyond description, one that it takes a lot of imagination to smell" (ibid). Bachelard (1969, 136) distinguishes between the clarity and sharpness of images, which easily conjure up a childhood memory, and the nebulosity of smells, which enable one "to penetrate into the zone of indeterminate childhood, into the childhood without proper names and without a history either". This also transpires in Proust's work which, in Benjamin's (1968, 214) view, requires the readers to tune accordingly, placing themselves in a disposition in which "the materials of memory no longer appear singly, as images, but tell us about a whole, amorphously and formlessly, indefinitely and weightily".

In the opening of her queer phenomenology about orientation as "feeling at home", Sara Ahmed (2006, 10) offers interesting observations about

---

94 Tellenbach 1981, 223.
95 For Bachelard, *this* odour is that of drying raisins.

relocating. Through smell, the contours between space and time become blurred and, thanks to it, a house can turn into a home:[96]

> Then I arrive, an empty house. It looks like a shell. [...] The familiar smell of spices fills the air. [...] I feel flung back somewhere else. I am never sure where the smell of spices takes me, as it has followed me everywhere. Each smell that gathers returns me somewhere; I am not always sure where that somewhere is. [...] Such memories can involve a recognition of how one's body already feels, coming after the event. [...] So we ask the question, later, and it often seems too late: what is it that has led me away from the present, to another place and another time?

As Nadia Seremetakis (2019, 128) argues in her anthropological investigation on memory as material culture through commensal practices, "[s]ensory memory is encapsulated, stored and recuperated in these artifacts, spaces and temporalities of consumption, sharing and exchange". Focusing on the rural and urban Greek environment with specific attention to women, she makes the case of a grandchild leaving the city to visit their grandmother in the country. During the trip by train, every station corresponds to a specific food and thus to a specific flavour; reaching the grandmother means crossing sensual substances. Once arrived, smells usher the entrance into another place. They combine and mingle, adhering to spaces and times:

> The fig is on the tree in the field one day, and next morning hundreds of figs are gathered and placed on bamboo mats on the beach, by the ocean to sundry. They look like pebbles and their strong sour taste blends with the smell of the sea. Then comes the olive season or the noodle making. For smells have seasons and each season smells. There is no watermelon in the winter, for instance, as in America. For taste has seasons too, and each season tastes (ibid, 30).

Space and time take on an atmospheric timbre also depending on the seasonality of ingredients, recipes, traditions and cooking methods. Gastronomy is indeed a great atmospheric generator, conveying memories, affections, sense of place and time. Indeed, "in smelling and tasting man

---

96 Dealing with the philosophical complexity of such a notion (from Husserl to Bollnow and Lévinas) would keep me from getting to the point of my contribution. Here and further on, I use the terms in a nontechnical sense, employing *home* when stressing the affective property of intimacy with space, regardless of geographical positions; *house*, when referring to material buildings, even if the distinction sometimes fades (see Griffero 2020a, 115-123). This topic is further investigated in ch. 2.

enters *the dominion of the moment* — but in such a fashion that past events may be implicitly contained in it, or more exactly, that the content of an atmosphere of a situation is simultaneously present" (Tellenbach 1981, 223). It is no coincidence that nostalgia for the homeland finds its most powerful remedy in food: like "[f]eta experienced abroad, the basil sniffed in a pot in London reminds the new migrant of 'Greece' in this instance, rather than any more localized association" (Sutton 2001, 85). However, this is not an allegorical reference but an osmospheric melting: more than other qualities, odours afford "a tuning or a fusion [...] of humans with their environment" (Griffero 2014, 67, [slightly modified]). Since "the smells do not adhere to definitive places; in respect to localization, they are characterized by a thoroughgoing vagueness" (Cassirer 1957, 129), they end up coinciding with an overall atmospheric ecology. Indeed, to the nostalgic of a bygone era, food inevitably used to taste better back then. The absent flavour condenses in the memory of an osmosphere which has gone but is felt as current and residual while tasting the osmospheric gap between the two. Pessoa (2003, 233-234) expresses it vividly in these lines:

> I'm walking down a street. The smell of bread from a bakery nauseates me with its sweetness, and my childhood rises up from a distant neighborhood, and another bakery emerges from that fairyland which is everything we ever had that has died. I'm walking down a street. Suddenly I smell the fruit on the slanted rack of the small grocery, and my short life in the country — I can't say from when or where — has trees in the background and peace in what can only be my childhood heart.

James (1981, 243) claims something similar by stating that "the feeling of an absence is *toto caelo* other than the absence of a feeling"; this especially applies to osmospheres. Given the atmospheric poignancy of food, the next chapter delves into food osmospheres, trying to understand food flavours as nodes of diverse affective relations.

2
Food Osmospheres

New York's air has recently been sweetened by the aroma
of honey-roasted peanuts.
Yu-Fu Tuan

2.1 *Flavours As Affective Foundations*

Flames, fire, oven: no matter how far our travels take us, we
must return home to the hearth, where the banquet is prepared.
Outside, the raw; in the kitchen, the aromas of a sublime
alchemy emanate from the grilled meat.
Michel Serres

The inescapable condition that the olfactory sphere constitutes "the very ground base of life" (Sacks 1987, 159) can be read in different ways. Sagacity suggests that we interpret it as a *foretaste*; indeed, smell possesses a sort of *foundational* nature also in the sense that it precedes the information provided by other senses, constituting the first perceptual clue we get from our surroundings. At the same time, smell plays a pivotal role in eating — like breathing, a fundamental need for life — and many of the olfactory stimuli that affect us on a daily basis are related to food. Food flavours are largely to be ascribed to cooking and food processing, hence to the use of fire or fermentation as the benchmark of humanity. The contrast between raw and cooked, as posited by Claude Lévi-Strauss (1964), has an osmospheric value as well, since the cooked and the fragrant are symptoms of humankind in its path to differentiating itself from animals, whereas the raw, often less aromatic, is the primordial stage of humans as mammals.

One can also infer a further meaning of smell's foundational role. In the first stages of our life before and immediately after our birth, smells are cardinal points in the affective and cognitive maps. Smell constitutes the basic, fundamental or primary tool during the early stage of development, laying the foundations for the shaping of our personality. Our aerial rooting is without exception but, in a way, paradoxically counterintuitive, given the solid association between the image of the root and the chthonic dimension of the soil, the earth as flesh and mother that provides support and nourishment. Tellenbach already suggested in 1968 something that is viewed as a key point in food psychology today, namely that the affective impacts of smell and food can be traced down taking into account the relationship children establish with their mothers. Since the first instants of a newborn's life, the maternal scent has coincided with her emotional atmosphere and the food she has been offering. In the child's experience, the mother is firstly her aroma, which is intertwined with her emotional irradiation and the sense of trust and care related to food. Put another way, flavour *inaugurates life*: the "mother's emanations are the nucleus of our first experience of the world" (Tellenbach 1981, 222). Moods, flavours and nourishment, being concurrent and permeated with affection, trust and protection, acquire an interchangeable atmospheric value. Kinship, just like the domestic sphere, corresponds with an osmospheric dimension that coincides with the general mood which "is condensed into taste" (ibid, 226). An unexplored but perhaps promising topic is the nexus between the olfactory sphere and eating disorders. In other words, the latter might partially be explained by detecting a primordial osmospheric distortion which pours into food as a vital element that embodies the affective relationships with others.

As prenatal studies prove, smell is already active during intrauterine existence: receptors and the nasal organ begin to develop in the embryo from the eighth week of gestation. The foetus, ingesting and expelling the amniotic fluid, savours the food eaten by the mother. As rightly posited by Shusterman (2011b, 316), our somas are thus modelled by food even in our mother's womb. The importance of the maternal diet is attested not only in physiological and medical terms, but also in aesthetic ones. Already in intrauterine life, food flavours seem to concur in the shaping of the child's future food preferences.[1] To summarise, the smell of food has very deep roots: it is the first stimulus that puts humans in touch with the world, and its effects last throughout our existence.[2] If it is true that odours are the "first evidence of our fusion with the world" (Bachelard 1969, 136),

---

1   Holley 1999, 2006; some updated research articles include Todrank, Heth, Restrepo 2011; Ustun *et al.* 2022.
2   Kohl 2012.

it is even more so in the case of food flavours. Therefore, when defining an atmosphere as a "qualitative-sentimental *prius* [...] of our sensible encounter with the world" (Griffero 2014, 5), the atmospheric primacy accorded to smell we have sketched in the first chapter finds a degree of legitimacy in ontogenetic terms as well.

It is almost superfluous to recall the centrality of olfaction in savouring food during — but also before, after, and even regardless of — its ingestion. To resume a vivid metaphor by the godfather of gastronomy Jean-Anthelme Brillat-Savarin (1994, 41), the mouth is the laboratory whereas the nose acts as its chimney. In the appreciation of a meal, the olfactory component — either of the food itself or of other elements — plays a fundamental role. In the act of eating, taste and smell intimately cooperate, mingle and overlap, giving rise to *flavours,* which are precisely the complex combination of them. Indeed, it is worth underlining that, without smell, it is impossible to distinguish one food from another if they share their basic taste (sweet, salty, bitter, etc.). If one has a strong cold or plugs one's nostrils properly, a candy will only taste sweet, but one cannot recognise whether it is strawberry, raspberry or banana flavoured. For the anosmic, even discriminating between an orange and a lemon, between an apple and a sweet potato, between tea and coffee, etc., can be very difficult. Indeed, "where the sense of smell is lacking, the sense of taste is also badly missing", Kant (2006, §28, 61) observes. It is no coincidence that many of those who have lost their sense of smell experience a sensation of unfamiliarity toward previously "cosy" foods.

As a confirmation in the reverse direction, we can recall another covid-induced olfactory complication. *Parosmia*, smell distortion, makes eating extremely problematic. Food is commonly perceived as bland or awful; "rotten", "chemical" and "burnt" are the most frequent adjectives used to describe its flavours. In turn, this "acquired" disgust gives rise to a deep consternation (Parker *et al.* 2022), as if an intimate bond was suddenly broken. For that reason — together with eating disorders or unhealthy dietary behaviours — nostalgia, depression, sadness, unsociability and melancholy take over (Burges Watson *et al.* 2021, 10). The "ways that moods and thoughts affect eating, drinking, and digestion, and the ways these latter reciprocally affect our mental states" (Shusterman 2008, 184) are a key point in the philosophy of taste and food as well.[3] Here, the affective influence of flavours plays a fundamental role. Once food flavours are compromised, the whole act of eating takes on a negative

---

3   The literature is quite wide; see, for instance, Shepherd, Raats 2006; Kaplan 2012.

import, deeply affecting everyday life and psychic well-being. As inferable from many news articles published during or after the pandemic, holidays are the worst moments for the parosmic person, in that food constitutes the glue and excuse for gatherings. Indeed, gastronomy embodies human celebrations and rituals; as Bachelard (1964, 15) points out by considering the action of fire, it "does not confine itself to cooking; it makes things crisp and crunchy. It puts the golden crust on the griddle cake; it gives a material form to man's festivities". But whereas food makes festivities tangible and concrete, its osmosphere makes them emotional, symbolic, punctuating time and the relationships within a community. Parosmic people agree that this condition "really affects mental health" (Burges Watson *et al.* 2021, 12): on the one hand, the joy of conviviality and socialisation permeated by food disappears; on the other hand, from a spontaneous and positive act, nutrition turns into a psychological and perceptual torture. Cooking then becomes one of the most difficult tasks, and this can even cause a sense of guilt due to the impossibility of caring for others.

The act of smelling implies a deeply tangled somatic-sentimental intertwining, to the point that it suggests the impression of assimilating — even of *eating* — the odorous source.[4] Commenting on Baudelaire's poetics, Sartre (1950, 174) describes such a radical mingling as follows:

> The smell of a body is the body itself which we breathe in with our nose and mouth, which we suddenly possess as though it were its most secret substance and, to put the matter in a nutshell, its nature. The smell which is in me is the fusion of the body of the other person with my body; but it is the other person's body with the flesh removed, a vaporized body which has remained completely itself but which has become a volatile spirit.

The perception of atmosphere is therefore very similar to the assimilation of food. Indeed, as pointed out by Tellenbach (1968, 55), although the atmosphere emanating from someone appears to be a "surface phenomenon", it actually originates from deep inside them and affects those who are under its influence, striking their innermost chords. To put it differently, "the perception of an atmosphere knows the shortest way to reach my mood and to rouse here the most immediate resonances — 'resonances' because, by means of the same atmospheric itinerary, they reflect on the other who feels rejected or accepted" (ibid).[5] Not incidentally, some osmospheres are exemplified by resorting to food aromas, like sweet

---

4   On sense-making through the case of smell, see Waskul, Vannini 2008.
5   See Griffero 2020b for an account on the notions of *resonance* and *responsivity*.

memories that smell of pastries. As strong mood-shaping stimuli, often connected to old memories, food flavours emblematically provide space and time with a featuring atmospheric tone. Premised on the foundational affective nature of the food osmosphere, this chapter unfolds by illustrating this acquisition in its various forms. After an inquiry into how food flavours affectively qualify spaces and seasons, the investigation focuses on two cases. The first scrutinises food osmospheres in Italo Calvino's poetics, which elicits different perceptual possibilities and affective timbres that further problematise osmospheric experiences. The second looks into the relationships between flavours, atmospheres and gender.

2.2 *Scent Of Place, Scent Of Season*

> A special joy of travel is to acquaint oneself with the
> geography and microcosm of smells and tastes. Every city has
> its spectrum of tastes and odours.
> Juhani Pallasmaa

Cities can be understood as osmospheric successions, where food scents follow one another in spheres of influence. Tuan (1995, 64) provides us with an example by writing these lines:

> In a sophisticated metropolis, a shaded street, lined by a variety of shops, can offer a real treat to the connoisseur of fragrance. Strolling along, we may pause by a fruit-and-vegetable stand to inhale the tangy aroma from the crates of oranges and lemons, mixed with the earthier odors of cabbages and potatoes; next to it, a tray of secondhand books exudes a papery and faintly musty scent of inexplicable charm to the bibliophile; a coffeeshop spills samples of its aroma into the open air of the sidewalk, as does a shoe shop when its door swings open to admit customers; and from the well-dressed and coiffed women on an upscale street we catch whiffs of expensive perfume. Vendors contribute significantly to a great city's olfactory ambience.

More centred on food in its ecology, the following description by Juhani Pallasmaa (2012, 59) evokes what can be called the food osmospheric *genius loci* of a place:

> Sales counters on the streets are appetising exhibitions of smells: creatures of the ocean that smell of seaweed, vegetables carrying the odour of fertile earth, and fruits that exude the sweet fragrance of sun and moist summer air.

The menus displayed outside restaurants make us fantasise the complete course of a dinner; letters read by the eyes turn into oral sensations.

Given that smells "enable us to identify places and to identify ourselves with places" (Böhme 2017b, 125), our being-in-the-air takes on an osmospheric timbre depending on the smells the air is permeated by. Understood as an ephemeral but identitarian feature,[6] the *spirit of a place* is often condensed in an osmosphere. In *If on a Winter's Night a Traveler*, Italo Calvino (1981, 10) describes the olfactory *aura* of the train station, which is characterised by "a passing whiff of station café odor". After all, stations "are all alike", with their special odour "after the last train has left", together with "the odor of the platform [and] the odor of wet sawdust in the toilets, all mixed in a single odor which is that of waiting" (ibid, 11).

That a "city without smell is like a person without character" (Böhme 1998, 51) is a shared osmospheric experience. However, just as a person without character *has* a character, namely that of having no character, in the same way an odourless city has its own osmosphere. In other words, olfactory absence is a *deeply affective presence*. Annette Stenslund has devoted many studies to this perceptual phenomenon, for instance by observing the scentless aura surrounding an artwork mimicking a hospital, which actually *evokes* a harsh atmosphere (Stenslund 2017).[7] The same transpires by considering the osmosphere pervading the recent pandemic, specifically when lockdown measures were enforced: according to the peculiar odours of given places, their absence conveyed the atmospheric tension of the period. Louisa Allen makes the case study of a nondescript town in New Zealand. In this circumstance, during her "smellwalks", she noticed that the "absence of normal smells such as petrol, rotting food and rubbish signal an atmosphere of dis-ease" (Allen 2022, 273). If smells, and specifically food scents, are experienced as traces of existence, hence *lines of habitation*,[8] we can explain the profound sense of alienation triggered by the gap between the absent osmosphere and the usual one. Each hour of the day, for example dinnertime, brings with it a specific osmosphere which, if absent due to restaurant closures, still *pervades* the atmosphere or, better, still *is* an atmosphere. The absence of cooking aromas during the pandemic bout could be smelled. Conversely, the "return of people and routine activities created a plethora of hot food smells like the yeasty smell of bread from the bakery" (ibid, 274) that emphasised the osmospheric gap.

---

6   See Pallasmaa 2019.
7   For a "re-humanisation" of hospitals through smells, Perullo, Tonatto 2021.
8   See also Ngamcharoen 2021, 36.

Many people complain about a sense of unease caused by deodorised places, especially when this applies to food and gastronomy. This scentless osmosphere can be temporary, as we have just seen, or more generalised. There are several testimonies concerning the U.S. food osmosphere. Descriptions of New York's osmosphere are plentiful. For instance, Andy Warhol (1975, 152-153) provides us with an interesting and detailed osmospheric report of the Big Apple where food is the dominant element. Yu-Fu Tuan (1995, 64), in turn, notices that "New York's air has recently been sweetened by the aroma of honey-roasted peanuts"; similarly, according to Yuriko Saito (2017, 19), "New York City's 'sense of place' cannot be separated from the smell of burnt pretzels and chestnuts". On the contrary, the anthropologist Edward Hall compares the fragrant osmospheres lingering in various European towns to the odourless North American ones, which would lack olfactory diversity.[9] Unlike the latter, the former would be pervaded by nuanced smells which are mostly food-related; considering the "typical French town, one may savor the smell of coffee, spices, vegetables, freshly plucked fowl, clean laundry, and the characteristic odor of outdoor cafés. Olfaction of this type can provide a sense of life; the shifts and the transitions not only help to locate one in space but add zest to daily living" (Hall 1966, 47). As Böhme (2017b, 125) puts it, smells "are that quality of a surroundings which most intensely allows us to sense through our disposition (*Befinden*) *where* we are".

A correspondence can be found with Serres's (2008, 185) harsh invective against the U.S. food model — "America eats mush". Overseas, according to the French philosopher, the "mustard is insipid, tasteless; the beer, almost non-alcoholic, is flavourless; spices are bland, coffee weak and barely roasted, fruits and vegetables monotonous to the point of sameness. We can only differentiate between foods by the name and price on the label. Wine has been transformed into milk — white" (ibid). What is of interest to us is the parallel Serres draws between a tasteless, bland, monotonous, odourless food and a community whose bodies and minds become like the food they eat. Thinking and feeling, distinguishing and remembering, knowing and savouring (in Latin *sapere*, "to know", "to taste" and "to have/perceive flavours" coincide): all these actions and abilities correspond to the quality of the food by which they are sustained. Thus, humans, like their food — aseptic, without fragrance, taste and consistency — and its osmosphere, become *undifferentiated*: the human being turns into *homo insipiens* (ibid). The lack of flavours is reflected in

---

9   J. Douglas Porteous has the same opinion; Porteous 1996, 36-37.

the incapability of savouring and, hence, of knowing. Therefore, as Serres puts it, a general anaesthetisation takes place, exacerbated by the language, the only means, together with price, by which to discern among otherwise indistinguishable industrial ingredients. However, anaesthetisation has to do not only with the total absence of stimuli, but also with their excessive emphasis, intensity or homologation. As Ivan Illich (1985, 49-50) points out, most of us have "lost the ability to imagine the geographic variety that once could be perceived through the nose. Because increasingly the whole world has come to smell alike: gasoline, detergents, plumbing, and junk foods coalesce into the catholic smog of our age".

There is no need to spend many words on the identity value of food and cuisine; many scholars have investigated such a correlation, which is also the very basis of food studies in general.[10] What I would like to insist on here, instead, is the relationship between a food osmosphere and the affective experience of a place, the *genius loci* as a transitory yet persistent essence. Cultural studies and sensory history, both fields in great expansion and with much research on smell, have shed light on odour control strategies in city planning throughout the ages.[11] Besides, the notion of *smellscape* or, in French, *paysage olfactif*,[12] has also been adopted in relation to space and gastronomy.[13] Indeed, an important role is commonly played by the variety of food smells; not only those wafting from markets, restaurants and private kitchens, whose osmospheres reveal culinary customs, key ingredients, traditional dishes and different habits including meal times and frequency, but also those of food, crop and livestock industries.[14] In a mutual relation, olfactory sensitivity as well as the aesthetic value of odours at a given time and place are moulded by their connection to spaces. Cities create food smells, while food

---

10   One of the first accounts is Fischler 1988. To give just one example, Simone de Beauvoir (1962, 71) tells us that, according to Gilde, "to drink a cup of hot Spanish chocolate was to hold all Spain in one's mouth". The topic of identity in osmospheric and socio-aesthetic terms is developed in ch. 3.

11   Since antiquity, the aromatic profile of buildings has been considered paramount (Tuan 1995, 64-65). The literature is wide: Corbin 1986; Drobnick 2005; Barbara, Perliss 2006; Bradley 2015, in particular Koloski-Ostrow 2015. See also Toner 2016.

12   Fraigneau 2019, Hassine *et al.* 2021.

13   Dulau, Pitte 1998.

14   Henshaw 2014, 85-112. See http://goodcitylife.org/smellymaps/ for olfactory interactive maps of different cities, designed by computer scientists. Food flavours constitute a specific category that can be isolated from other olfactory classes such as emissions and nature.

smells physically shape cities. This is evident in urban planning projects based on odour-producing industries, and the value of neighbourhoods depending on the osmosphere they are surrounded by. For instance, slaughterhouses in Europe, strong-smelling places as they are, before modernity used to be located near the city centre or spread over several locations. In the second half of the 19th century, slaughterhouses in Paris were concentrated in a specific area, "La Villette", together with abattoirs, markets and warehouses. This positioning change was the result of the new urban middle-class aesthetic sensitivity, which reflected the desire to conceal "the ugly side of human existence out of sight and smell" (Claflin 2005, 58).

As Janus-faced stimuli, food smells can trigger a sense of belonging as well as of strangeness, of pleasure or disgust, of comfort or discomfort: food osmospheres are not always positive *ipso facto*. In reality, they are often intertwined with social issues and contrasts. As we shall see, food osmospheres are diversified, sometimes putting a strain on social coexistence. Moreover, their aesthetic value cannot be distinguished from the space where they linger; hence, their quality is always contextual. Just as a joyful atmosphere is disturbing if it occurs in a painful circumstance or in a space that requires reserved seriousness, in the same way a food osmosphere, albeit usually pleasant, turns negative if mismatched to the location it pervades. Endless examples could be given. As Saito (2007, 122) observes, "the smell of turkey roasting in the oven, the indispensable ingredient of the American celebration of Thanksgiving Day, will not be appreciable if it is wafting through an operating room in a hospital"; similarly, the "strong smell of coffee that we enjoy in a Starbucks cafe is not going to be positively experienced if it permeates a small Japanese *sushi* stand" (ibid).[15]

However, the reverse is also true, and "bad" food odours can give rise to positive atmospheres. Saito provides the example of the stench of rotten eggs, revolting on almost any occasion except when diving into a volcanic sulphureous wind. To evoke the air lingering in a ghastly party, Woolf (2003, 205) notes that there was "an atmosphere so repellent that it became, like the smell of bad cheese, repulsively fascinating". Conversely, in a comic episode of *Three Men in a Boat* by

---

15   It is precisely based on the logic of congruity and non-contradiction between smell and place that *scent marketing* designs its products, an aspect which concurs in corroborating the inherent "atmosphericity" of smells. Scent marketing, addressed in ch. 4, has several synonyms, such as olfactory/aroma/smell marketing; I will use them interchangeably.

Jerome K. Jerome, the stink of cheese causes profound embarrassment and even anger in those forced to endure it, only to eventually — once allocated somewhere else — turn into something highly appreciated. When discussing the food supply for their two-week boating holiday, the three men agree not to include cheese among the foods to be stored because it "makes too much of itself. There is too much odour about cheese" (Jerome 1960, 50). At this point, the narrator tells of the time when a friend of his asked him to take to London some cheeses he had bought in Liverpool. "Splendid cheese they were, ripe and mellow, and with a two-hundred horse-power scent about them that might have been warranted to carry three miles, and knock a man over at two hundred yards" (ibid). He then describes his journey accompanied by this osmospheric presence, first in a carriage and then by train, with several humorous events caused by the smell. From the horse dragging the carriage, which bolted as soon as it got a whiff of the odour, and which could only be calmed by plugging its nose, to the different reactions of the passengers sharing the same train compartment (and, complaints aside, the undeniable advantage of getting everyone to leave). Even the most stoic of wagon-mates, who remained seated after mocking the exaggerated drama of others, "grew strangely depressed" (ibid, 52) and, after being offered a drink as an apology for the osmospheric disturbance, got into another carriage. After arriving with the cheeses at the house, following further vicissitudes, including his friend's wife deciding to go to a hotel to avoid the smell, the narrator recalls that his mate eventually managed to get rid of them by burying the cheese wheels in the beach of a seaside town. Like the smell of rotten eggs carried by a sulphureous wind, it "gained the place quite a reputation. Visitors said they had never noticed before how strong the air was, and weak-chested and consumptive people used to throng there for years afterwards" (ibid, 55). The hilarious journey recounted in the novel by Jerome finds parallels in real stories, such as non-fictional tales in the 20th-century memoirs of Jews settled in the Mississippi and Arkansas Delta. Jewish women would load ice coolers into their cars on their way to different cities, especially New York, to bring kosher food back home. One woman remembers her grandfather bringing back to Paragould, Arkansas, foods such as bagels, lox, corned beef, and dark loaves of pumpernickel bought in St. Louis. Whereas on the outward train journey he sat with his friends, on the return journey he was left alone "because the smell of salami and pastrami was too strong for his companions" (Ferris 2018, 314).

Indeed, every cuisine has its own osmosphere; we dwell in urban osmospheres, navigating our way through an amalgam of food flavours. Often, we become attached to places precisely because of their olfactory *qua* atmospheric welcoming quality. De Beauvoir used to be partial to German cuisine, with a particular predilection for red cabbage, smoked pork and *Bauernfrühstück*. But what she especially liked was the osmosphere hovering in some places: "I was not attracted by the *Konditorei*, which were rather like teashops; but the brasseries, with their big, solid tables and rich aroma of cooking, I found extremely comfortable, and we often lunched in them" (de Beauvoir 1962, 146). Sartre, too, had preferences based on food osmospheres; in fact, he adored the Brasserie Demorie precisely for "its heavy smell of beer and sauerkraut" (ibid, 19). As an artistic case based on the rendering of national food osmospheres in images, it is worth mentioning the hand-painted postage stamps of fictional nations by American artist Donald Evans. His fictitious geography is a visual diary of feelings and experiences created in order to preserve the affective qualities of places. As Calvino notes in his short essay *Stamps from States of Mind*, "it was above all through food that Evans established his relationship with countries, catching their most typical flavours and aromas during his travels" (Calvino 2013a, 141). Indeed, the series of the country "Mangiare" was created after a journey in Italy; stamps illustrate a wide variety of ingredients, dishes and seasonings such as "pesto alla genovese", evoking the actual, rather than fictional, food osmosphere the artist smelled in the visited regions and remembered as an affective condensation.

Together with places, food osmospheres provide periods of time with an affective character. "During World War II in France", Hall (1966, 47) maintains, "I observed that the aroma of French bread freshly removed from the oven at 4:00 A.M. could bring a speeding jeep to a screaming halt". During conflicts, a food osmosphere is the symbol of times of peace, hence of life as opposed to death. In the prewar period, when the prodromes of World War II are *hovering*, de Beauvoir reports something similar, treating the air of Paris as the carrier of smells *qua* feelings. She remembers, while walking back to Montparnasse, a "wonderful autumn morning: the fresh smell of carrots and cabbages along the Boulevard Sébastopol..." (de Beauvoir 1962, 304). But when she comes out of the cinema in the afternoon, the air has changed, it is now *heavy*: Nazi Germany prepares to invade Poland and the outbreak of war, long feared, becomes impending; the food osmosphere leaves room to something undefined but frightening. The contrast between the reassuring air full of the smells of vegetables, evidence of normal life going on, and an air weighed down by omens on the point of becoming reality demonstrates to what extent food qualifies an osmosphere by connoting it in an affective sense. In this case, the air that smells of food has in itself a vital meaning that contrasts with an imminent danger.

The dense pages devoted by Bachelard (1969, 116) to seasons as "the fundamental mark of memories" take it as a given that each recollection recalls a season and a flavour: "pure memory has no date. It has a *season*" (ibid). Given the close connections between smells, food, childhood and memory, if each recollection has a season, every season has a flavour. Food osmospheres are significant sources of time as a dimension that persists in its change. As Lefebvre (2004, 21) puts it, "smells are a part of rhythms, reveal them: odours of the morning and evening, of hours of sunlight or darkness, of rain or fine weather. The rhythm analyst observes and retains smells as traces that mark out rhythms". Each season, despite increasing homogenisation, is characterised by specific foods, which are linked to the availability of raw materials, traditional recipes and procedures that mark the cyclical nature of each season, with its celebrations and rituals.[16] Spicy sweets condense the atmosphere of winter and Christmas festivities, whereas a whiff of roasted chestnut is not simply an aroma; rather, it is the osmosphere that carries within itself the quality of autumn. Keller (2003, 42) depicts a beautiful image when she says that autumn smells of persimmon trees, "the odour of which pervaded every nook and corner of the wood — an illusive, fragrant something that made the heart glad". Anything but heartening is instead the autumnal food osmosphere redolent of stale sausages and turnips experienced by Marcovaldo, the protagonist of the eponymous novel by Calvino (subtitled: *Or, The Seasons in the City*). After a more general introduction, what follows is, starting from *Marcovaldo*'s episode "The lunch box", a brief analysis that investigates some of Calvino's works where episodes about food flavours have a bearing on the plot or show the affective power of food osmospheres.

---

16   For an anthropological case on seasons and rhythm, Krause 2013.

2.3 *Flavours In Italo Calvino*

> But on reading *schoëblintsjia* you are ready to swear to the
> existence of *schoëblintsjia*, you can taste its flavor distinctly
> even though the text doesn't say what that flavor is, an
> acidulous flavor, partly because the word, with its sound or
> only with its visual impression, suggests an acidulous flavor to
> you, and partly because in the symphony of flavors and words
> you feel the necessity of an acidulous note.
> Italo Calvino

Unlike Proust, Calvino's poetics is anything but eminently olfactive: smell is systematically addressed only in *The Name, the Nose*, which is discussed in the next chapter. Nonetheless, there are still scents lingering in his literary imaginary. From *The Argentine Ant*, where everything is infested by ants and saturated with their odour, to the *Italian Folktales*, in which flavours are often triggers to food cravings for poor and hungry people. In *The Baron in the Trees*, food aroma is even a narrative device, since the protagonist confines himself to a life on the trees encouraged by his aversion to the flavour of a dish of snails cooked by his creepy sister. *Invisible Cities* opens up with a sense of emptiness conveyed by "the odor of the elephants after the rain and the sandalwood ashes growing cold in the braziers" (Calvino 1974, 5); in addition, the smell of fish in the city of Eudoxia is just one of the aesthetic elements that draws attention to the partial perspective of the perceiver. The same smell, in the *Cosmicomics*, wafts in from the underbelly of the Moon, conveying *her* feminine and maternal olfactory code,[17] reinforced by the tart flavour of her milk as sensuous counterbalances to a highly abstract narration. Leaving aside further olfactory examples, there are some episodes where eating, flavours and gastronomy play a relevant role, and food osmospheres are used in such a peculiar way as to make them interesting for our inquiry. Respectively, *Marcovaldo* shows the extent to which the emotional value of food osmosphere depends on the relationship between the eater and the person who prepared the food. In *Under the Jaguar Sun* and *Palomar*, the core issue lies in the intertwining between sensing and knowing, and in the role of sight and words in perceiving and expressing flavours. Finally, *Theft in a Cakeshop* opens up to speculations on the contradictory affective

---

17   See Cavallaro 2010, 54.

values inherent in the same food osmosphere. Let us investigate them in this order.

In "The lunch box", the pleasure of eating is chiefly spoiled by the familiar atmosphere of Marcovaldo, the tragicomic personification of a human being in the capitalistic society who, as an inveterate dreamer, craves to experience nature in its seasonal variation in an urban and hostile environment.[18] Every day, the proletarian Marcovaldo goes to work and, to save time and money, eats his noon meal brought from home outdoors, near his work place. Describing the flow of Marcovaldo's (sometimes opposing) moods and perceptions, bodily movements and reflections, Calvino sketches a kind of detailed phenomenology of the experience of food consumed from the lunch-box.[19] "The joys of that round and flat vessel [...]", the incipit reads, "consists first of all in its having a screw-on top" (Calvino 1983a, 31), being this very action preparatory to foretaste its content, all the more so when one does *not* know what food is served. In this case, it is always prepared by his wife Domitilla. A sense of mystery is the key ingredient in this initial phase of pleasure,[20] but Marcovaldo's expectations are almost invariably disappointed. At that stage, after having opened the box, he quickly sniffs the aroma, and then pokes the food with the fork to make it more visually attractive. However, such an operation, while embellishing the lunch, often reveals its small amount; Marcovaldo resolves to carefully measure the timing of each bite, chewing as slowly as his hunger allows. Once the food enters his mouth, the "immediate sensation is the sadness of eating cold food, but the joys promptly begin again as you find the flavors of the family board transported to an unusual setting" (ibid, 32). While eating, a thought looms up: "Why am I so happy to taste the flavor of my wife's cooking here, when at home, among the quarrels and tears, the debts that crop up in every conversation, I can't enjoy it?" (ibid). The question is rhetorical; however, there is an additional reason: Marcovaldo realises that these are the leftovers from the night before. Right away, "he is immediately seized again by discontent, perhaps

---

18   Cantarin, Marino 2018.
19   On the aesthetics of the Japanese lunchbox, Ekuan 1998.
20   Something similar can be found in the novel *In Praise of Shadows* by Jun'ichirō
      Tanizaki (1977, 15), that reads "Remove the lid from a ceramic bowl, and there lies
      the soup, every nuance of its substance and color revealed. [...] What lies within
      the darkness one cannot distinguish, but the palm senses the gentle movements of
      the liquid, vapor rises from within forming droplets on the rim, and the fragrance
      carried upon the vapor brings a delicate anticipation. [...] A moment of mystery, it
      might almost be called, a moment of trace". I thank Yuriko Saito for introducing
      it to me.

because he has to eat leftovers, cold and a bit soured, perhaps because the aluminum of the lunch-box gives the food a metallic taste" (ibid). However, this is not so much a gastronomic issue but, rather, an affective one: "but the notion lodged in his head is: The thought of Domitilla manages to spoil my meals even when I'm far away from her" (ibid). Like a clearing mist, the concern is then replaced by appetite, which increases as the food quantity diminishes and eventually ends; then sorrow takes over again.

In this humdrum routine, the monotony is paradoxically broken up when Domitilla serves sausages and turnips for three dinners and as many lunches. Again, Marcovaldo ascribes his repulsion to the food itself instead of gustatory boredom and the feeling of being neglected. The sausages taste like dog meat, especially due to their unbearable stench; turnip is indeed the only vegetable he dislikes anyway. However, naïve and absent-minded as he is, for three days Marcovaldo repeats the above sketched ritual, in an unchanged sequence of expectancy and frustration; on the fourth, after smelling the same disgusting odour, he starts roaming around inattentively, carrying his untouched lunch with him. The episode ends with Marcovaldo gladly enjoying a plate of fried brains, the result of a food exchange with a child confined to his room and looking out of the window of an elegant villa, punished because he had refused to consume his meal. To the child's exchange proposal, "Marcovaldo looked at the dish on the sill. There were fried brains, soft and curly as a pile of clouds. *His nostrils twitched*" (ibid, 34 [my italics]). Thus, both greedily eat the food of the other, "declaring they had never tasted such good food" (ibid).

Here, gustatory pleasure seems corroborated not so much by the aesthetic qualities of the food itself; rather, by the wealthy atmosphere of the household and, most of all, by the lack of negative connotations ascribable to the affective traits of food. In other words, while eating sausages and turnips, Marcovaldo *savours* his existence made of a noisy and crammed house in an industrial grey city in northern Italy, and of financial difficulties worsened by six children and Domitilla, whose pragmatism dissuades Marcovaldo from sharing his dreamy world with her. The osmosphere of her cuisine, her atmosphere, is absorbed as well. Unlike the usual co-implication of food, flavours and the atmosphere of love, comfort and care that often crystallises around the female figure who cooks the domestic meal, Domitilla's food is therefore stale and disturbing.

Different is the osmospheric relationship between the main characters of *Under the Jaguar Sun*, whose plot is quite simple: an Italian married couple — the protagonist/narrator and Olivia — goes on a trip to Mexico to discover the country through its cuisine and to revive a lengthy relationship that has been gradually cooling down. *Sapore, Sapere*[21] is the pun originally chosen by Calvino for what is known today as *Under the Jaguar Sun*, the essay on taste that entitles the whole book,[22] ideally designed as a collection devoted to the five senses though published posthumously and incomplete. The issues of knowledge, the senses, body and thought, which punctuate Calvino's whole *corpus*, are here key points. In fact, the aesthetic *as* epistemological quality of the trip comes to light in the middle of the story: "the true journey, as the introjection of an 'outside' different from our normal one, implies a complete change of nutrition, a digesting of the visited country" (Calvino 1988, 12). In order to *know/taste* a place "authentically",[23] one has to *sense* its flavours in the first person, carrying out an exercise of presence. The impossibility for odours and flavours to be transferred also entails that this presence can be replaced neither by mediatic transposition nor by a recreation of the original setting, such as exotic restaurants in big cities. To properly savour a place and its cuisine, we have to dive into its air, its osmosphere. However, despite claiming the necessity of first-hand engagement and a perceptual attunement, Calvino largely draws on a mediated, mainly *optic*, experience of food flavours. Indeed, their *visual* rendering is a recurrent aspect of Calvino's poetics, and *Under the Jaguar Sun* is permeated by a multiplying kaleidoscope effect. In a nutshell, the reader savours the osmospheres through the protagonist as he observes his wife Olivia perceiving them. Her facial expressions and the rhythmical movements of her lips and eyes reveal the unfolding of the aromatic experience. The observation of her nose plays a pivotal role:

> I followed the tension as it moved from her lips to her nostrils, flaring one moment, contracting the next (the plasticity of the nose is quite limited [...] and each barely perceptible attempt to expand the capacity of the nostrils in the longitudinal direction actually makes them thinner, while the corresponding reflex movement, accentuating their breadth, then seems a kind of withdrawal of the whole nose into the surface of the face) (ibid, 9).

What Calvino describes in "extroverted" terms, has important "introvert" causes and consequences. Flavours change according to the

---

21   I have already pointed out the semantic overlap between "to savour/taste, to have flavour" and "to know".
22   Biasin 1993, 97.
23   The complexity of this notion cannot be unravelled here; in relation to exotic food and travelling, see Heldke 2005, Koczanowicz 2017.

actions performed by the eater: the same food or beverage tastes different if it is chewed slowly or rapidly and barely, if it is gulped down or held at length in the oral cavity, if it is sucked, munched, sipped, ruminated, or chomped. In reverse, the actions correspond to the aesthetic value of what is perceived while eating. We usually assume that a food is disgusting if we see that it is nibbled hesitantly, or it is swallowed in one gulp to taste it as little as possible; on the contrary, a delicacy is slowly savoured to prolong the pleasure, or avidly devoured. The respiratory movements of the eater tell us whether its flavours are appreciated or not. Hence, the body works as a resonance chamber, concurrently expressing its experience. Eating is therefore a social act in its most radical sense: observing the other, one can grasp the bodily stirrings which mirror the inner sensations. The relationship between Olivia and the protagonist heavily relies on this osmospheric, albeit reflexive, sharing:

> What I have just said might suggest that, in eating, Olivia became closed into herself, absorbed with the inner course of her sensations; in reality, on the contrary, the desire her whole person expressed was that of communicating to me what she was tasting: communicating with me through flavors, or communicating with flavors through a double set of taste buds, hers and mine (ibid).

Calvino's reflexivity opens up an aesthetics of eating that moves from a mainly self-centred inquiry to an other-directed investigation, therefore exceeding the borders of the individual. To put it differently, *Under the Jaguar Sun* shows well that, in "the universe of taste, everything [...] is caught in the same spiral of fluid transformation, in a relentless whirl of melting and flowing processes, and hence defined by a drastic rupture of conventional barriers between self and other" (Cavallaro 2010, 180). Rather than a sort of taste at a distance, or a visual savouring by proxy, Calvino sheds light on the importance of attuning proprioception to mirrored perception, showing in what ways sight conveys flavours. As the jingle goes, food tastes better when shared, but this story offers an original extroverted aesthetic understanding of such a pleasure: Olivia's and the protagonist's subjective selves "find their amplification and completion only in the unity of the couple" (Calvino 1988, 10). In this sense, Calvino goes even further. As a first step, the sexuality of the couple is replaced by the aphrodisiac power of Mexican cuisine whose peculiarity lies in stimulating desires "that sought their satisfaction only within the very sphere of sensation that had aroused them — in eating new dishes" (ibid). This self-referential and solipsistic orientation blurs the boundaries between chaste and carnal love, because of the "experience of flavors gained through secret and subtle complicity" (ibid, 11).

The two characters do not have the same aesthetic and osmospheric attitude. Olivia is "more sensitive to perceptive nuances and endowed with a more analytical memory" (ibid), paying great attention to subtle sensations, almost stopping her movements, concentrated and concerned, "as if reluctant to allow an inner echo to fade" (ibid, 8) — an evident homage to the Proustian madeleine episode. She tensely inquires of her husband, assuming they are having the same experience: "Did you taste that? Are you tasting it? […] Is it *cilandro*? Can't you taste *cilandro*?" (ibid, 9). Olivia acts as a "nose", the person who gains, through education, an *organ* which is able to distinguish the slightest olfactory shades. Condensing in one sentence a re-elaboration of Condillac's philosophical system, Serres writes that the "intellect is empty if the body has never knocked about, if the nose has never quivered along the spice route" (Serres 2008, 163), and, as Bruno Latour (2004, 207) aptly maintains, perceptual skills imply that the body learns to be affected; in his words, "body parts are progressively acquired at the same time as 'world counter-parts' are being registered in a new way". In so doing, the person achieves *sapere* in its double meaning: the capacity of sensing, which corresponds to the ability of detecting and knowing hitherto unperceivable variations. As a counterbalance to Olivia's nose, the protagonist seems to be hindered by smell and taste obtusity, and tends "more to define experiences verbally and conceptually" (Calvino 1988, 11).

As he is presumably the counterpart to the writer himself, it is interesting to quote a passage where Calvino mockingly pinpoints the perceptual difficulties he encountered in the process of writing *Under the Jaguar Sun*:

> My problem in writing this book is that my sense of smell isn't very developed, I lack auditory attention, I'm not a gourmet, my tactile sensitivity is approximate, and I'm nearsighted. For each of the five senses I have to make an effort that allows me to master a range of sensations and nuances. […] [M]y goal is not so much to make a book as to change myself, which I think should be the goal of every human undertaking (Calvino 2023, 129-130).

Lamenting his perceptual dullness, Calvino suggests the existential potentialities of improving sensory skills and the sentient body, namely *that* kind of aesthetic cultivation in which many philosophical currents such as somaesthetics are rooted.[24] Nonetheless, as a writer, he digs into the depths

---

24   For a comparison between somaesthetics and new phenomenology, Griffero 2021b.

of language "in order to foreground the lunacy inherent in any attempt to grasp conclusively the mysteries of perception and communication alike" (Cavallaro 2010, 14). Calvino's lexical choices endeavour to express the very flavour of the referent, so that the reader can savour it. Although Calvino never systematised an aesthetic theory, he "considered the medium of literature as both an intellectual and a sense-simulating instrument" (Ricci 2001, 91). In the effort of extending the perceptual effects of literature, Calvino creates a synesthetic language. Every word, with its sound, has a flavour, which corresponds to its osmosphere. This arises in connection with *gorditas pellizcadas con manteca*, the name of meatballs through which the protagonist "eats", in a sort of metaphorical cannibalism, Olivia's osmosphere. Similarly, in the second incipit of *If on a Winter's Night a Traveler*, the question emerges in relation to *schoëblintsjia*. Even if readers do not know what kind of dish *schoëblintsjia* is, they "can taste its flavor distinctly even though the text doesn't say what that flavor is, an acidulous flavor" (Calvino 1981, 35).[25]

Inversely, Olivia accuses his husband of being *insipid*. Her nose seems to get provisionally used to the intrusive osmosphere of Mexican food; her husband is *insipid* inasmuch as Olivia's smell cannot taste/know the flavours dulled down by violent stimuli. It is the problem of overstimulation: the exaggeration of aesthetic stimuli generates not only problems of attention but also an elevation of the perceptual threshold, followed by an anaesthetisation which smooths out those subtle differences. Here, Calvino's poetics gives an anticipation of the main aesthetic problem our century is suffering from, supporting the urge of an aesthetic education to fully appreciate experiences that are not necessarily extraordinary. Indeed, the protagonist protests by claiming that "there are ranges of flavor more discreet and restrained than that of red peppers. There are subtle tastes that one must know how to perceive!" (Calvino 1988, 25). Similarly to the case described in *Marcovaldo*, the charge of being insipid is the result of an osmospheric relationship which is unbalanced and unsatisfactory to Olivia. Again, the gustatory domain transcends food and the act of eating, qualifying the sensual atmosphere of a marriage.

Like the senses-themed collection *Under the Jaguar Sun*, the writing process of *Palomar* can also be considered a kind of aesthetic exercise carried out by Calvino himself. Despite his personal lack in observatory and descriptive skills,[26] sight is the perceptual modality that dominates

---

25 Salvatori 1986, 207-208.
26 Calvino 2023, 128-129.

the book, even when food and flavours are involved. Mr. Palomar, albeit near-sighted and astigmatic, takes his name from the Palomar astronomical telescope in California, implying the aspiration to escape subjectivity and to describe isolated things as they *appear*.[27] However, the more the experiential field is circumscribed, the more it multiplies and becomes leaky and complex, hindering Mr. Palomar in his anxious pursuit of the truth as a single and absolute principle. Seeking the *essence* of what he observes, his ontological inquiry invariably ends up in failure. In *Mr. Palomar Does the Shopping* and, specifically, in the episodes "Two pounds of goose fat" and "The cheese museum", this occurs with respect to food osmospheres.

"Two pounds of goose fat" takes place in a charcuterie in Paris at Christmas; Mr. Palomar is queuing, surrounded by delicacies. His attention is caught by the glass jar that contains goose fat, and he tries to remember the flavour of cassoulet, a French stew of meat and beans. In a visual metaphor, the goose limbs immersed in their fat can only be half-seen like a dark shadow in a fog of memories. However, contemplating the jar, "neither his palate's memory nor his cultural memory is of any help to him" (Calvino 1985, 67). Instead of being taken by an overall osmosphere, and then possibly circumscribing or analysing it, Calvino seeks to walk the reverse path: he tries to evoke it from distinctive elements. All the foods displayed in the shop window are described in their visual appearance: tapestries and coats of arms are just some of the analogies adopted to optically convey the edible diversity in front of him — a vivid variety in contrast with the grey opacity of customers. Indeed, it is precisely Palomar's *voyeurism* that prevents him from recalling the osmospheres he would like to perceive. The conflict between sight, smell and recollection recurs here: when Mr. Palomar *looks around*, expecting to feel "the vibration of an orchestra of flavors" (ibid, 69), everything keeps silent: the "delicacies stir in him imprecise, blurred memories; his imagination does not instinctively associate flavors with images and names. He asks himself if his gluttony is not chiefly mental, aesthetic, symbolic. [...] [H]is gaze transforms every food into a document of the history of civilization, a museum exhibit" (ibid, 69-70).

Something similar occurs in "The cheese museum", set in a Paris cheese shop. Here, too, Mr. Palomar has an ocular (and nomenclative)[28] approach: he *sees* names, concepts, meanings, histories, contexts and psychologies of

---

27   Wood 1994, Heaney 2001, Baldi 2019.
28   The cheese shop appears to Mr. Palomar also as a *dictionary*, with appellatives, lexical variants, synonyms, etc. of all the cheeses.

cheeses, fully aware that even the most detailed classification of cheeses according to their forms, textures and ingredients "would not bring him a step closer to true knowledge, which lies in the experience of the flavors, composed of memory and imagination at once" (ibid, 73). Though not a gourmet, Mr. Palomar knows, but without *savouring* it, that, among other things, behind every cheese there are "meadows caked with salt that the tides of Normandy deposit every evening; meadows scented with aromas in the windy sunlight of Provence" (ibid).

Elsewhere, Calvino (2013b, 118) states that "the retina is a peripheral portion of the cerebral cortex", venturing that "the brain begins in the eye" (ibid, 119). In spite of Calvino's renowned fascination with the visual, it would be wrong to blame him for the naïve belief that sight is a passive, unfiltered and neutral detection of objective facts. As emerges from Mr. Palomar's inquiries, *seeing* is a complex action attuned to a broad spectrum of circumstances and situations, and depending on the *use* of the gaze.[29] In contrast to *Under the Jaguar Sun*, where sight is employed as an affective and transmodal medium, Mr. Palomar's way of scrutinising, aspiring to be a mirror of the reality as an isolated object, noticeably inhibits the affective *reciprocal relationship* (Calvino 1985, 72) between him and the food, seeking the self-sufficient, crystallised and icastic "image" of flavours, hence impeding their osmospheric disclosing. For that reason, Mr. Palomar cannot create "a scale of preferences and taste and curiosities and exclusions" (ibid, 73) that would help him choose his cheese amidst the proliferation of potentially endless options. Lost in his ruminations and trying to memorise each visible dairy product, he starts to sketch in his notebook a categorisation system through names and visual details. At this point, taken by surprise when the salesgirl calls him, he gets confused, and the "elaborate and greedy order that he intended to make momentarily slips his mind" (ibid, 74-75), ending up opting for the most trivial and advertised cheese, the result of *visual* conditioning by mass media.

Whereas in *Palomar* the food osmosphere is craved but eventually not felt, in *Theft in a Cakeshop* the food osmosphere generates an uncontrollable craving that cannot be fully satisfied. Set in poverty-stricken post-war Italy, this short story describes the misdemeanour of

---

29 As philosophers have largely argued, despite the traditional superiority of sight as the sense of "disinterest", "science", "knowledge, even of "mind", it is not possible to sharply dissociate the cognitive from the affective. The mind itself has acquired the shape of "a bodily-affective instrument oriented to the 'knowing-how' (*pathos*), whose realizations are at least partly due to bodily-environmental structures and processes" (Griffero 2017b, 71).

three miserable thieves slipping inside a pastry shop to steal the cash. Here, the primacy of smell comes out from the very beginning, when the leader of the gang, Dritto, employs his nostrils to show the way to his cronies: Baby, the most important character of the story, and Uora-Uora, the lookout. To ease the way for Dritto and break into the shop, Baby has to climb up onto a window. In that moment, "he became aware of the smell; he took a deep breath and up through his nostrils wafted an aroma of freshly baked cakes. *It gave him a feeling of shy excitement, of remote tenderness, rather than of actual greed*" (Calvino 1983b, 98 [my italics]). This positive emotion is coupled with a sense of frustration due to the fact that it "was years since he had eaten a proper bit of cake, not since before the war perhaps" (ibid). Using his hands to make his way into the pitch-black laboratory to let Dritto in, Baby finds himself surrounded by cakes: in an alternation of tactile disgust, olfactory seduction and gustatory impulse, horror and pure happiness, he is so engrossed in this intrusive, sweet and sticky presence that he forgets about his task. The reader immediately *smells* that the situation is doomed to get out of control. Indeed, when Dritto lights up the darkness with his torch, Baby's ambiguous and somewhat repulsive contact with sweets converts into a bottomless optic yearning. In front of that abundant and splendid "land of milk and money" (ibid, 100), Baby gets overwhelmed with anxiety, worrying about time pressure in contrast to the urge to sample everything. Whereas the osmosphere of sweets inspires a delicate feeling in him, the touch and then the sight of them lead him to violently throw himself headlong into them. So he begins bingeing

> *without even tasting them*; he seemed to be battling with the cakes, as if they were threatening enemies, strange monsters besieging him, a crisp and sticky siege which he must break through by the force of his jaw (ibid [my italics]).

"In gluttony", Benjamin (1999, 358) observes, "two things coincide: the boundlessness of desire and the uniformity of the food that sates it".[30] This is a *compulsive indifference* to taste (Perullo 2016, 101-102) that, conversely, takes on the traits of the food's tactile and visual salience. If

---

30   Benjamin's episode takes place in Naples, where he is buying plenty of colourful figs. As the seller has no wrapping paper, he is compelled to squeeze them all into his pockets, hands, and mouth. The description has manifold perceptual similarities with Calvino's story, since smell, taste, sight and touch acquire conflicting values.

taste and smell fade, the haptic and optic dimension prevails, to the extent that Baby "still felt a kind of frenzy he did not know how to satisfy; [...] he would have liked to lie down in those tarts, cover himself with them" (Calvino 1983b, 101), becoming again repulsive. So Baby

> found that he no longer had any desire for cakes, in fact a feeling of nausea was beginning to creep up from the pit of his stomach, but he refused to believe it, he simply could not give up yet. And the doughnuts began to turn into soggy pieces of sponge, the tarts to flypaper and the cakes to asphalt. Now he saw only the corpses of cakes lying putrifying on their marble slabs, or felt them disintegrating like turgid glue inside his stomach (ibid, 102).

An inquiry on disgust as the extreme stage of food pleasure would probably devote much attention to touch, which represents the ambivalent and almost simultaneous fluctuation between voracity and repletion, delight and nausea, not to mention conflicting impulses which transform into physical tensions towards incorporating the "foe" or pushing it away. Differently, smell usually acts in order to prevent ingestion; in the extreme cases in which such dramatic gluttony overwhelms the eater, flavours give way to the substantiality of food and its frictions. If "the smell of a good dinner greets the nostrils and tempts the taste-buds" (Brillat-Savarin 1994, 323), it can also lead to an unbridled voracity that often ends up overlooking the very stimuli that set it in motion.

For Baby, in the osmosphere of sweets a positive affection initially coexists with a negative one, as if through the aromas of baked goods he also perceived poverty, social inequality and crime. The way he gobbles food and attends to his tactile reactions unveils the complexity of bodily stirrings he person is assailed with. Moreover, the osmospheric contrast is exacerbated by the gap between the type of food — delicate sweet products, each with a name that conveys traditions, crafts, human geography, rituals, etc. — and its dramatic and feral consumption. This takes on erotic nuances in the epilogue which plays on the classic intertwining among sweet food, gluttony and sex. The story ends with Baby grabbing some sweets and squeezing them under his shirt to bring them as a gift to his girlfriend. In the final scene, she and he are "lying on the bed licking and picking at each other till they had finished the last crumb of cake and blob of cream" (Calvino 1983b, 104). A further interpretation might be as follows. The aroma of baked cakes, which conveyed to him "a feeling of shy excitement, of remote tenderness" (ibid, 98), osmospherises a sense of security and *maternal* care that Baby — *nomen omen* — yearningly seeks as a compensation for his existence filled with risks and insecurities.

2.4 *Food Smells, Gender And Home*

The snoring, the rain, and Mama's hair
that smells like bread.
Sandra Cisneros

Philosophy could be reproached of overlooking gender issues when discussing atmospheres, a subject — the so-called *retail atmospherics*[31] — which is inversely much explored by consumer science for its effectiveness in "emotional marketing".[32] Several scented commodities are precisely designed in order to convey gendered food-related atmospheres, which are symptomatic of the collective imagination around food, cooking, gender and "sense of home".[33] Certainly, thinking of "feminine" and "masculine" in terms of deep unconscious principles of the subject would betray and misrepresent a theory whose main purpose is, at least in Schmitz's view, to de-psychologise emotional life proposing an anti-introjectionist conception of atmospheres. However, "externalising" sexualised principles and understanding them as *affordances*[34] in the relationship between the dweller and the environment, allows one to test the opportunity to integrate theories on atmospheres with intuitions on genders as spatial tendencies. While discussing the coextensivity of sexuality with human life, Maurice Merleau-Ponty (2012, 172) describes it as an atmosphere that radiates like "an odor or a sound from the bodily region that it occupies most specifically". By sketching an exploratory investigation on gendered osmospheres, I will try to illustrate how food flavours are irreducibly linked not only to the phenomenological experience of being placed, *housed*, but also to gendered values. Given that food and gastronomy are strongly gendered domains,[35] *eo ipso* the perception of food osmospheres always seems blended with gender imagination, claiming a specific phenomenological investigation that is still lacking. Hence, I will speculate on the phenomenological intertwining of food osmospheres and "sense of home" by mentioning just a few symptomatic examples of olfactory devices. Since their explicit purpose is to endow space with an emotional

---

31 Kotler 1974, Spangenberg *et al.* 2005, Krishna *et al.* 2010.
32 Borges *et al.* 2013.
33 On the idea of home, Rybczynski 1986.
34 On atmospheres and affordances, Griffero 2020a.
35 Bordo 1993.

aura, I am here particularly interested in room sprays and scented candles, anticipating the main concerns of the next chapters.

From different perspectives, the debate on male/female olfactory oppositions in relation to bodily secretions, perceptual sensitivity and cosmetics assumes that smell has a tight relationship with the gender issue.[36] According to de Beauvoir (1956, 158), women use jewels, makeup and especially perfumes to conceal their flesh and odour, which are symbols of the animality that confines them in their biological nature as subjugated to the needs of the species. As a market that, until recently, was strongly (hetero)sexualised,[37] perfumery itself has for a long time been "polarized into a male and female type: she smells of violets and roses and he of leather and tobacco" (Illich 1985, 62).[38] Nowadays, consistently with the social and political rejection of binary genders, endorsed by artistic perfumery as well, unisex fragrances seem to be the new frontier.[39] Nonetheless, relics of olfactory gendered stereotypes firmly persist. As sketched in the previous pages, smell and the affective dimension of food are rooted in the primordial stages of life when, through maternal scent, moods and nourishment acquire an interchangeable osmospheric value.

The aesthetic link between female identity and food is not limited to biological or psychological instances; cultural paradigms largely contribute to settling and reinforcing it. The issue is well-known and widely debated. In many societies including the Western one, women have been expected to look after kids, to cook, to do chores, house cleaning and laundry; men to hunt and, in general, to run their activities outside the household. According to such a vision, while the masculine occupies the public and

---

36   Among others, Le Guérer 1994, 3-22; Reinarz 2014, 113-143; Diaconu 2022b, 67-69. On literature, Fjellestad 2001. In olfactory terms, menstrual blood is certainly the most discriminating element between the two sexes. Commonly tabooed and taken as a symbol for female impurity, menstruation ended up provoking disgust and shame in the menstruating woman herself, specifically towards the "stagnant odor emanating from her — an odor of the swamp, of wilted violets" (de Beauvoir 1956, 512). The issue of menstrual smells is entering art as a provocation to raise awareness on the female condition. Some examples are *Menstruation Bathroom* (1972) by Judy Chicago and, more recently, *Menstrual Garden* (2022) by Jiabao Li. In *You Can Call Me F* (2015), artist Anicka Yi questions patriarchy by releasing a scent which is the result of bacteria grown from the samples taken from the mouth or vagina of 100 women.

37   Kjellmer 2021a, 150-151; Grand-Clément, Ribeyrol 2022, 11.

38   See Tullett 2014 for Macaroni's perfume as a male antitype in 18th-century England.

39   Ellena 2013, Graham 2006.

mundane space,[40] the feminine is placed in the intimate sphere of the house, devoted to the everyday, ordinary and domestic family management.[41] As Carolyn Korsmeyer (2004, 83-104) and other scholars have extensively argued, the long-lived marginalisation within the academic discourse of food, the domestic and the "lower senses" can be reasonably attributed to their connection to female activities: if "the business of preparing meals is the job of women, servants, slaves (and of course women are in all those categories), then food, the sense of taste, and gustatory appetites reside in the wrong social place to merit much notice" (Korsmeyer 1999, 36). It is not by chance that these topics have been gaining philosophical interest thanks to female (or feminist) scholars, in conjunction with the challenging of gendered hierarchies or with an interest towards marginality as such.[42] Just to mention a few philosophers, Emily Brady, Mădălina Diaconu and Chantal Jaquet have sought to introduce smells and tastes in aesthetic appreciation for decades. Olfaction has been gradually entering academia at the same time as it opened up to women.[43]

Despite political and social changes directed at dismantling rigid demarcation in areas of responsibility, or at recognising a wider array of sexual identities following queer theories, food, especially when domestic, still has a privileged relationship with the feminine. This justifies and explains why my investigation is unbalanced towards the female pole: in osmospheric terms, "home" seems to coincide with womanhood. Indeed, the *domestic kitchen* as a female domain is a *topos* which ranges from paleoanthropological insights to the most worn-out male chauvinist

---

40   Tuan 2013, 23.
41   Locke 2007, 55. In general, public as well as private spaces themselves undergo
      gendered differentiations according to their function. In this respect, smells
      are both causes and consequences: architectural arrangement has followed and
      concurrently shaped olfactory sensitivity. In modern times, for instance, the
      smoking room, a male territory, "was distanced from the rest of the house [...]
      because of the smell of cigars" (Spain 1992, 114). The installation *Smoke Room*
      (2015) by Peter de Cupere — three-dimensional evolution of previous "paintings"
      such as *Cigarette Bacon-Smoke Painting* and *Please Smoke* (1999-2010) — is
      made of more than 750,000 cigarette butts, and recreates such osmosphere with
      implicit gendered clues (Vv. Aa. 2022, 68-71). Indeed, contrary to what visitors
      might believe, the smell does not come from the cigarettes, but is a fragrance
      evoking a mix of exhaust smoke, asphalt and smoked bacon (de Cupere 2016, 36,
      83-84).
42   Saito 2007, 4. Some pioneering studies are: Curtin, Heldke 1992; Telfer 1996;
      Perullo 2006; Boisvert, Heldke 2016.
43   Brady 2005, 2012; Diaconu 2005, 2006a, 2006b; Jaquet 2010, 2015a, 2015b,
      2018.

rhetoric. "Wife in the kitchen. Whore in the street" (Agrest 2000, 368) is, to put it mildly, an extremely reactionary formula based on the parallelism between female identities (the "angels of the hearth") and cooking duties, concurrently suggesting an equation between spatial localisation and moral respectability. As opposed to professional cooking, where the male majority is evident,[44] household cooking is a female prerogative that can even become the yardstick to assess the self-fulfilment of a wife/mother. These lines written in 1879 by an Italian woman render this idea very clearly: "The kitchen! It is a sacred place to me! The stove is an altar and the smell of *sfritticcio*[45] is the incense offered to the tutelary goddess of the domestic Lares Familiares" (cit. in Muzzarelli, Tarozzi 2003, 140). Japanese artist Maki Ueda plays on these stereotypes in *Eau de Parfum: Perfect Japanese Woman* (2008), an installation that revolves around the social expectations of Japanese women. It includes four fragrances: tatami, soap and two other food-related aromas. One is described as the "scent of motherhood" and is made of *nukamiso*:[46] when a woman is said "to stink like nukamiso" it means that her femininity has been lost in favour of her complete dedication to the family. The other is "the scent of a woman in the kitchen", specifically *miso soup*,[47] satirically aimed at pleasing the family and especially the husband.[48] Although in different ways, such a sexualisation of food, preparations and flavours is still fully in force today.

Grandma's Kitchen candles can be considered as iconic examples of interior environmental fragrancing through feminine food. For instance, the "Homesick"[49] branded candle is designed to recall warm apple pie with ice cream and fresh-baked snickerdoodles, the olfactory transposition of the idiom "sugar and spice and everything nice",[50] from a 19th-century

---

44 Rendell 2000; Perullo 2013; 2017, 38-40.
45 *Sfritticcio* is probably a malapropism meaning "soffritto", mirepoix. However, given the lack of sources, this is just a hypothesis.
46 Salted rice bran to prepare pickles, added with other ingredients such as garlic, ginger, sake.
47 The national dish, a soup made of dashi stock, miso paste and various ingredients according to taste, season and region.
48 https://www.ueda.nl/index.php?option=com_content&view=category &layout=blog&id=101&Itemid=792&lang=en. See Diaconu 2022b, 68.
49 *Homesick* (https://homesick.com/) is famous for its candles reproducing the osmosphere of American states and cities. As the company's name suggests, scents are designed to soothe nostalgia and "sense of place"; a similar product is made by Spain-based and themed company *Govalis* (https://govalis.com/).
50 https://homesick.com/products/grandmas-kitchen-candle.

nursery rhyme to typify girls' character.[51] Although variations are manifold, perceptual and emotional *qua* spatial leitmotifs are palpable. A recurring description reads: "No one can bake like Grandma. Her love of making people happy fills each recipe and her entire home with a comforting, warm scent that feels like a hug. It's a spicy, sweet happiness". The osmosphere revolves around baked goods, often sweets (pies, biscuits, etc.), together with spicy and fruity notes such as vanilla, cinnamon, apple. The goal is to trigger cosiness and warmth: a hugging osmosphere which folds the space inwards.

Before delving into this point, which raises interesting phenomenological concerns, let us set forth a diametrically opposite case. "Homesick" has also designed the *Bud Light Tailgate* air freshener,[52] which embodies a typically masculine food-related event. Tailgating is an American way of open-air partying where people — not exclusively but mostly males — drink alcohol, have a barbecue and share mainly meat-based food; it usually takes place in parking lots, before or after sport events or music concerts. Vehicle tailgates are used as stoves or tables, hence the name. The olfactory nuances are, among others, smoked charcoal, lawn chairs, grass, old pigskin and hops, evoking an outdoor barbecue and traditionally male sports. Manhood is therefore expressed through woody and musky tones.[53] The osmosphere is extroverted and exposed; the space unfolds outwards, taking on an *outgoing* character in any possible way: the advice is to "add crispy boys" when burning it, so as to have a full experience of tailgating also in its social and light-hearted dimension. Broadly speaking, the same applies to cookout-themed fragrancing devices that, among the various "home fragrances", have a more eccentric than hedonistic function, epitomising a sort of inherent inconsistency with the domestic sphere as

---

51   Although increasingly unisex, many food-scented objects in the toy market are mostly female-targeted. As Varney (1996) argues, fruity and sweet smells (strawberry, vanilla, raspberry, marshmallow, etc.) would symbolise the female olfactory code, exemplifying the features a woman should have according to sexist stereotypes, namely being attractive and pleasing.

52   Previously also in candle format, but no longer available.

53   https://homesick.com/products/bud-light-tailgate-air-freshener; similarly: https://homesick.com/products/budweiser-backyard-bbq-candle. There are many analogies with the Parisian maison Diptyque's description about the pairing of its *Juniper* and *Wood Fire* candles, which translates the English club in osmospheric terms: "The masculine atmosphere of club chairs and aged wood paneling. We hear the sound of muffled voices and the clink of cocktail glasses before a roaring fireplace. The smoky scent of wood fire enhances the bitter burst of spice"; https://www.diptyqueparis.com/en_eu/p/juniper-candle.html.

such, not only with regards to its spatial dimension, but also to its mood. This gendered osmospherification can be interpreted as a myth set up by the paternalistic view that, claiming woman for the hearth and home, "defines her as sentiment, inwardness, immanence" (de Beauvoir 1956, 261).

Gendered food osmospheres seem characterised by suggestions of motion and felt-bodily stirrings, to use Schmitz's terminology. These are spaced between the two poles of contraction and expansion. I suggest distinguishing between *unfolding* and *folding* food osmospheres. The former are characterised by various levels of expansion, therefore vastness; they are "masculine" in the sense that their orientation is centrifugal, promoting a sense of spatial extroversion, as in the case of "Bud Light Tailgate" fragrances and the like. The latter, instead, suggest contraction, hence narrowness; they are "feminine" as they are centripetal, affording the intimacy of inhabiting an introverted, "uterine" space. The *Grandma's Kitchen* kind of olfactory devices evidently fall into this second category. *Feminine* and *masculine* osmospheres are therefore to be understood as motosensory tensions through which an olfactory quality is perceived. They do not coincide with the gender of the perceiver, but their opposition has to do with different *oriented* intimacies. Psychoanalytically speaking, both (indeed, many) sexual instances coexist in the same personality. From a phenomenological perspective, it is possible to speak of a "sexed nose" that experiences the "sexual space" in its olfactory connotations, rephrasing and adapting Merleau-Ponty's insights on the body to our specific case. Sexuality as "the subject's general power of adhering to different milieus, of determining himself through different experiences, and of acquiring structures of behavior" (Merleau-Ponty 2012, 161) can be formulated as an existentially structured space which is inhabited according to its affordances, namely gendered osmospheres.

Noticeably, some edible items and cooking methods are perceived as more feminine than others, and scented commodities largely rely on these categorisations. This would confirm the conclusion to which many scholars have come: meat and other animal products are masculine, whereas plant-based foods are feminine.[54] In this respect, ethno-anthropological

---

54 Bentley 2005; Kaplan 2020, 47-48. The contrast is implicitly present in some linguistic expressions. In Italian, the term *finocchio* (verbatim "fennel") — an offensive epithet for an effeminate man — seems to originate from the practice of using this vegetable as an olfactory camouflage during persecution: once thrown into the fire of the stakes in which witches and homosexuals were burned in the Renaissance, its scent would conceal the stink of burning human flesh (Federici 2004, 197).

investigations highlight strong similarities among different societies.[55] Moreover, roasting and baking/boiling are not gender-free (Montanari 2006, 49), embedding opposite gendered osmospheres. Implying different bodily engagements, timing, occasions, settings, instruments and matters, they are dense with sexualised symbolism. This could be narrowly ascribed to the contexts the activities of roasting and baking normally take place in: the former outdoors, the latter indoors. Otherwise, roasting is masculine because it requires mainly fire, high heat and, as a rule, little time; food gets *crunchy*.[56] Recollecting his childhood, Bachelard remembers his grandmother cooking eggs indirectly under the ashes, or potatoes and a soggy bread soup in a pot in the fireplace. Interestingly enough, when it comes to the crispy *gaufre*, which is cooked "violently", the femininity of the grandmother is linguistically concealed by the use of the impersonal voice, which then turns into the masculine form for the gender of fire and of the waffle iron:

> on days when I was on my good behavior, they would bring out [in French: "on apportait"] the waffle iron. Rectangular in form, it would crush down ["il écrasait"] the fire of thorns burning red as the spikes of sword lilies. And soon the gaufre or waffle would be pressed against my pinafore, warmer to the fingers than to the lips. Yes, then indeed I was eating fire, eating its ["son"] gold, its ["son"] odor and even its ["son"] crackling while the burning gaufre was crunching under my teeth (Bachelard 1964, 15).

Earth, air, water and fire, *gynandromorph* if considered as static ideas, undergo sexual differentiation according to their performative actuality. Cooking itself involves varied levels of cooperation among the elements, together with diverse thermic dynamics; in calorific terms, "the sexual distinction is quite clearly complementary" (Bachelard 1964, 53). Whereas the masculine is centred, active, abruptly brutal, the feminine pertains to "surface and outer covering, a lap, a refuge, a gentle warmth" (ibid).

---

55   Pollock 1998.
56   It is notable that in *Swann's Way* the smell of roast but *tender* chickens is the condensation of François' virtues for Marcel. The passage reads that "meanwhile François would be turning on the spit one of those chickens such as she alone knew how to roast, chickens which had wafted far abroad from Combray the savour of her merits, and which, while she was serving them to us at table, would make the quality of sweetness predominate for the moment in my private conception of her character, the aroma of that cooked flesh which she knew how to make so unctuous and so tender seeming to me no more than the proper perfume of one of her many virtues" (Proust 1998, 169).

Baking, together with boiling, is feminine as it is gentler and slower.[57] Ingredients mingle; as a rule, they become softer. The process, as well as the gustatory result, is sweeter.[58] Indeed, working the dough is a complex process of elemental generation[59] — "a feminine labor", Bachelard (2002, 34) parenthetically pinpoints — which implies the creation of a new "ecosystem". Baked foods find their osmospheric counterpart in a feeling of closeness which rarely entails virile traits. A parallel can be drawn between such folding orientation and food by pondering the symbolism of the *placenta*, which is related to baking in many respects (the mammalian organ takes its name from a cake with honey and cheese from ancient Greece and Rome). A key aspect is discussed by Sloterdijk (2011, 377) in the rich pages devoted to it, where he explains that, because of ancient midwifery traditions, "the dough baking in the maternal oven was not so much the child itself as that mysterious placental cake on which the child evidently fed *in utero*". Therefore, the womb during pregnancy was conceived as a *twofold workshop*: "a placenta bakery and an intimate child kitchen. While the child itself is prepared in the uterine cauldron, the mother's second work, the flat cake, ensures the appropriate nutrition during the longest night" (ibid). Seremetakis (2019, 27) highlights that baking is an operation in which raising and sleeping alternate; the same applies to the maker and to food itself: "[i]t is often said after a dish has finished cooking, 'Let it sleep now, let it rest.' The cook also rests at this point; most of the time she does not eat the food she prepares for others, for she is 'filled with the smells'".

Understandably the essence of the feminine as an enveloping shelter is easy to grasp — like a mother's belly, or the protective smell of the nest (*der Nestgeruch*) described by Tellenbach — when we read this Bachelardian (2014, 66) recollection, albeit void of any gastronomic specification: "The house clung close to me, [...] and at times, I could smell her odor penetrating maternally to my very heart. That night she was really my mother". Indeed, if every "dwelling has its individual smell of home" (Pallasmaa 2012, 58), an osmospheric topoanalysis of the domestic would likely reveal that we are primitively *housed* while sniffing baking aromas. Unfortunately, Bachelard (1969, 141) did not fulfil his "urge to collect all the warm bread to be found in poetry", in that the fragrance of freshly baked bread, *domestic* bread, in his words, condenses celebration, gratitude

---

57 Shapiro 2001.
58 On sweetness, softness and crispness as gendered textures, Borsato 2023, 69-72, 87-88.
59 de Beauvoir 1956, 439-442.

and joy.[60] Had he done that, with all likelihood he would have considered the poem *Not for a Nation* by Edna St. Vincent Millay (1956, 555), where the smell of bread *is* an osmosphere of belonging, tenderness and safety. I will quote a few verses from it:

> I know these elms, this beautiful doorway: here
> I am at home, if anywhere.
> A natural fondness, an affection which need never be said,
> Raises from the wooden sidewalks warm as the smell of new-baked bread
> From a neighbour's kitchen. It is dusk. The sun goes down.
> Sparsely string along the street the thrifty lights appear.
> It is pleasant. It is good.
> I am very well-known here; here I am understood.

Likewise, when Elsa Morante (1979, 417) writes: "The tepid air, especially in the sun, smelled of bread", she is rendering the vital, maternal and welcoming quality of the air through the flavour that incarnates the idea of "home". Curiously, a trick to easily sell a house would precisely consist in baking some bread before potential buyers visit it.[61]

Nowadays, we dwell in spaces which are massively food-scented. Naively, one could explain this *osmospheric foodification*,[62] as I call it, as a counterbalancing aesthetic strategy, given the decreasing time we devote to cooking. In this sense, by relying on take away or delivery services, the eventual removal of the kitchen from apartments is foreseeable; as Federici (2012) argues, this is in line with the disaccumulation of capital in the home and of the services provided by households, a focal point in gender studies and Marxist feminism. I suspect, however, that the reasons are different, somehow deeper and darker. Since odours are *qualia* that characterise such a felt, not isotropic, and oriented space, the emotional *qua* spatial disorientation which follows olfactory disorders becomes even clearer; an anosmic person describes this situation as follows: "I feel discombobulated — like I don't exist. I can't smell my house and feel at home" (Burges Watson *et al.* 2021, 11). However, smell loss or malfunctioning is not exclusively a medical condition, it is also a daily reaction as a result of olfactory fatigue. The more the osmosphere is

---

60   Different food osmospheres can even enhance each other: as Bachelard recalls on this occasion, the odour of roosters cooking on a spit was ancillary to that of fresh baked bread, glorifying it.

61   Pollan 2013, 208.

62   On *foodification*, Bourlessas, Loda, Puttilli 2022. See also https://www.foodification.it/.

saturated, the higher the possibility of anosmia becoming chronic, even ontological.[63]

Sloterdijk (2002, 95-96) warns that the germ of consumer society was born in 19th-century over-perfumed arcades,[64] but late capitalism is taking such embryonic osmospheric aestheticisation to the extremes.[65] The link between late capitalism and postmodernism is interesting in olfactory terms, since the latter, as some have noticed,[66] finds its allegorical sense in smell because of the dismissal of normativity, also in relation to gender, in favour of *fluidity*, a characterising aspect of odours in many respects. Designed scents no longer linger exclusively in shopping malls, urban streets, etc., but they invade private houses, making them "home". As will be discussed further on, this is the latest frontier in scent marketing, where fast-food chains, with their flavoured merchandising, are representative promoters. The evolution of the "aroma-technical modification of the atmosphere" (Sloterdijk 2002, 92), besides revealing an obstinate addiction to market seduction, seems to be somehow infected by the ecological thought, as Timothy Morton (2010, 19) would put it. In this sense, osmospheric dwelling and ecological thought can be woven together.

As a matter of fact, the gaseous atmosphere today is brimming with the ghosts of ecological crisis, climate change, pollution and viruses. We are having a global and first-hand experience of this — air is *the* space of co-existence, but co-existence is not necessarily harmonious and safeguarding. It has to do with an unavoidable familiarity with the unfamiliar, potentially dangerous, deeply sinister and uncanny. It implies the full, ecological awareness that we share our very *Heim* with *das Unheimliche*. Apparently, as *(aerobe)beings-in-the-air*, humans still carry the memory of when, in the Paleoproterozoic era, most of the life on Earth underwent its first mass extinction due to the so-called "Oxygen Catastrophe". Humankind started thriving at the expense of other species; the fear is that something similar could happen again, but this time to our detriment. More than the ground under our feet, we are basically losing our breathing space, an imperceptible milieu that is becoming increasingly salient today. Hence, osmospheric foodification could be seen as an aesthetic strategy to make air familiar, folding, controllable, maternal, "uterine" and substantially life-sustaining once more.

63 Philippopoulos-Mihalopoulos 2021.
64 Borch 2011.
65 Lipovetsky, Serroy 2013.
66 Classen, Howes, Synnott 1994, 203-205; see also Graham 2014, 55.

Ultimately, it would be an attempt at taming it through *domestication*. Thanks to olfactory technology, the domosphere is designed, quite literally, like a *pregnant womb as a twofold bakery*. In Morton's (2016) words, it is *human-flavoured*.

3
OSMOSPHERIC SOCIETIES

> The social question is not only an ethical one,
> but also a nasal question.
> Georg Simmel

3.1 Smell And Civilisation

> When we see we remain who we are, when we smell we are
> absorbed entirely. In civilization, therefore, smell is regarded
> as a disgrace, a sign of the lower social orders, lesser races,
> and baser animals.
> Max Horkheimer and Theodor W. Adorno

The aesthetic but also epistemic, moral and social values of the senses are affected by the posture of the body and thus by their position with respect to the ground. In broad outline, the hierarchy among the senses — where traditionally smell is at the lowest rung of the ladder[1] — is rooted in the long-lasting Western contraposition between high and low, hence between superiority and inferiority, elevation and degradation. Societies are indeed used to mistreating smell precisely because it is the depositary of "the old nostalgia for what is lower [...], the longing for immediate union with surrounding nature, with earth and slime" (Horkheimer, Adorno 2002, 151), hence becoming "a disgrace, a sign of the lower social orders, lesser races, and baser animals" (ibid). What is high has to do with culture, spirituality and detachment from the mortal and animal nature of humans. Such a distinction applies to the body as well. The upper parts, the chest, the hands and in particular the head, are symbolically and osmospherically opposed to the lower ones (from the belly down, with genitals, intestines

---

1   Korsmeyer 1999, 11-37.

and feet), which are connected to carnality, hunger, roughness and filth. The Hegelian partition of the face responds to this same logic: the forehead is where theoretical activity occurs, whereas the mouth governs physiological functions; the nose is the junction point. However, even if in-between, the nose still belongs "to an animal need, for smelling is essentially connected with taste and this after all is why in the animal the nose is there in the service of the mouth and feeding" (Hegel 1975, 729). For all these reasons, smell has suffered from the stigma of uncivilised animality for a long time.

According to Charles Darwin, olfaction is almost useless, in that, as *The Descent of Man* reads, humans inherited it "in an enfeebled and so far rudimentary condition, from some early progenitor, to whom it was highly serviceable and by whom it was continually served" (Darwin 1871, 24). This view was for a time dominant, interpreting smell as an evolutionary relic or part of the oldest layers of the brain.[2] Although these diversified but still long-standing theories have been increasingly criticised,[3] the underlying idea has led to the deterministic definition of smell as "primitiveness".

By bringing into focus society as an organised body, the well-known Freudian observations establish a direct link between olfactory inhibition and the raising from the ground which smoothed the path for civilisation.[4] Bodily odours are *intermittent* stimuli, instigating promiscuity. Deemed regrettable in a society based on the stability of the family, smells are replaced with visual excitements, whose effects are instead permanent, as argued by Freud (1962, 46 n. 1). However, eroticism still largely relies on strong olfactory stimuli wafting from genitals and fluids; Freud observes that, even in Europe — where an olfactory and hygienic revolution in terms of deodorisation has occurred since the 18th century[5] — there exist "people among whom the strong genital odours which are so repellent to us are highly prized as sexual stimulants and who refuse to give them up" (ibid, 53 n. 3).

The central position of smell in animal mating has been scientifically proven since the 19th century: in biochemistry, with the discovery of

---

2   Shiner 2020, 51-53, 82-86.
3   For instance, in the 1960s, the neuroscientist Paul D. MacLean proposed the model of the "triune brain", which is based on the evolution of the vertebrate forebrain. According to this theory, judged by many scholars as an oversimplification (Steffen, Hedges, Matheson 2022), the brain would be composed of three complexes: the reptilian (basal ganglia), the paleomammalian (limbic system) and the neomammalian (neocortex). Olfaction is pivotal in the first and second systems (MacLean 1990).
4   Freud 1962, 46-47 n. 1, 52-53 n. 3.
5   Corbin 1986.

pheromones in insects and mammals;[6] in psychiatry, with the investigation of sexual perversions and regressions in humans.[7] For instance, Ambroise Tardieu (1878, 206) calls *renifleurs* (sniffers) those who are excited by the smell of urine. Notably, different cases are included in *Psychopathia Sexualis* by psychiatrist Richard von Krafft-Ebing. The nexus between smell and sexual behaviours is not just evident in the "love of certain libertines and sensual women for perfumes" (Krafft-Ebing 1933, 32),[8] but also in pathological paraphilias such as fetichism, masochism and coprophilia.[9] Playing a pivotal role in attraction,[10] odours disclose ethical and social issues especially in cultures and religions where the body is treated as a danger. Indeed, body-hatred and smell-hatred are two sides of the same coin; people "who despise smell are the same that endorse a rigid morality: the contempt of odours is proportional to the disgust towards the body" (Chaumier 2003, 93).

Even further, the very passage from quadrupedalism to bipedalism, in both the phylogenesis and ontogenesis of human beings, implies a postural elevation — from crawling to standing and walking — which brings about dramatic consequences in the olfactory sphere. On the one hand, hominids seem to have evolved from primates; the evolutionary process entailed multiple anatomical, cognitive, linguistic, perceptual and social adjustments, including a considerable change in the nasal organ and in the role of smell (Straus 1952). On the other hand, whereas adulthood is the age of reason, infancy and childhood are considered pre-verbal and instinctual, not dominated by intellect and ethics. Erect standing is in fact at the basis of *humanity* in its manifold meanings; as Merleau-Ponty (2012, 174) argues, "the reasonable being is also the one who stands upright". The vertical posture would enable humans, among other things, to escape the state of nature, developing sight as the prime sense at the expense of smell, and various abilities such as abstraction.

The contrast between smell and reflection has been addressed in various ways, being one of the main causes at the basis of the philosophical

---

6   Mucignat-Caretta 2014; for humans, Grammer *et al.* 2005.
7   Brill 1932.
8   For some insights on perfumes in the erotic arts, Shusterman 2021.
9   Borloz 2019.
10   On this aspect, many studies have been published: Le Guérer 1994, 7-14; Reinarz 2014, 113-143. As Serres (2008, 171) maintains, "[w]e do not love unless our senses of smell find themselves in improbable accord, a miracle of recognition between the invisible traces which scud over our naked skins, as air and clouds float above the ground".

marginalisation of smell. A case in point is the opening of Étienne Bonnot de Condillac's *Traité des sensations*. To trace the genesis of the mind and its faculties through sense impressions, the sensualist philosopher first endows his famous imaginary statue with the sense of smell. Rather than a destigmatisation of olfaction, this strategic move aims at resting the whole system on the most difficult epistemological precondition to demonstrate.[11] So, if it is possible to represent the development of cognitive activities *even* by starting from smell — which "seems to contribute the least to the knowledge of the human mind" (Condillac 1982, 171) —, the hypothesis that the intellect is formed by the senses is fully corroborated and is true *a fortiori* for all the other senses. The distance from abstraction can also be found in cases of hyperosmia (heightened sense of smell), where the world is perceived at variance with theoretical analysis and categorisation, since it appears "overwhelmingly concrete, of particulars, [...] a world overwhelming in immediacy, in immediate significance" (Sacks 1987, 157).

What I have said so far finds interesting correspondences with the cases of *enfants sauvages*, namely children raised in the wild by animals, or isolated from human groups, who develop peculiar perceptual set-ups where smell is often very influential.[12] Similarly, "uncivilised" or primitive societies are usually depicted with a keen sense of smell whose hedonic responses are often opposite to those of "civilised" people.[13] Rousseau (1979, 157) provides various examples: "Canadian savages, from their youth on, make their sense of smell so subtle that, although they have dogs, they do not deign to use them in the hunt and act as their own dogs", and a Tartar "must catch the scent of a stinking quarter of a dead horse with as much pleasure as one of our hunters catches the scent of a half-rotten partridge" (ibid, 156).[14] A kind of archaism of smell seems corroborated by Bachelard (1964, 103) when he asserts that a "psychology of primitiveness must devote a good deal of attention to the olfactory psychism". This connection also becomes evident in relation to archetypical enchantments mentioned by Max Horkheimer and Theodor W. Adorno (2002, 56), who observe that "[m]agic and countermagic in the metamorphoses of Odysseus's companions are linked to herbs and wine, as intoxication and waking are to the sense of smell, which is increasingly suppressed and repressed and is closest not only to sex but to the remembrance of prehistory". As is clear,

---

11   See also Biscuso 2000, 14.
12   Classen 1990a, 1991.
13   Sacks 1987, 158.
14   For similar remarks, Henning 1916, 388.

the relationships between smell and civilisation are diverse and complex. To further retrace the evolution and imaginary of olfaction with respect to civilisation, I will draw, firstly, on Calvino's story *The Name, the Nose*; secondly, on José Saramago's novel *Blindness*, in that both show, putting the emphasis on different aspects, how societies shape and are shaped by (food) osmospheres.

As a short but accurate synopsis that transliterates scientific findings into literary form, *The Name, the Nose* covers what scholars have largely discussed on smell.[15] It consists of three tightly interrelated stories which are thematically analogous but transposed to different eras and settings. Indeed, the "I", coinciding with the narrator, is captured in a dizzying journey through time and space. The common thread is the male protagonist's struggle to reach the female fragrant source, as well as the epilogue, where the craved odour mixes with the whiff of death epitomising the life cycle.[16] The "I" takes three shapes, respectively (following an "ascending" order instead of the plot): a nondescript prehistoric ancestor who evolves into a primate and a hominid; a 20th-century English punk-rock drummer; and Monsieur de Saint-Caliste, a 19th-century wealthy Parisian hedonist.

Calvino centres the story of the animal and its process of turning into human on the above-mentioned olfactory switch. Locomotion and smell functions correspond, mutually affecting each other. When environments were perceived as "a network of smells" (Calvino 1988, 71), bodies were oriented downwards: heads and noses hung low to track trails and clues, hands stayed in contact with the ground to move and run along. As animals, "[w]e understood whatever there was to understand through our noses rather than through our eyes" (ibid), to the point that "everything [was] first perceived by the nose, everything [was] within the nose, the world [was] the nose" (ibid). Once hands were freed from the necessity to climb trees or to support motion, the nasal organ, suspended in the air, raised from the ground. This had manifold consequences, including a loss in the information achievable by sniffing the earth. There are still some benefits: the "nose is drier, so you can pick up distant smells carried by the wind, and you find fruit on the trees, birds' eggs in their nests. And your eyes help your nose, they grasp things in space" (ibid, 80).[17] Nonetheless, before this

---

15 Cavallaro 2010, 187-191.
16 Stamelman 2006, 272-273.
17 Correspondences with Calvino's *The Baron in the Trees* can be found here. Being an interstitial identity between a civilised human and a wild animal living in the trees, the protagonist uses his nose as a compass to orient himself amidst the thick green foliage where sight is ineffective.

stage, smell was primarily involved in triggering sexual arousal. Calvino insists on this point by describing the protagonist's attraction to a female of the herd. However, their mating turns into a chaotic herd orgy where bodies and odours mingle.[18]

Such an archaic but still lingering memory is rooted in the story of the player, the second "I" that composes the triptych. Calvino renders moral lowness through the episode of a hungover rocker, surrounded by intoxicated people sleeping or fornicating on the floor of a concert room in a stinky London district after a night of revelry. Here, debauchery has a specific postural and olfactory dimension: sweaty and stinky, the drummer crawls on a carpet soaked with alcohol and vomit, keenly sniffing dirty groupies scattered around. Even if "in a big tangle of bodies" (ibid 1988, 75) and befogged by a gas leak, he is lured by a redolent trail that differentiates itself from the general stench; he imagines a ginger girl's white and freckled skin. Once he finds her thanks to his nose, they have sexual intercourse while semiconscious. What was sketched so far also shows the Janus-faced status of smell. Its link to sexual arousal, while justifying suspicion, simultaneously corroborates its importance for the survival and propagation of the species. In this sense, olfaction would constitute the evolution of the first chemical communication put in place by primordial aquatic organisms in order to reproduce and hence, *in nuce*, the embryo of civility and of thought: "[w]e *think* because we *smelled*" (Ackerman 1990, 20). However, disgust arose "when, with the adoption of the upright stance and the greater distance from the earth, the sense of smell, which attracted the male animal to the menstruating female, fell victim to organic repression" (Horkheimer, Adorno 2002, 193).

Calvino's episode of the third "I", Monsieur de Saint-Caliste, can be interpreted as a sublimation of smell which occurs specularly. The story begins in a luxurious *parfumerie* on Champs-Elysées, where the protagonist, a loyal customer, desperately asks for help in identifying the languid and elegant essence let out by a mysterious woman he had smelt during a masked ball. Olfaction is *elevated* firstly through the culturalisation of its stimuli,[19] which are connected to perfumery instead of bodily secretions. Not by

---

18   Hume 1992, 41.
19   Culturalisation also involves food preferences which come in succession or fluctuate throughout an individual's lifetime (Perullo 2016). In the ninth incipit of *If on a Winter's Night a Traveler*, Calvino uses a complex flavour to draw the reversal ontogenesis of a human being. While eating spicy meatballs prepared by the woman the protagonist suspects is his mother, his lips are burning "as if that flavor should contain all flavors carried to their extreme" (Calvino 1981, 226),

chance, the precious jars containing the rare essences are on the highest shop shelves, and salesgirls have to use ladders and *climb* to reach them. By using fragrances, sexual instincts are dressed in an olfactory refinement which corresponds to aesthetic cultivation. The long history of perfumery testifies and follows the fluctuations in olfactory sensitivities as well as the status of smell. Purity and candour are traditionally assimilated to delicate odours or even to their absence; on the contrary, animal or intense perfumes correspond to licentiousness and deceitfulness. Plautus' *Mostellaria* reads that old tarts soak themselves with perfume and cosmetics to conceal their physical flaws. Nonetheless, when they sweat, "they smell as if the cook had poured in every flavor in the kitchen" (Plautus 1955, 14). On the contrary, *mulier recte olet, ubi nihil olet* — "a girl smells nicest when she doesn't smell at all" (ibid) — a formula that has become proverbial. Among others, Michel de Montaigne (1948, 277) recalls it, adding that "[t]o smell good is to stink", which, in turn, is a rephrasing of *non bene olet qui bene semper olet* by Martial (1919, 116).[20] Such olfactory values lingered long in European culture, taking on further moral nuances related to deception. Indeed, at least from the second half of the 19th century, "[g] ood taste forbade the young girl to use perfume; this indiscreet solicitation might reveal her ambitions for marriage too crudely" (Corbin 1986, 182).

The characters' postures in *The Name, the Nose* follow the evolution of humanity in its anatomical and moral sense. Interestingly, Calvino adapts his lexicon and syntax to the respective stage: the complexity of expressions is inversely proportional to the vicinity of the nose to the ground. According to the evolutionary view, even language would depend on raising from the ground and on the partial dismissal of smell, since facial muscles, instead of being used for sniffing or prehensile tasks, are employed to articulate speech. The drummer and the primate's stories are rendered through colloquialisms and have almost no punctuation marks, whereas Monsieur de Saint-Caliste's episode is characterised by sophisticated vocabulary and proper punctuation. Here Calvino insists on the issue concerning the verbalisation of odours (the so-called *tip-of-the-nose* state),[21] often considered problematic for their imprecision and emotional nature. Indeed, many agree with Simmel (2009, 577) when he asserts that odours cannot be described objectively, and they "are not to be projected onto the level

---

eliciting "an opposite but perhaps equivalent sensation which is that of the milk for an infant, since as the first flavor it contains all flavor" (ibid).

20   Kaiser 2022, 62-77.
21   Lawless, Engen 1977; Jönsson, Stevenson 2014.

of abstraction".[22] However, the poverty of olfactory vocabulary, as recent research suggests, seems to be culturally-driven rather than a universal truth.[23] The same applies to the alleged weakness of human olfaction that, at least since Aristotle, has been a fundamental aspect in Western thought.[24] As anticipated, smell was even understood as a vestigial organ doomed to disappear,[25] the hypothesis underlying the opening of *The Name, the Nose*: "Epigraphs in an undecipherable language, half their letters rubbed away by the sand-laden wind: this is what you will be, *O parfumeries*, for the noseless man of the future" (Calvino 1988, 67).[26] As the next example will now reveal, this prediction could even turn out to be positive in a dystopic time to-come.

The antithesis between humanity and bestiality, respectively exemplified by vision and smell, is masterfully represented by Saramago's *Blindness*, which revolves around the idea that, in all likelihood, "humanity will manage to live without eyes, but then it will cease to be humanity" (Saramago 2017, 241). An epidemic of "white blindness" symbolises a sort of ontological indifference affecting society that "has lost its sense of compassion and solidarity" (Frier 2001, 105); the allegory pertains not only to past and future holocausts[27] but, in general, to human egoism and brutality. The "atmosphere of oppression and death" (Seixo 2001, 214) coincides with its unbearable osmosphere. Elsewhere the Portuguese writer clarifies the connection with olfaction, recollecting a blind man he, as a child, used to dislike in particular for his smell, "a rancid odor of cold, sad food and ill-washed clothes, a smell that would be associated forever in my mind with blindness and which probably resurfaced later in my novel" (Saramago 2011, 103). Indeed, the novel is steeped in suffocating miasmas, from the reek of decomposing flesh to the stench of excrements — contradicting Roland Barthes (1989, 137), we could say that, even if written, shit *does* smell —, in a peculiar contrast with the milky visual fog in which blind

---

22 The problematic labelling of smells (and a critique to this idea) spans from anatomy and neurology to psychology and, of course, philosophy, from Plato to Locke and Cassirer. See Keller 2016, 117-133; Winter 2019; Barwich 2020, 73-103, 264-302; Shiner 2020, 103-116; Dubois 2022.

23 Majid, Burenhult 2014; Barkat-Defradas, Motte-Florac 2016; Cimatti *et al.* 2016; Alač 2017; Majid *et al.* 2018; Jędrzejowski, Staniewski 2021.

24 Shepherd 2004.

25 McGann 2017.

26 Today there is an increasing trend in olfactory training (often to treat smell disorders as side-effects of coronavirus), in olfactory environmental exploration, and in using food flavours to improve health.

27 Monteiro 2001, xxv.

people are trapped, so much so that the "atmosphere was charged with unpleasant odours, making the invariable whiteness of the objects absurd" (Saramago 2017, 213).

At the outbreak of the mysterious pandemic, infected people are isolated in a ramshackle mental hospital, with "dingy latrines, a kitchen that still reeked of bad cooking" (ibid, 38). During the quarantine, the asylum is the scene of ethical as well as physical decay, gradually transforming into a sewer. The story focuses on an exceptionally virtuous tiny community, not fortuitously led by the doctor's wife, the only person who preserves her sight. Olfactory parallelisms to hell are manifold, since "pestilential stench is the worst thing condemned souls have to bear" (ibid, 256). The floor covered in "an endless carpet of trampled excrement" (ibid, 126) epitomises not so much, as Sloterdijk (2014, 321-333) would put it, the *latrinocentrism* of the sedentary society that finds its very identitarian spirit in its "merdocratic space", but an "abject reality" (Saramago 2017, 129) that invades the nostrils:

> Some of the blind internees were stirring in their beds and, as every morning, they were relieving themselves of wind, but this did not make the atmosphere any more nauseating, saturation point must already have been reached. It was not just the fetid smell that came from the lavatories in gusts that made you want to throw up, it was also the accumulated body odour of two hundred and fifty people, whose bodies were steeped in their own sweat, who were neither able nor knew how to wash themselves, who wore clothes that got filthier by the day, who slept in beds where they had frequently defecated (ibid, 128).

We might say that the compulsive eradication of bodily smells dictated by the ideal hygienist dream that has dominated Western society since the 17th century is here brutally desecrated, vividly representing why every smell, after all, "is primordially the smell of shit" (Laporte 2000, 86). *Blindness* also discloses interesting insights on the issue of individuality that, from the sphere of vision, infiltrates the olfactory domain. People have no proper names; they are simply labelled by their profession (in this situation, obsolete) or physical qualities, paradoxically invisible to all except for the doctor's wife. The permeating stench overshadows personal osmospheres; such an olfactory anonymity contributes to making the characters even more *faceless* and indiscernible.[28] Depersonalisation

---

28   Interestingly, Marshall McLuhan (1964, 147) postulates that the attenuation or elimination of the olfactory sphere is more likely found in highly literate societies; indeed, bodily odour, "the unique signature and declaration of human

concerns food preferences as well: there is no room for personal tastes, because each palate is the same. Eating is indeed problematic, especially when infected people leave the asylum and discover that the whole city has been affected by the pandemic. Whereas the terrible stench was initially circumscribed to the internees, now it spreads adhering to everything. The blind, like competing animals, rely on their nose to find whatever is edible. Since "hunger has always had a keen sense of smell, the kind that penetrates through all barriers" (Saramago 2017, 216), olfaction makes urban hunting and gathering possible by detecting the smell of food even when packaged in air-tight cans.

Another trace of inhumanity is detectable in the absence of cooking: ready-made or raw, food is consumed carelessly. If we accept that "[c]ooked meat represents above all the overcoming of putrefaction" (Bachelard 1964, 103), and that, "[t]ogether with the fermented drink it constitutes the principle of the banquet, that is to say the principle of primitive society" (ibid), the society depicted by Saramago lacks the very precondition for being considered as such. The brutal osmosphere is here likely to be the illustration of an age pre or post the control of fire, which is "*all-purifying* because it suppresses nauseous odors" (ibid). It is in cooked food, and especially in gastronomic and unnecessary pleasures, like dessert, "that fire shows itself a friend of man" (ibid, 15). Interestingly enough, the rancid scent of rotten sweets constitutes the odour the doctor's wife sniffs at first when foraging for supplies. In this savage dystopia, "the aroma of a chunk of stale bread" (Saramago 2017, 224) condenses life itself.

Many details suggest that the author, especially through osmospheric cues, is depicting a reversion of the evolutionary and civilisation process. The reminiscence of humanity is further symbolised by the odour of the doctor and his wife's apartment — "simply that of a flat in need of a good airing" (ibid, 255) —, by a decorous meal eaten around a table, and by the smell of soap once the group gets to wash. While intensifying the surrounding stench, the fragrance of detergents and clean bodies becomes the metaphor of human existence, the "actual yardstick of civilization" (Freud 1962, 40). Even the last, violent olfactory episode centres on the subversion of the boundaries between humanity and bestiality. In the basement of a supermarket, the doctor's wife finds many corpses in an advanced stage of decomposition, probably trampled to death by a stampeding crowd sniffing food. Dancing will-o'-the-wisps are the visual

---

individuality, is a bad word in literate societies. It is far too involving for our habits of detachment and specialist attention".

rendering of an oppressive tang which even her fellow dog cannot endure, causing him to whimper and whine. As a result, the smell of food ended up blinding already blind people.

3.2 *The Nasal Question: Food And Identity*

> The ingesta, that is, air, food, and drink,
> regulated the excreta and therefore
> individual odor.
> Alain Corbin

There is plenty of evidence, including phraseologies, that the "social question is not only an ethical one, but also a nasal question" (Simmel 2009, 577). Whereas Germans adopt the formula *jemanden nicht riechen können*, "not to bear one's odour", to mean that one cannot stand someone else, the same is expressed by the French idiom *avoir quelqu'un dans le nez*, verbatim "to have somebody in the nose". In general, a sociological inquiry about osmospheric spaces cannot overlook the relationships between population density, physiography, human geography and built environment. The very sociability of national characters would depend on the weather and its repercussions on gathering settings — hence the axiom by Simmel (ibid, 579) that establishes a directly proportional equation between social skills and temperate climate. On the contrary, unsociability and isolation would be typical of colder countries where people, meeting indoors, should be forced to cope with intrusive olfactory annoyances. Given that "the modern notion of society implies the interactions among the deodorized in the olfactorily neutral space (human rights are preceded by the zero smell hypothesis)" (Sloterdijk 2014, 325), it comes as no surprise that, in this framework, the "word 'odor' itself nearly always connotes bad odor", as observed by Tuan (1974, 9).

Many pages have been written about the operativeness of odours with regards to social dynamics and political attitudes.[29] What generally emerges is that smell has a strong socio-political authority in that it always acts affectively, governing the relationships between individuals while inducing acceptance or, more often, rejection. The *xenophobic* attitude

---

29   Diaconu 2005, esp. 223 ff.; Inbar *et al.* 2011; Liuzza *et al.* 2018; Liuzza 2020; Carnevali 2020, 154-159; Hsu 2020, 2022; Kettler 2020; Lynn, Parr 2021; on Arabs, Hall 1966, 149-150.

of smell can be assimilated to its neophobic inclination towards food; scholars hypothesise that the distrust of unfamiliar smells has to do with a conservative force since the unknown is always potentially perilous.[30] After all, as already pointed out, the act of smelling implies a tightly tangled somatic and sentimental intertwining to the point that it suggests the impression of internalising, even of *ingesting*, the odorous source. For that reason, not only any flavour, but also the scent of a person, as their unique atmosphere, "penetrates, so to speak, in the form of air, into our most inner senses" (Simmel 2009, 578). The common fact that people tend to be more lenient towards their own bodily odours verifies the aforesaid conjecture. "That *we dislike in others things which we tolerate in ourselves* is a law of our æsthetic nature about which there can be no doubt" is the incisive conclusion James (1981, 1051) comes to by considering the offensive smell of a dirty comrade.[31]

Kant (2006, §22, 51) defines smell as less social than taste, maintaining that olfactory disgust is more frequent than pleasure since malodorous elements prevail over fragrant ones, *especially in crowded places*. According to Simmel, it is the *dissociating* sense *par excellence* because it discriminates. Examples are countless: Alexander von Humboldt (1811, 50) remarks that Peruvian Indians can distinguish races just by relying on their nose, so much so that they have olfactory terms to indicate the specific odours of European, Indian American and African people. Often, demarcating differences coincides with spurning others: the "olfactory signature, elevated to a *principium individuationis* has (unfortunately) often suggested regarding social difference as a prejudicial matter of odour" (Griffero 2022a, 85). However, the reverse is also true: olfaction also promotes sharing, recognition and belonging. Osmologically speaking, freedom and constraints, mixing and social distinction, play a pivotal role. If "[t]he boundary is not a spatial fact with sociological effects, but a sociological reality that is formed spatially" (Simmel 2009, 551), in the axis of proximal distance set by smell, the very idea of *boundary* is simultaneously strong and faulty. Understood as a demarcation line meant to separate and safeguard, such an osmospheric border appears as a binding and concurrently unattainable instance. The lack of spatial freedom, of *Spielraum*, turns into a pneumatic substantial experience. Merleau-Ponty (2012, 339) remarks that it sometimes happens that "the lived distance is at once too short and too wide [...] I can literally no longer breathe".

---

30   Pliner, Salvy 2006.
31   The same is supported by Thomas Hobbes (1969, 32).

Interestingly, he also refers to the pathological experience described by Minkowski in relation to hallucinations and space.[32] The French psychiatrist reports a case of spatial hallucination in which odour is central. One of his patients had told him that one day, while lying in bed with the windows closed, she had clearly smelled roasted chestnuts, describing it as a *suggested sensation*. In other words, she claimed that another person in the same mental state as her was standing outside in front of a roast chestnut vendor. A kind of psychic link had been established between her and this other person, overcoming the barriers of space and revealing itself through an osmospheric experience.

Social identities are not osmospherically sealed but mutually absorbable, epitomising *transition*. This is evident in many rites that communities perform to "integrate" a stranger: ritual baths and various re-odorising practices are precisely aimed at removing impurities, that is, olfactory differences.[33] Something similar can be found in the third incipit of Calvino's *If on a Winter's Night a Traveler*, where the protagonist is listening to the dialogue between the patrons in a tavern. A prison guard is talking about a perfumed rich lady visiting a convict every week: "when the visiting hour is over, the young lady comes out with the stink of jail on her elegant clothes; and the prisoner goes back to his cell with the lady's perfume in his jailbird's suit" (Calvino 1981, 64). And as a drunkard, he adds: "I'm left with the smell of beer. Life is nothing but trading smells" (ibid). At that point the gravedigger comes in: "Life and also death, you might say [...]. With the smell of beer I try to get the smell of death off me. And only the smell of death will get the smell of beer off you, like all the drinkers whose graves I have to dig" (ibid). The notions of self and the other reveal their elusiveness but also, on an empirical level, their effectiveness, so much so that they become nodal and prescriptive in the unfolding of collective life: "[f]rom a culture-climatological perspective, a settled ethnic unit is above all a group that smells itself and finds a spherically extended criterion of identity in its own smell" (Sloterdijk 2014, 322).

How food contributes to creating levels of reality has been widely analysed. Olfactory geographies are largely to be ascribed to food; likewise, social, cultural and perceptual idiosyncrasies mould and are moulded by food aromatic variants, which convey tastes, common ingredients, culinary techniques and eating habits. Although each olfactory identity is

---

32 Merleau-Ponty refers to Minkowski 1932, which in turn refers to a clinical case described extensively in Minkowski 1927.

33 Howes 2008.

unique, both in the receptive and active sense, biological and biographical variability is transversally crossed by diet, which is the ground shared by a given group.[34] This mechanism is incisively summarised by Alain Corbin (1986, 39), maintaining that the "ingesta, that is, air, food, and drink, [regulate] the excreta and therefore individual odor". As already said, studies addressing the various correlations between food and identity are too extensive to list here. In a sense, odour is the impalpable veil which makes someone precisely who they are. This smell arouses, in turn, particular feelings and opinions. Indeed, as argued by many philosophers and made clear by Hannah Arendt (1992, 66), "only taste and smell are discriminatory by their very nature and because only these senses relate to particular *qua* particular".

Besides its thermoregulatory function, sweating expels through the skin some of the substances introduced by eating. As Shusterman (2011a, 153) puts it, "[s]tyles of diet are likewise recognized not only through the smell of the food itself but through the odoriferous traces they leave on our skin and breath". In this respect, he remembers arriving at his mother-in-law's village in rural Japan and being told that he smelled like a Korean; clearly, the garlicky dinner consumed in Seoul the previous day "was still producing its somatic scent" (ibid). It emerges that olfactory somatic style fluctuates between stability and permeability. Olfactory selfhood has to be understood, borrowing a Deweyan concept, as *transactional*; indeed, the body subsists and is nourished by what, at first, is external to it. Hence, the osmospheric self, rather than an essence that originates from an internal nucleus, finds its roots in food, a portion of the outer world that, once ingested, assimilated and internalised, radiates and externalises the self outwards. In this perspective, food perfectly stands for the idea that one's very identity is shaped by one's relationships, questioning the assumption of an isolated organism.[35]

In its most recent outcomes, often drawing on biology, food philosophy encourages precisely to think of the "I" as the result of multi-species and ecological relationships, instead of as a self-contained individual.[36] In this sense, Calvino is well-known to have racked his brain over the conundrum of individuality, developing a poetics imbued with the porosity of beings, understood as a fleeting structural stasis within an ever-mingling flux of materials. *T Zero*, for one, discloses fruitful insights to our investigation.

---

34   Reinarz 2014, 91-94.
35   Mol 2008.
36   Heldke 2018; Perullo 2022a. For an interesting anthropological case, Meigs 1988.

The unpronounceable palindromic protagonist, Qfwfq, is the emblem of an open-ended entity in endless morphogenesis, evolving throughout the terrestrial eras similarly to the "I" of *The Name, the Nose*. By creating this character, Calvino wants to highlight the impossibility of drawing the neat boundaries of selfhood.[37] This objective is masterfully achieved in "Priscilla", a long chapter devoted to Qfwfq's beloved one. The ontological problem lies in "the fact that from one moment to the next I am no longer the same I nor is Priscilla any longer the same Priscilla, because of the continuous renewal of the protein molecules in our cells through, for example, digestion or also respiration which fixes the oxygen in the bloodstream" (Calvino 1969, 76-77). Priscilla's way of being deeply depends on her embedded alterity, including the scent of her skin, which is a combination of genetic inheritance, physical and psychic features, socially and culturally driven habits and, most of all, the result of "everything she has eaten in her life" (ibid, 77). As Calvino (1985, 69) writes elsewhere, food is humans' "consubstance, flesh of their flesh". It might be said that one's odour is all but the intercurrent *osmospheric osmosis* between mingled bodies.

Having said that, a socio-aesthetic inquiry on osmospheres needs to be articulated considering, first of all, that one's olfactory identity is always indirectly subsumed by the aesthetic sensitivity of others. That is to say, olfactory self-awareness is mostly extroverted, in that personal scent is, in normal conditions, the *blind spot* of self-perception. It comes as no surprise that perceiving the osmospheric self is usually the symptom of some kind of *self-schism*:

> It is only in my bad smell that I see myself confronted with my own atmosphere. [...] The melancholic is forced to be their own neighbour with the least degree of freedom; and for this reason it emerges precisely from this that the melancholic cannot be at home when they are by themselves. A human being who perceives a bad smell on themselves immediately distances themselves from themselves, they are "outside themselves", above themselves [...] (Tellenbach 1968, 128).[38]

Given that one can neither taste nor smell themselves, in olfactory aesthetics the self and the other are tightly intertwined since the former internalises the latter's nose. Following Barbara Carnevali (2020), *appearance* is the unavoidable interface through which the selves manifest themselves,

---

37   Iovino 2014.
38   Leucadi 2001.

constituting the very precondition of social relationships. Given that aesthetic reflexivity presupposes a "double endogenous and exogenous structure" (ibid, 16), an inquiry on this doubling and its consequences on the osmospheric dimension is compelling; specifically, a socio-aesthetics of smell should wonder whether and how the *nose of the other* as the introjection of the other's olfactory judgement affects osmospheric self-perception.[39] Indeed, we can only grasp our osmospheric emanation by resorting to its resonance, i.e. *vicariously*; in other words, "[t]hrough the medium of atmosphere we continually acquire ourselves from others" (Tellenbach 1981, 227). Consubstantial with breathing, the sense of smell easily gets fatigued, keeping some prolonged stimuli below the threshold of conscious perception. The aroma of home strikes as soon as one enters it, fading soon after; that of one's own homeland becomes particularly salient in the memory of the expatriate. Somehow, smell encourages what can be called an *extroaesthetics*. One's personal scent is clearly unbalanced towards the indirect, extroverted and mediated pole of self-perception, same as when wearing a perfume. Of course, every adornment is always innervated by other people's appreciation; yet, the perception can also be direct: a jewel can be contemplated in its "objectuality". A fragrance, instead, does not only change considerably once matched with a specific skin smell (as perfumers use to say, the wearer's skin is an ingredient), but it also blends the latter into a prosthetic cloud that the person cannot directly smell. We willingly spend even a considerable amount of money for an experience of ourselves we can never directly achieve.

If no one is normally aware of their own olfactory identity, the latter must be deduced from the representation others make of it. Like moral standing, beauty and race, "one's smell seems to be in many ways a creation of the other" (Miller 1997, 247). This is why some osmo-sociological patterns get us to assume that olfactory qualities are constructed, that is, they *follow* a preceding judgement towards their source, taking on aesthetic values accordingly. Putting the emphasis on attitude and social character, Max Weber (1924, 485) explains the enslaving of African Americans (and not of Native Americans) by suggesting that the smell Yankees attributed to them (*der Negergeruch*) did not depend on their bodies; rather, their activism and political claims *made* them bad-smelling. This mechanism would explain why olfactory allegations are usually symmetrically reciprocal, suggesting that the human being is *zoon politikòn* also *qua* a *smelling* animal, both in the receptive and emanative sense; Andreas Philippopoulos-Mihalopoulos (2021, 97) calls *olflow* this "dense planetary swirl that leaves nothing outside". In order to detect a smell, a sort of friction

---

39   Mancioppi 2021a, 2021b.

between oneself and the outside/other needs to be established.[40] Nevertheless, immediately afterwards, the smeller gets lost "in identification with the Other" (Horkheimer, Adorno 2002, 151).

A last point is worth mentioning about the "nasal question", namely the nose's pantomimical sphere. The nasal appendix and its movements can convey feelings whose tone partially exceeds — but always takes root in — olfactory perceptions. Among other authors, Helmuth Plessner (1970, 62) did not ignore the fact that the slightest wrinkling, screwing up or holding of one's nose is an expressive code indicating a general sense of disapproval or superiority, revealing repugnance, disdain, or scorn. In so doing, humans effectively communicate the affective qualities of a situation or of a person that, from the olfactory level, transcend the sensory content. This has crystallised in various idiomatic expressions: in English, *to turn up one's nose*; in French, *lever le nez sur quelque chose*; or, in German, the saying *über jdn./etw. die Nase rümpfen*, which is analogous to the Italian *storcere il naso*. In a way, this supports Hegel's (1975, 730) observation that, since nasal movements express feelings and judgements exceeding odours but pertaining moral characters, smelling "becomes as it were a theoretical smelling — becomes a keen nose for the spiritual". Moreover, the very shape of the nasal organ has been interpreted as the sign of an inclination. A snobbish (toffee-nosed) bearing is commonly exemplified by an upturned nose; according to racist rhetoric, the flat nose with wide nostrils of black people indicates their animality no less than their alleged rank smell. Adorning the nose is also a common practice among "primitive" people; Serres (2008, 34) draws a parallel between the aesthetic and cosmetic sphere with respect to the sensuous cartographies of the bodies, venturing that "the reason why we do not have a ring hanging from our nose, as other peoples do, is that we have forgotten the sense of smell".

Since the Late Middle Ages, anti-Semitic iconography has depicted the Jews with big, hooked and downward-sloping noses, a caricatural trait indicating evil and an inclination towards vice.[41] And also, from Ancient Rome on, the *foetor judaicus*, also mentioned by Johann Kaspar Lavater and denounced by Arthur Schopenhauer (2009, 228, 235), has been vilified to attest the inferiority and immorality of the Jews.[42] Summarising Horkheimer and Adorno's (2002, 151-152) observations, it could be said that antisemitism

---

40 Diaconu 2010.
41 Lipton 2014.
42 Trachtenberg 1943, 47-50; Geller 1997.

rests on the act of *sniffing the repugnant*. Coherently, Nazism can be seen as sharp-nosed in its wish to detect and then eradicate the "Jewish stench". However, the feeling is mutual, so to speak: Ernst Bloch (1970) ascribes the odour of urine, blood and stale air to Nazi ideology; Benjamin (1972, 217) associates National Socialism with beer vapours since Hitler's followers used to gather in cellars, halls and restaurants. Even the miasmas exhaled by concentration camps can be reversely attributed to the perpetrators rather than to the prisoners themselves. In this case, the reek of brutalised bodies, repugnant food and decaying corpses so overwhelming in chronicles and memoirs[43] acquires a reflected moral value by osmospherising the cruelty behind the genocide. Exhaling the "odour of turnips and cabbages, raw, cooked and digested" (Levi 1959, 119), the camp smell, initially a torture for the prisoners, over time is absorbed and assimilated by the victims, becoming their very exhalation that, in turn, instigates Nazi revulsion.

Trying to shed light on this "silent game [that] plays a decisive role in constituting the individual 'self'" (Tellenbach 1981, 227), the following pages focus on food osmospheres as they draw maps crossed by social issues intertwined with the aesthetic and political state of affairs, both on the inter- (ethnic) and intra- (class) community level. Of course, such distinctions are for the sake of convenience, as a society does not necessarily coincide with national boundaries, and ethnic issues are often tangled with class ones. Simmel (2006, 577) claims that the "reception of Africans into the higher levels of society in North America seems impossible from the outset because of their bodily atmosphere". When, in 2007, Joe Biden declared that Barack Obama was a "*clean* and nice-looking guy", he was merely proving the osmospheric rule through its exception.[44]

3.3 *Ethnic Flavours*

> Working-class Italians smelled of fried peppers, and Greeks
> smelled of garlic and brilliantine, and, when they sweated,
> their underarms smelled of yogurt.
> André Aciman

The role of smell in the link between cuisine and osmospheric ethnic personality is stressed by André Leroi-Gourhan (1993, 292) when he

---

43   Rindisbacher 1993, 239-266.
44   See Parr 2021.

notes that, despite being united by the same staples, "no one can confuse a Malagasy rice dish with an Indian, Chinese, Hungarian, or Spanish one, for the simple reason that culinary processing entails the creation of a bouquet of smells and tastes peculiar to each culture". The potentially endless aromatic palette of existing cuisines corresponds to the most diverse *osmologies*,[45] with their symbolism, memory and material culture. For instance, André Aciman (1994, 104) maintains that Egyptians can be roughly divided in two groups: entirely Westernised Egyptians, who smell of aftershave, and just half-Westernised Egyptians, who smells of *hilfa*, "an Arab smell", as his father and grandmother used to say. Moreover, the latter "disliked all kinds of recognizable ethnic odors, [thinking] that the more Westernalized a family, the more odorless its home, its clothes, its cooking" (ibid, 105). However, corroborating the above hypothesis that the osmospheric self is a blind spot, the author comments:

> It would never have occurred to either of them that all homes bear ethnic odors, and that anyone born in Alexandria would just as easily have sniffed out a Sephardi household like ours, with its residual odor of Parmesan, boiled artichokes, and *borekas*, as they themselves could recognize an Armenian kitchen by its unavoidable smell of cured pastrami, a Greek living room by the odor of myrrh, and Italians by the smell of fried onions and chamomile (ibid).

Before expatriating to the U.S. due to the expulsion of his family from Egypt after the 1956 war, Aciman recollects a spring morning in Alexandria where a "smell of *ful*, the national bean breakfast, permeated the air" (ibid, 262), an aroma that, by instructing the family cook, he intentionally replaced with that of "eggs and bacon and of butter melting on toast wafting from the kitchen" (ibid, 305), as if preparing himself to the forthcoming forced exodus and ethnic osmospheric change.

Whereas eating in an exotic restaurant can function as a temporary surrogate to dive on purpose into an alternative and circumscribed ethnic food osmosphere, actual coexistence in multi-ethnic neighbourhoods often provokes complaints about unfamiliar odours, where gastronomy plays a pivotal role.[46] Indeed, "the food of immigrants, redolent of peculiar aromas and bursting with unfamiliar flavors, easily gets entangled in polemics that go well beyond the gustatory and touch on the political" (Parasecoli 2022, 158). It comes as no surprise that the associations between food flavours and racial hatred are conspicuous. The Japanese reserve the term *bata kusai*

---

45   Diaconu 2005, Breton 2017.
46   Manalansan IV, 2006.

(バタ臭い) — literally "smelling of butter" — for Westerners,[47] while Middle Eastern populations are commonly given an acrid smell due to their large use of spices. North Americans used to nickname Italian emigrants *garlics*, due to its widespread use in their cuisine. Intertwining with the distrust of a particularly closed ethnic group, usually poor and linked to the underworld, the garlicky aroma took on a denigratory value and fostered marginalisation; the same flavour was ascribed to the Jews in Poland. Revulsion towards the smell of garlic is actually long-lived.[48] Sidonius Apollinaris, in poem XII *To Catullinus*, also known as "Satire on the Burgundians", attributes his loss of poetic inspiration also to the Germanic tribe's reek he was forced to live with. The Barbarians' disturbing presence, besides their revolting voracity, is largely related to smell: the Burgundians not only sprinkle their hair with rancid butter, but relentlessly inundate the air with the smell of food rich in "garlic and foul onions" (Sidonius 1956, 213). However, bad smells can even be intentionally cultivated as weapons. In a fictional but effective image depicted by Martin Amis (2007, 78), the Mongol horde, while approaching the cities, was frightening for its smell, not so much that of unwashed bodies, but especially their breath, "further enriched by the Mongol diet of fermented mare's milk, horse blood, and other Mongols". These sorts of observations played a prominent role in "scientific racism". For instance, in 1915 French nationalist and doctor Edgar Bérillon (1915a, 1915b) tried to demonstrate the inferiority of the "German race" by diagnosing *bromhidrosis* (foul-smelling perspiration) and *polychexia* (excessive defecation) caused, among other things, by the diet largely based on animal fats and vegetables such as cabbages.

Metaphorically, these kinds of osmospheric relations can be described as two bubbles that touch each other without bursting. Two possibilities exist. The first: the two bubbles double the thickness of their respective membranes; here we have the olfactory prejudices that arise from a distorted and projected perception of the other. The second: the two bubbles overlap each other and, at the point of greatest contact, interpenetrate, thus containing the breath of both, in variable quantities; in this case, the thickness of the parting membrane is halved. The latter are olfactory discriminations due to a direct osmological exchange that, nevertheless, emphasises the alterity of the intersection in relation to the two macro-groups. Communities exist where such social osmologies are systematically codified and regulated,

---

47   Interestingly, the kanji 臭 means odorous, stinking, but also suspicious. I thank my colleague Maddalena Borsato for some olfactory insights she picked up during her stay in Japan.

48   Jenner 2000.

as many ethnographic and anthropological studies show.[49] An interesting case is that of various tribes in the Colombian Amazon.[50] Here, inter- and intra-tribal relations are strictly ruled by the odour of the community each member belongs to, which coincides with the respective dietary regime. Specifically, the Pira-Tapuya, the Desana and the Tukano, occupying adjacent areas, differentiate themselves and their territories through the sense of smell: the first, being a fishing society, smell like fish; the second, consisting of hunters whose diet is mainly based on game, smell like musk; the third have instead the odour of roots and vegetables since they are farmers. Spatial occupations, marriages, rituals and political dynamics are structured as food-osmospheric twines, combinations and subdivisions.[51]

Even without such configurations or prescriptions, it is the nose that usually navigates between the areas and inhabitants of a city.[52] Indeed, despite the massive osmospheric homologation of spaces occurring nowadays, "your nose can still tell you whether you are in East or West Berlin" (Böhme 2017b, 125). Sensory history provides many examples. For a white Mississipian, the "smell of overfried catfish and the hickory smoke smell of the barbecued pork chops" (Smith 2006, 80) drove the boundary line of black Columbus in the 1920s. Indeed, the dominant osmosphere can host many micro-osmospheres testifying to the sensual presence of ethnic minorities. It is worth mentioning "Little Manila" as well, an event that takes place in Hong Kong on Sundays, when more than 100,000 Filipino residents gather to eat, talk and feel "at home" in the city centre. Streets become a branch of their native osmosphere which saturates the air. While evoking a sense of belonging to the most populous minority, Filipino food smell causes a strong annoyance to the natives. This cyclical food osmosphere marks the temporal rhythm of a city whose osmosphere is otherwise quite homogeneous, given the low percentage of nonlocal inhabitants.[53]

When considering adjoining ethnic neighbourhoods in a metropolis, osmospheric foams are in order. Early in the 20th century, in the densely populated East Harlem, food smells served to justify intolerance between diverse groups: because of the smell of garlic, Irish immigrants could not

---

49 Skinner-Petit 1976; Almagor 1987; Classen 1990b; Classen, Howes, Synnott 1994, 98-122.
50 Classen 1993, 81.
51 See also Classen 2005, in particular the case of the Ongee, hunter-gatherers living in Little Andaman Island.
52 Wicky 2022.
53 On this, see Law 2001. For a study on smell in the Philippines, Beer 2007.

tolerate cohabitating with Italian neighbours who, in turn, complained about the odour of herrings in brine given off by Jewish grocery stores.[54] Conversely, in Little Italy, the "reassuring fragrance of warm bread, the heady aroma of roasting coffee, the musty smell of wooden barrels filled with wine, the pungent odors of ripe olives and anchovies in brine, of gorgonzola and provvolone [sic] cheese and hanging salami" (Sermolino 1952, 25) heartened Italian immigrants who managed to breathe the osmosphere of their own land. Protected by a micro-osmosphere suspended in a macro-osmosphere that has its own roots in pluralism, these cases suggest the image of an osmospheric food melting pot. Sloterdijk calls *plural spherology* the most characteristic form of thought and of society today, characterised by the proliferation of multiplicity, and co-isolation.[55] Foam bubbles, that is, couples, households and survival communities, are, in his words, "self-referentially constituted microcontinents. However much they might purport to be connected with other and outside things, they initially round themselves off purely in their respective selves" (Sloterdijk 2016, 56). Societies are then configured as entities that inhabit and shape osmospheres, sensual and affective topographies from which the very community emerges, pouring into them.

The various problems arising from the co-existence of multi-ethnic osmospheric foams can nevertheless turn into aesthetic and socio-political potential, as well as sources of artistic inspiration. On the one hand, they concretise some of the spatio-temporal peculiarities of olfactory perception, hence stimulating a deeper investigation. On the other hand, they encourage one to reflect on the osmospheric value attributed to food and spaces, where perceptual qualities become the bearer of ethical instances and racial prejudices clearly conveyed by the verbal expressions used to describe them. Both elements are present in the work of U.S. artist Brian Goeltzenleuchter, one of the pioneers of olfactory art whose research on smell I will tackle further. Here, two of his projects deserve brief mention: *The Olfactory Present: By Means of Smoke* and *Sillage*.

The Olfactory Present: By Means of Smoke (2022)[56] is the result of Goeltzenleuchter's collaboration with four women, different in nationality but equal in cookery skills. The project consists of a series of ethnographic reviews, a cooking school, watercolour paintings and a forthcoming cookbook. In a nutshell, it aims at investigating food as a tool for

---

54   Cinotto 2013, 85.
55   In general, Bonaiuti 2022.
56   See https://www.bgprojects.com/home/2022/10/31/the-olfactory-present-by-means-of-smoke.

transmitting knowledge and recipes as scores that the performer can only hybridise. That said, as the title suggests, the focus lies on the notion of *olfactory present*, a common thread of the artist's poetics which, in this case, revealed itself to him in the guise of a composite but simultaneous multi-ethnic food osmosphere. This happened while he was walking through a park in San Diego flanked by apartments mainly inhabited by immigrants. As Goeltzenleuchter explains:

> I had been thinking about the spatiality of smell in these tight domestic settings, where residents often have to deal with their neighbors' cooking smells, which are diverse and can be quite "exotic", euphemistically speaking, to others. Members of many of these various communities were grilling food for outdoor picnics. As I breathed, I could smell overlapping cuisines. It made me think of what I call the *olfactory present*: in *that* moment, in *that* space, literal migration and atmospheric migration brought together a mixture of gastronomic traditions, which shook me (and presumably others) awake to the similarities and differences in which cultures experience the present. Whereas most of my work attempts to define or locate the present through the sense of smell, this project fleshed out the idea in relation to postcolonial temporalities.[57]

This example sheds light on the sensory concurrence of alterities that materialises in osmospheric food perception, at the same time putting in place a valorisation of the gastronomic melting pot by fostering sharing and a sense of community beyond diversities.

Goeltzenleuchter's *Sillage*, staged in Los Angeles (2014) and Baltimore (2016), seeks instead to show the latent but stubborn osmospheric fragmentation operating between the neighbourhoods of a city as a foam, where the aesthetic and linguistic connotations can be ascribed to broader socio-economic dynamics. The artwork, which does not concentrate exclusively on food, is performed by the visitors who, at the exhibition, wear the perfume corresponding to the city area they live in. To sniff the other scents, people are encouraged to smell each other, which often leads to conversation about urban patterns and political issues. The artist creates the fragrances according to data from a survey conducted beforehand on the patrons of the hosting museum, which ask them to associate each city neighbourhood to an odour. Considering only the gastronomic aspects, answers reveal, first of all, which areas are the most foodified.[58] For our purposes, the case of Baltimore discloses

---

57 Personal communication with Brian Goeltzenleuchter, whom I thank infinitely for the stimulating exchange, as well as for his kindness and generosity.
58 See Goeltzenleuchter 2018, 255-258; https://www.bgprojects.com/home/2017/9/5/sillage-los-angeles. For instance, in Los Angeles, East/Northeast Los Angeles,

fruitful insights.[59] In addition to the Northeast being associated with roasted coffee, the East and Southeast are described through food osmospheres in such a way as to reveal socio-economic disparities and how this translates into aesthetic values and lexical choices. Recurring odours for East Baltimore are trash and mildew; verbal labels include nomenclature such as "skunk weed" (the negative expression for the smell of marijuana) and "pit beef", a peculiar way of cooking meat connected to low-income African-American communities. Although this dish is widely appreciated and consumed, most people judge negatively the city areas affiliated with it. Southeast Baltimore is instead pervaded by an osmosphere characterised by "undertones of gentrified, white or hipster Baltimore",[60] which fully corresponds to its reputation as an old-fashioned but charming neighbourhood. Associated with freshly baked bread because of the presence of a historical bread factory, the word cloud lists flavours like Old Bay Seasoning (a blend of herbs and spices marketed throughout the U.S. but originally from Baltimore), beer, ice cream, pizza, cinnamon, raisin, fish, coffee and tacos. As is clear, the osmosphere of ethnic popular gastronomy is persistently coloured by a hostile pitch, whereas local dishes (or ethnic ones, but assimilated and adapted to North American taste) contribute to the positive idea of a clean and quiet place.

Food osmosphere can even symbolise the temporary power of a minority over another one: as a bullied Puerto Rican living in an Italian block in Harlem, Piri Thomas (1967, 27) recalls, with a certain sense of pride, that "Momma was cooking, and the smell of rice and beans was beating the smell of Parmesan cheese from the other apartments". Another example is Porta Palazzo in Turin, the largest street market in Europe, which embeds an osmospheric micro-foam in a multi-ethnic district: food flavours follow one another evoking gastronomic cultures from all over the world. Their salience fluctuates depending on the time of the year. During Ramadan, the Islamic osmosphere stands out when the daily fast is broken, and pots of *harira*, a North African soup, "bubble all afternoon, and the scent of coriander and ginger wafts out into the streets" (Black 2012, 107).

Going even further, one's very self can be structured as a "multi-ethnic foam", where the different food osmospheres one identifies with keep more or less conflicting relations. The sense of belonging to assorted worlds can be qualified by collision, friction or cohesion. The literature by second-generation immigrants opens up to interesting considerations. An example

---

Hollywood and San Fernando Valley are respectively associated, amongst other non-food smells, to Mexican food, cotton candy, and rosemary/melting bubble-gum.

59   Goeltzenleuchter 2021; https://www.bgprojects.com/home/2017/9/4/sillage-baltimore.

60   Personal communication with the artist.

is *Pecore nere* (Black Sheep), a collection of autobiographical stories by four women united by a hybrid ethnicity.[61] The osmospheric and, especially, gastronomic sphere is an incisive means to exemplify it. According to their effects, food flavours represent either a remedy to homesickness, an obstacle to a complete integration, or a barrier to the acceptance of their original identity. Whereas the aroma of spices soothes the homesickness suffered by Laila Wadia, born in Bombay and transplanted in Italy when she was twenty, that of pork sausages is unbearable to Igiaba Scego, an Italo-Somali and Sunni Muslim, despite her efforts to overcome such a disgust in order not to be split in two ethnic halves anymore. Finally, once landed in Adras for the first time, Gabriella Kuruvilla, born and raised in Milan by her Italian mother and Indian father, feels almost asphyxiated by the Indian atmosphere. Here, ethnic smells take on the perturbing tones of a journey to discover intimate unknown roots; she finds relief just in a stateless, westernised and air-conditioned luxury hotel, osmospherically hermetic and gastronomically homologated.

Within the theme of ethnic issues, gastro-chauvinism plays a part as well.[62] As an example, Serres (2008, 166) acknowledges his difficulties in "understanding that other culture, of boiled food, more Nordic or puritanical, hidden beneath the smell of cabbage". To explain and validate his rejection, he adds: "I have lived downwind of a fast food restaurant long enough to know how disgusting it is to be lacking in culture" (ibid). Indeed, many pages could be devoted to the odour of cabbage as an osmospheric stereotype in xenophobic or classist discourses. Reading *The Diary of a Young Girl* we can smell the omnipresence of fermented kale in Dutch cuisine, whose offensive stench forces Anne Frank (1997, 212) to protect her nose with a handkerchief soaked in pre-war perfume. In *The Nonexistent Knight*, Calvino (1962, 50) imbues the opposing regiments in the Crusade with the odour of cabbage soup exhaling from the field kitchens. Here, however, the annoying smell *bridges* ethnic differences.

Getting over gastronomic flag-waving through revolting ingredients and their flavour is at the basis of the concept of the *Disgusting Food Museum*. Based in Malmö (Sweden), its stable exhibition displays 80 repulsive foods

---

61   Kuruvilla *et al.* 2005.
62   "Demon 79", the last episode of the sixth season of the series *Black Mirror*, is set in an extremely racist and intolerant Northern England in the late 1970s. The protagonist, an Indian sales assistant, is invited by her boss to opt for sandwiches for her lunch break, or to eat her Indian meals closed in the basement of the shop, as her British (and conservative) colleague complains about the stench permeating the room after she has eaten her food.

from all over the world. Visitors, noticing that such gastronomic foulness also includes some of their own traditional foods, are likely to realise that "alien" is a relative term, and that disgust, being largely culture-driven, is not only a double-edged sword, but also a potentially educational tool to question ethnic prejudice.[63] Indeed, as a prosthetic projection of the self in the public space, smell can cause deep humiliation to the person exhaling it. We have already tackled something similar when considering Father Terrier's discomfort and sense of violated nakedness when Grenouille, still nursing, seems to scrutinise his deeper self through his nostrils. Embarrassment for one's own food osmosphere often leads to the attempt to conceal it. Moved from North India to New Jersey as a child, journalist A. Mitra Kalita (2003, 2) recalls: "Before friends came over, I sprayed several rounds of air freshener to rid our house of its pungent cooking odor; I never smelled the scent my brothers and I dubbed 'IFS,' for Indian Food Smell, but knew it existed because my classmates told me so". The person who smells feels an "atmosphere of external shame, delocalised and emblematically embodied in a kind of anonymous gaze" (Griffero 2014, 140); like in the atmosphere of shame — but, in this case, apparently without guilt in the strong sense —, contraction is the predominant sensorymotor tension. Osmospherically, we might talk of the wrinkling nose of the *Doppelgänger* that reveals the self to itself, in a reflected game of mirrors.

3.4 *Smelly Classes*

> Cabbage was always a depressing reminder of the leaner
> years of my childhood and I suffered silently whenever she
> served it, but this was the third time within the week and it
> dawned on me that Mary must be short of money.
> Ralph Ellison

The osmospheric timbre lingering in ethnic conflicts operates in a similar way in the class hierarchy. As pointed out by Corbin (1986, 142-160), "the stench of the poor" became one of the most monitored elements and, at the same time, one of the most repeated classist accusations against low-income people, in conjunction with the rise of the bourgeois class in the 19th century before Pasteur's theories. Indeed, it is significant that what Corbin calls *olfactory revolution* took place during the 18th century, the *century*

---

63   On this, Spaid 2021.

of taste, to borrow George Dickie's (1996) well-known expression, which saw the birth of aesthetics in its modern sense, and also of gastronomy as a socially recognised practice of cultural performance, with the invention of restaurants as public eating places, as well as of museum institutions. According to Corbin, the reasons for the 18th-century olfactory turn were mainly twofold: the first was the relationship between diseases and smells (and hence, the hygienic imperative); the second was the bourgeoisie's desire for distinction. The new social class, in fact, aimed to differentiate itself also from an olfactory perspective, englobing itself in an osmosphere dissimilar both from the vulgar olfactory excesses of the masses, and from the stratified perfumes of the nobility. This change was reflected, on the one hand, in the art of perfumery which, instead of the essences of animal origin that had hitherto been more popular, increasingly used vegetable products divorced from intense physical secretions; on the other hand, in gastronomy. The taste for delicate foods and gentle flavours was a middle-class paradigm, which ended up corresponding to "elegant" cuisine.

I have outlined elsewhere the main combinations between food and aromas throughout history.[64] Retracing the changes affecting culinary paradigms in terms of olfactory stimuli, whether incorporated into the food itself or released into the environment, would deserve a separate study, which would presumably help understand the varied aesthetic values attributed to food osmospheres according to gastronomic models and class power. I'll only note that two major patterns can be distinguished: *food/smell discrepancy* and *food/smell correspondence*, each coinciding with the specific cultural-dietary system of the time it is in force.[65] The former is identified, on the one hand, by the massive use of condiments and seasoning in order to conceal food flavours; on the other hand, by strong ambient scents spread throughout the spaces where food is eaten. The discrepancy between food and its smell is a feature of the "synthetic" model of gastronomy, in force in Europe roughly from antiquity until the 17th century, privileging mixing, artifice, accumulation and aromatic stratification, the latter recurring in the banquets for the rich. On the contrary, the latter is characterised by the idea of "purity": to be appreciated, a food has to keep *its* specific smell. This style, coeval with the olfactory

---

64 Mancioppi 2022a, 138-141.
65 Within this framework, a third, very recent and niche model can be extrapolated: *no-food/food smell*, which emphasises the olfactory dimension to the detriment of the ingestion of food as an edible matter. As we shall see, it finds its roots in Futurist cuisine, with many variations in the contemporary world.

revolution fostered by the middle class, dates back to Modernity, having to do with the "analytical" turn of cuisine and taste.[66]

Simultaneously, *class-specific odours* have also taken the shape of an instrumental means to describe the miserable conditions of working classes in cities or of peasants in the countryside.[67] "Stinking potatoes fouled the land,/pits turned pus into filthy mounds:/and where potato diggers are/you still smell the running sore" is Heaney's (1980, 22-23) denunciation of the life conditions Irish potato diggers had to endure. Osmospheres can call into question the political establishment, as the large presence of olfactory depictions in social novels shows.[68] In this respect, it is worth mentioning Charles Dickens' works.[69] As emblematic examples, both *Oliver Twist* and *Great Expectations* are dotted with notations on smells that can be read as status symbols. In the former, one description of the filthiest and overpopulated London slums reads: "Jostling with unemployed labourers of the lowest class, ballast-heavers, coal-whippers, brazen women, ragged children, and the raff and refuse of the river, [the visitor] makes his way with difficulty along, assailed by the offensive sights and smells from the narrow alleys [...]" (Dickens 1992, 381). With reference to the latter book, among many other, the rich fragrances of scented soap and sweet cakes can be opposed to the poor odours of beer, stale air or soot; on their part, the prisoners give off "that curious flavour of bread-poultice, baize, rope-yarn, and hearthstone" (Dickens 2002, 225). Interestingly, the uncle of the protagonist Pip, Mr. Pumblechook, being a corn-chandler, smells of seeds and corduroys (ibid, 52) — a commonly used textile by both country gentlemen and workers —, satirically representing the commercial classes whose personality traits (in this case, osmosphere) correspond to the qualities of material goods through which their prosperity was acquired.

If the smell of dirt and sweat can metaphorise the industriousness and the dignity of a humble origin, it can also act as "a premeditated ostentation of poverty, a demonstration of trade unionism" (Gadda 2017, 128). Indeed, the *venerable perspiration of work* often constitutes an insurmountable obstacle even for those of the upper strata who are willing to "make considerable sacrifices of personal comfort and do without various preferences and enjoyments in favor of the disinherited" (Simmel 2009, 577). In this sense, smell can sometimes act as an inhibitor of social responsibility, preventing the well-off from putting into practice

66   Flandrin, Montanari 2000.
67   Illich 1985, 59.
68   Carlisle 2001.
69   Reinarz 2014, 22.

humanitarian acts and charity, sharpening class struggle. Needless to say, the previously discussed contraposition between the high and the low in olfactory terms also applies to classes, which differ according to their position in the vertical axis. Whereas the lower classes incarnate the lowest parts of the social body, hence the material sphere, the upper ones symbolise the detachment from the most urgent and basic needs. Both correspond to the respective osmospheric-topological values, which are obviously aesthetically constructed by those who hold the power. In fact, stench is more often attributed to the oppressed and outcast ones.

The osmospheric class conflict is evident in the movie *Parasite* (2019, directed by Bong Joon-ho), where the antithesis between the above/wealth/fragrance and the below/poverty/pong is precisely aimed at conveying the economic tensions and class disparities of South Korean society. The Parks, emblem of the well-off, live in airy villas on the hills; they are clean and candid in moral terms too, since they don't need to resort to ploys to survive. On the contrary, the poor — the Kims, who succeed in being hired by the Parks under false pretences by concealing their kinship — find their place underground, in narrow basements. Whereas the second-born of the Park family is the only one who notices that the new employees smell the same, his father, Mr. Park, is only tormented by the annoying odour of the chauffeur, Mr. Kim. "You must have smelled it. That smell that wafts through the car, how to describe it?" says Mr. Park to his wife, who replies: "An old man's smell?". And Mr. Park: "No no, it's not that. What is it? Like an old radish? No. You know when you boil a rag? It smells like that. Anyway, even though he always seems about to cross the line, he never does cross it. [...] But that smell crosses the line. It powers through right into the back seat". Finally, casting about to find an effective analogy, he adds: "It's hard to describe. But you sometimes smell it on the subway. [...] People who ride the subway have a special smell".

As is well-known, George Orwell (1965, 129) ascribes the rooted conviction that *the lower classes smell* to the middle-class upbringing.[70] Sketching the traits of a true socio-aesthetics of smell, in various essays he stresses what I tried to posit earlier, namely that one's odour is irreducibly deduced reflexively, where the "other" can be the result of an array of axiomatic conventions. Class smell seems to be a matter of principle, partially or entirely independent of the actual odour, affecting the latter in a performative way. As a member of the scholarly class, Orwell (1981, 37-38) recollects of his youth:

---

70   See Sutherland 2017.

I had no money, I was weak, I was ugly, I was unpopular, I had a chronic cough, I was cowardly, I smelt. [...] But a child's belief in its own shortcomings is not much influenced by facts. I believed, for example, that I "smelt," but this was based simply on general probability. It was notorious that disagreeable people smelt, and therefore presumably I did so too.

Impressive cases of class-specific odours can be found by considering the Indian millenary and still latent caste system. From the Hindu funeral rites[71] to the olfactory qualities of each profession,[72] the osmosphere interlaces with sharp distinctions between classes. Food plays a relevant role. The dark misery of the Pariahs of the Madras Presidency can be inferred reading some lines by Abbe Dubois, a French Catholic missionary. He recorded that they are particularly despised for what (and how) they eat and smell:

> Attracted by the smell, they will collect in crowds round any carrion and contend for the spoil with the dogs, jackals, crows and other carnivorous animals. They then divide the semi-putrid flesh and carry it away to their huts, where they devour it, often without rice or anything else to disguise the flavour [...]; and though the Pariahs themselves do not seem to be affected by the smell, travellers passing near their village quickly perceive it and can tell at once the caste of the people living there (cit. in Kapoor 2022a, 30).

In spite of that, a depressing food osmosphere can concur with a social disgrace that is shared by an entire community, while simultaneously recalling past opulent times. The misery that grips the peasants of the Friulian countryside after a famine is rendered by a 19th-century Italian patriot and writer as follows: "hunger and discontentment settled on every hearth; and at sunset, when all courtyards used to smell of steaming pork chops, or tasty soups, a melancholic perfume of boiled turnips wafted through the districts" (Nievo 2010, 468).

Although class partaking can be the result of an individual's choice, especially in societies that grant social mobility, social inheritance tends

---

71 Commonly, pyres for the upper classes are sandalwood-scented, whereas the lower-class ones use fainter aromatic substances. In general, as evidenced by places of burnt offerings, each emanation is functional to propitiate divinities. In Italian, *incensare*, which etymologically means "to burn resins, incense", has also taken on the meaning of "to praise, to flatter" (Frisk 1960, 694-695). In a proportional relationship, the more intense the flattery, the more generous the benefit, also in Indian culture.

72 On smell, social order and caste, Lee 2017; with respect to leatherworking in tanneries, Kapoor 2022b.

to characterise one's olfactory portrait lifelong. That's why the *parvenu* is often represented as suspicious also in osmospheric terms. The parvenus live in a social limbo: even if economically comparable to those of the upper classes, their recently acquired status still reminds of the bottom from which their social climbing started. The upstart is often snobbish, which is also described as being "sniffy". In Italian, a "snobbish attitude" is rendered through the olfactory idiom *avere la puzza sotto il naso*, verbatim "to have the stench under the nose", meaning a generalised repugnance. Think of the very archetype, the freedman Trimalchio as described by Petronius in the famous episode of the banquet in *The Satyricon*. Whereas his personal scent is not mentioned, overwhelmed by the most luxurious foods and balm perfumes, the stink of his slaves is the reason why he has allotted each diner an entire table (Petronius 1997, 25). Formerly a slave himself, he evidently despises his own social background as a bad smell.

Tasteless wealth can even constitute the osmosphere of a period. This is well express by Orwell (1981, 33) when he compares the odour of English upper and upper-middle classes in the decades before 1914 to "a smell of the more vulgar, un-grown-up kinds of luxury, a smell of brilliantine and créme de menthe and soft-centred chocolate — an atmosphere, as it were, of eating everlasting strawberry ices on green lawns to the tune of the Eton Boating Song". This proves that, in contrast with the old saying *pecunia non olet*, money *does* smell: it stinks when linked not only to greed, crime, colonisation,[73] but also to inelegance. Woolf (1977, 528) declares: "first class travellers are always old fat testy and smell of eau de cologne, which make me sick". Indeed, considering the recurrent inclination to an excessive use of perfume, the enriched seem to aspire to concealing their own smell. "It smells of cheap perfume in here" (Chekhov 2010, 83) the aristocratic Gaev scornfully remarks with regard to the parvenu Lopakhin, vulgarly Patchouli-smelling in *The Cherry Orchard*. Indeed, a fragrance is generally considered elegant if diluted and worn with sobriety; tacky if too harsh. From a socio-aesthetic perspective, quantity and intensity are both aspects that, more than determining the pleasantness or unpleasantness of one's perfume, hint at the undisguised desire to hide one's personal odour and social position. In this case, parvenus and lower classes are osmospherically similar, in that both aspire to removing olfactory prejudicial attributions by overloading osmospheric traits, with the result of reinforcing them. William Ian Miller (1997, 247) puts it very accurately:

---

73   Branco, Mohr 2018; Hsu 2020, 177-179.

One wonders if the heavy use of colognes and aftershaves by lower-class men is a reflex of these beliefs. Their belief is that one cannot smell bad if one smells good, but in fact this is a misreading of the code that governs the relation of smell to class. The true rule is that one does not smell bad if one does not smell. So the aftershave, sure enough, begins to stink. [...] So those low who care enough about how they are seen by the high come to mistrust their senses and admit "the general probability" that they smell.

Interesting Orwellian insights on the osmological social problem in relation to food can be found in *The Road to Wigan Pier*, a sociological cross section of the life condition of English miners in the 1930s. Here, the social osmosphere is not just characterised by the dirt and the overcrowded housing, but also by the diet, since a "human being is primarily a bag for putting food into" (Orwell 1965, 92). A healthy and balanced diet is directly proportional to income; the logic is that "the less money you have, the less inclined you feel to spend it on wholesome food" (ibid, 96). This is why only a "millionaire may enjoy breakfasting off orange juice and Ryvita biscuits [light rye-based crispbread]; an unemployed man doesn't" (ibid). Poor people eat junk food not so much for its lower cost, but because it represents the only appealing and affordable comfort in an otherwise miserable life. White bread and margarine, canned food, potatoes, powdered milk, fish and chips, corned beef and sugared tea are ordinary staples; in turn, this dietary regime determines physical decay, bodily smell and perceptual sensitivity. Thus, poor people would lose their ability to detect decent food: in line with Serres (2008, 185-186) and his critique of modern food industry, Orwell (1965, 202) maintains that in the "highly mechanised countries, thanks to tinned food, cold storage, synthetic flavouring matters, etc., the palate is almost a dead organ". The contemporary revival of "peasant foods" — dishes that today are treated as delicacies, whose humble ingredients are appreciated for being "traditional", simple, genuine and nutritional — proves to be, more than a destigmatisation of lower-class meals, a bourgeois socio-gastronomic construct which essentially renames middle-class diet through an idealisation and illusory elevation of the subordinate's tables.

Going back to the social class pyramid, food itself has suffered from discrimination according to its position in the environment throughout history and in particular in the Middle Ages. Hegemonic classes deserved high-placed foodstuffs, namely fruits and game birds; underclasses, on the contrary, low-placed ones such as tubers and vegetables like onion, potato and cabbage,[74] the latter an osmospheric insignia of poverty. Another work saturated with status-symbol osmospheres is Émile Zola's *The Belly of Paris*. Among other foods and flavours, piles of cabbages tower in the book, and their odour wafts through Les Halles where, early in the morning, all the hungry people flock to eat a cabbage soup that gives off "a terrible smell" (Zola 2009, 23). It is curious that people in need as well as the malnourished or underfed masses are often described as smelling of what they eat. Reversely, food class-specific osmospheres are rarely attributed to wealthy people. As the architecture and location of the rooms in rich ancient Roman houses seem to suggest, food smells and cooking odours were considered particularly unpleasant. The kitchen was usually placed in the furthest wing of the building, away from the dining room and close to the toilets and the slaves' quarters.[75] Moreover, it is not surprising that the bourgeois osmosphere is detached from food if we consider, on the one hand, its mid position between the high and the low, and, on the other hand, its historical connection to the tactics of deodorisation.

As many recipe books testify, middle-class gastronomy is based on the value of *delicacy*, hence the preference for non-pungent ingredients or for culinary processes aimed at tempering flavours. The famous cookbook by Pellegrino Artusi, *Science in the Kitchen and the Art of Eating Well*,[76] shows it very clearly, being explicitly addressed to Italian middle-class households. The adjective "delicate" (together with the Italian *gentile*, "gentle, fine") abounds, often associated with ladies' refined taste.[77] Suffice it to mention the recipe of salted codfish Mont Blanc style, where codfish "loses its vulgar nature, becoming very delicate and worthy of gracing an elegant table" if accurately prepared (Artusi 2003, 115). Exceptionally, in the recipe of country-style spaghetti, garlic is reclassified, not just for its medicinal properties but also for its flavour, as long as it is cooked properly. Quite a few people, according to Artusi, "have a horror of garlic merely because they can smell it on the breath of those who have eaten it raw or poorly cooked. As a result, they absolutely ban this plebeian condiment

---

74   Montanari 2010, 38.
75   Potter 2015, 127; Nissin 2022.
76   The original work (1891) was punctually followed by new editions updated by the author. The last version dates back to 1911, when Artusi passed away. The publication period of Artusi's book coincides with the years of greater expansion of the middle class.
77   Giacomo Leopardi (2013, 814) observes that people, and especially women, can no longer tolerate intense odours, which were conversely accepted by former generations and also by the Greeks and Romans, ascribing this "taste for insipid and delicate flavors" to civilisation.

from their kitchens" (ibid, 108). An emblem of rusticity since the classical
era, garlic has traditionally been treated as a food for the lower classes:
Martial (1919, 343) describes the osmosphere of a poor family's house
mentioning garlic and onion; the same occurs in Indian culture.[78] It is even
the *pars pro toto* for stinky food[79] or coarse dishes qualifying the vile-
smelling effluvia of 19th-century sailors.[80]

Leaving aside the exceptional nature of the revaluation of garlic, such
a gastronomic model derives from the medical theories of that time which
"assigned different digestive and assimilative powers to stomachs belonging
to people of different social origin" (Ballerini 2003, lx). In other words, each
person would be equipped with a sensitivity and bodily constitution which
correspond to their position in the pyramid: higher and middle classes are
not able to bear intense flavours and to digest heavy and popular foods,
which are instead enjoyed and consumed by peasants and labourers. Given
one's social position, one has to eat accordingly. Not coincidentally, Artusi
(2003, 73) observes that it "is said, and rightly so, that beans are the meat of
the poor". The manual labourer who cannot afford a piece of meat to feed
his family, "often finds in beans a healthy, nourishing and cheap alternative.
Moreover, beans take some time to leave the body, quelling hunger pangs
for a good while" (ibid). When giving the recipe for lentil soup, he expands
such an opinion writing that "lentils seem more delicately flavored than
beans in general, and [...] less dangerous than common beans" (ibid, 75).
With respect to our socio-aesthetic perspective, this assumption fossilises
osmospheric discriminations and classist representations.

In conclusion, I would like to emphasise a peculiarity of egalitarianism
which arises when it comes to smells. Whereas the taste of food is
exclusive (to eat and savour food, one must possess it), its odour, as it
spreads, is more "democratic". Referring to an episode of *Perfume* by
Süskind, the poor Jeanne Bussie, the umpteenth nanny who wants to get
rid of Grenouille, acknowledges that he lacks the peculiar sweet scent of
a baby's head which is similar to caramel. "Caramel? What do you know
about caramel? Have you ever eaten any?" (Süskind 1986, 13), Father

---

78   McHugh 2012, 265 n. 114.
79   Robinson 2020.
80   Forget 1832, 127. *Garlic Soap* (1994-2015) by the artist Oswaldo Maciá rests on
      the opposing symbolic values ascribed to this ingredient, deemed at the same time
      magical and repugnant. The sculpture consists of a soap bar made of garlic oil and
      displayed on a blue and white soap dish, reflecting "on the languages, peoples
      and beliefs that have been eradicated in the name of cleaning". See https://www.
      oswaldomacia.com/garlic-soap.

Terrier asks her sardonically. "Not exactly", she replies, "But once I was in a grand mansion in the rue Saint-Honoré and watched how they made it out of melted sugar and cream. It smelled so good that I've never forgotten it" (ibid). Thomas McLean's "Charity tubes"[81] also revolves around this olfactory peculiarity. The strip is a satirical illustration of London in the Industrial Revolution; it depicts labourers inhaling some smoke coming out of pipes guarded by a man in livery. As explained by the caption, this would be a charitable act: the philanthropists, enriched thanks to the new machinery, *offer* the scent of their rich tables. Yet this is evidently an act of *un*charity which, rather, constitutes a tormenting ostentation. As a status symbol, the food osmosphere nourishes the self-satisfaction of those who emanate it, not the belly of those who sniff it.

A further point is worth mentioning with respect to torture through food smells. The penances reserved for gluttony sinners in various Christian representations are emblematic. Dante's *Divine Comedy* depicts two opposite ways to chastise through odours in line with the logic of *contrapasso*, according to which sinners are sentenced to a punishment fit (by similarity or contrast) for the committed offence. In *Inferno*, Circle III symbolises the negative overturning of the feast's typical sensory pleasures. Gluttons, commonly well-off people, instead of being delighted by music and comforts, are deafened by the barking of Cerberus and mauled by its sharp nails. Furthermore, damned souls are tormented by the stench of mud in which they lie, the osmospheric transposition of the perfumes, redolent balms, mouth-watering flavours, delicious dishes and flowers they excessively enjoyed in life. The verses read: "Snow, massive hailstones, black, tainted water/pour down in the sheets through tenebrae of air./The earth absorbs it all and stinks, revoltingly" (*Inferno*, canto VI, vv. 10-12).

In Dante's *Purgatorio*, the osmosphere does not undergo any qualitative change and, precisely because of this, it rather carries out a quantitative deformation which causes tribulation. Circle VI is saturated with the "good and sweet" (*Purgatorio*, canto XXII, v. 132) perfume of fruits hanging from two trees. The penitents are extremely slender and famished; they are plagued not only with unbearable hunger, which is sharpened by the scent of fruit they cannot eat, but also with thirst, which is analogously worsened by the odour of water they are not allowed to drink. Sinners are condemned to the agony of being *unceasingly* tickled by tempting food they are unable

---

81 Part of the "Living made easy" series (January 1830), *Science Museum*, London.

to ingest; this gap transforms food aromas from an invitation to a torment.[82] What occurs is the twisting of the normal alternation between olfactory content and its specific *formed vacuum*. Speculating on the formed vacuum inherent to every sense as posited by E. Straus, Tellenbach (1981, 223) claims that "the formed vacuum of the oral sense must be relatively large, considering how rarely smelling and tasting occur in comparison to seeing and hearing. This is an important point, because under certain psychotic conditions it can be reversed". Whereas smell perception usually establishes the predominance of its absence, the preeminence of its salience, on the contrary, breaks the normal aesthetic-experiential rhythm of the olfactive. Hence, olfactory punishments are literally *tortures* in that they constitute atypical perceptual torsions. The fact that some forms of psychosis imply an imbalance towards the pole of continuous olfactory saturation corroborates the exasperating penitence reserved for the gluttons.

The sense of smell plays a pivotal role because of the tight relationship between pleasant scents, desire and the pull towards consumption. In this widely acknowledged mechanism lies the problem of dissatisfaction. Many philosophers and poets have pointed this out. In his *Zibaldone*, Giacomo Leopardi (2013, 715) notes that "[v]ery fragrant things that are also good to eat generally overwhelm the taste with the smell and the taste never quite lives up to the expectation that the smell had left us with". Food smell acts as a propulsive power, a driving stimulus that converts into an active impulse. And when, in this progression, an interruption occurs, olfaction turns into torture. No less importantly, in the afterlife, the pervasiveness of the food osmosphere that those who overindulged enjoyed in life becomes equally distressing as the food shortage suffered by a person in need.

---

82 Olfactory tortures are manifold; think also of the spoiled food served in jails or of the food left to rot in the cells of prisoners who refuse to eat. See Drobnick 2006a; Jones 2017. For the food situation in American prisons: Soble, Stroud, Weinstein 2020. Along these lines, Proust provides a case of osmospheric workplace bullying ante-litteram, perpetrated by Marcel's aunt against her kitchen-maid. Marcel recalls that "many years later, we discovered that if we had been fed on asparagus day after day throughout that summer, it was because their smell gave [her] who had to prepare them such violent attacks of asthma that she was finally obliged to leave my aunt's service" (Proust 1998, 173).

3.5 *Excursus 1: Truffle And Class*

> Truffle oil is the tomato ketchup of the middle class.
> Anthony Bourdain

Truffle is an interesting subject when dealing with the intersection of smell and class. Its complex history shows that gastronomic prestige often coincides with diplomatic dynamics and the economic power of the nations where it grows, with notable fluctuations in its imaginary.[83] Indeed, the truffles eaten in Ancient Greek and Rome were not the same as those consumed today worldwide (mostly, but not exclusively, European); rather, they were "desert truffles" (*terfezia arenaria*), another species, more similar to a vegetable, from Africa.[84] Neither doctors nor naturalists have agreed on the humoral nature of the truffle. Medical theories have been oscillating between harmfulness and wholesomeness; even its proverbial aphrodisiac effect has been occasionally doubted. Whether truffles are roots, plants, seeds, tubers, animal products, earthy protuberances, or the result of humidity, rotting wood, rain and lightning is a thorny issue which has protracted until modernity,[85] when they have been categorised as mushrooms, in conjunction with the recognition of the fungi kingdom as distinct from the plant and animal ones, in parallel to the developments of mycology in the 18th century.

From Mediaeval times, winter truffles have been considered the noblest ones, specifically *tuber melanosporum* Vitt., or "prized black truffle", and *tuber magnatum* Pico, "prized white truffle". The gastro-chauvinism between Italy and France, and consequently the alternating superiority attributed to the respective truffles, has kept pace with the political influence of those nations. The rivalry still persists today; interestingly, when extolling truffle scent, Serres (2008, 162) specifically refers to those from Quercy,[86] since he regards the white Italian ones as *hypocritical* (I will resume this point shortly). In any case, truffle's strong smell has traditionally distinguished

---

83 Rittersma 2010, 2011.
84 Hall, Brown, Zambonelli 2007.
85 Pliny the Elder, Dioscorides and Nicander are just some of the prominent thinkers who questioned the nature of truffles. See Bock 1522; for an overview, Nowak 2015.
86 As a child in Quercy, the geographer Paul Claval remembers that "he was enchanted in winter by the smell of the truffle ragouts brought by his classmates and which were warmed up all morning in bowls on the stove of the school where his mother was a teacher" (cit. in Pitte 1991, 20).

aristocratic tables. Bartolomeo Scappi, a famous Italian Renaissance chef who cooked for prominent personalities, cardinals, and led the Vatican kitchen, gives many recipes involving the use of truffle. It is used in various pies, in stuffed pullets and in the "thick soup of truffle with chicks and other ingredients" (Scappi 2008, 245), where he parenthetically expresses his preference for Italian black truffles. Leaving nationalist quarrels aside, truffle holds a high stature; Dumas (1873, 1034) refers to it as the *sacrum sacrorum* of gastronomes. However, an ambiguity lingers, seemingly resting on the inconsistency between its humble origin and its social position (even if subterranean, it is an icon of opulence), not to mention the contrast between the inebriating aroma and its visual appearance similar to an irregular potato-shaped lump. In a notable description of cheeses, Zola (2009, 211) draws a parallel between the princely air and fat veined face of *roqueforts* and the ailing look of rich people who suffer from diseases caused by excessive consumption of truffle.

In French, *truffe*, "truffle", also means "mockery, fraud, deceit".[87] As is well known, in 1664 Molière entitled his comedy *Tartuffe ou l'Imposteur,* which is a sharp critique of 17th-century society. Here, Tartuffe impersonates the false devotee who strives to gain the trust of others for personal gain through eloquence and persuasiveness. On the contrary, the "truffled" are those who fall for it. "Truffle" has thus become synonymous with fraud, impostor and liar. Such a personification recurs in further political pamphlets and writings in France and Italy. According to Antonio Gramsci, *Tartufo* is the conformist, the pietist who makes the socialist coincide with the demagogue; Tartufo thus "modifies the vocabulary and determines a certain fortune to words" (Gramsci 1917), rehabilitating what is politically incorrect.

The ability of truffle "to embellish everything it touches" (Dumas 1873, 928) insinuates from the gastronomic domain into human psychology, acquiring a negative connotation. Indeed, its being hypogeous implies its hypocrisy: an elusive entity which grows underground. Its low-born nature is in contradiction with its high reputation obtained by means of its seductive smell. In many respects, truffle is analogous to the social climber. The mushroom proliferates by charming fungivore animals with its aroma; likewise, its personification acts opportunistically to achieve his ambitions; hence, the air of dishonesty which surrounds truffles. The

---

87 Quitard 1842, 662; Bloch, von Wartburg 1964, 653, 654; Picoche 2002, 562. Funnily enough, one of the most famous pamphlets on truffles published in the 16th century is by Alfonso Ceccarelli, who was a counterfeiter himself (Ceccarelli 2018).

"disgust for the smell/of truffles, the money that came your way" is a poetic image by Montale (2012, 479) to criticise the hypocrisy of intellectuals — in this case, the target is Pier Paolo Pasolini — who earn a profit from ideological and homologated positions. The strong and peculiar smell of truffle coincides with shady money also as a metaphor for reputation.

Given the economic value of truffles, adulterations have been (and still are) recurrent, contributing to the association between truffle and deception. Of course, frauds and sophistication techniques take advantage of the difficulty in discerning added odours. A systematic truffle forgery dates back to 1881, when a factory in Paris was caught red-handed while producing fake truffles made of rotten potatoes dyed black and flavoured with fennel essence. Similar cases have then multiplied. The newspapers of the period speak of "truffles" made of earth and spoiled turnips, reporting various cases of food poisoning. A few years later, people were intoxicated by a liqueur used to provide truffles with the peculiar aroma of the Périgord ones. Detected and arrested, the head of the factory declared that he had bought a "patent" from a man who had a large number of customers.[88] Today, sophistication is often obtained by adding synthetic flavours to unripened truffles or less precious species.

The characteristic note of the *tuber melanosporum* (black truffle) is ascribable to *dimethyl sulphide*, whereas that of *tuber magnatum* (white truffle) to *bis(methylthio)methane*. Both are today synthetically created from petroleum-derived products, and added to a wide variety of foods such as oil, butter, pasta, rice, sauces, chips, cheeses, cured meat and even preserved truffles. Truffle-flavoured foodstuffs are sold at an increased price (even ten times higher than the unflavoured versions) which is unjustified: if real truffle is present at all, the quantity is negligible, and for visual rather than aromatic purposes. The spread of synthetic truffle flavourings has had notable repercussions on truffle's aura. Again, in *The Belly of Paris*, the odour of truffles is the quintessence of the delicacies that spread their aroma in the streets. The "scent of truffles, the keenest aroma to be found anywhere in the neighbourhood" (Zola 2009, 167), lingers especially in the Rue Coquillière, where "there was a large provision merchant's that exhaled such a strong perfume that Cadine and Marjolin, when they closed their eyes, could imagine that they were eating the most exquisite foods" (ibid).

Despite truffle flavourings having "vulgarised" the status of truffles, they always *enrich* what they are associated with. The truffle osmosphere

---

88   Bruni 1891.

seems to sway between two poles. On the one hand, it retains its prestige; therefore, synthetic flavourings give rise to a process of *gentrification* of the edible substances to which they are added. On the other hand, truffles are no longer perceived as rare, perishable and, even less so, site-specific and seasonal, since flavourings have *democratised*, homologated and made their osmosphere everlasting.

3.6 *Smells, Law And Prohibition*

> West Madison Street in Chicago, from the edge of the
> Loop to Halsted Street and beyond, smelled like a distillery
> throughout the dry era.
> Herbert Asbury

Smell and law are ambiguously connected. Given the intrusiveness of odours, they are daily subjected to a wide corpus of taboos and rules *lato sensu*.[89] Nonetheless, in the juridical field *stricto sensu*, the regulation of olfactory emissions, especially when harmless to human or environmental health, is particularly tricky.[90] On one side, the diversity in sensitivities undermines the possibility of establishing a unanimous "intolerability";[91] on the other, the hedonic tone of a substance varies in unpredictable ways, depending on manifold variables such as concentration and air composition.[92] Not least, the spatiality to which smells conform is a thorny legal issue. A first friction between law and smell is terminological: the norm as a "legal precept" is a metaphorical derivation from the Latin *norma*, meaning the "carpenter's square" used to measure right or perpendicular angles.[93] As can be easily inferred, since smells inhabit and tinge a volume that is difficult to limit and measure, having neither sides nor borders nor edges, the ontological status of the two seems to clash. Smell disputes, amongst other things, "one of the most fundamental Western jurisprudential and social principles: property" (Mandic *et al.* 2018, 6).[94]

---

89   A case in point is that, depending on the culture, certain bodily emanations are considered extremely shameful.
90   McCartney 1968, 107-120.
91   Marusek 2018.
92   Nicolay 2006, Bonasoni *et al.* 2022.
93   Onions 1966, 614; Klein 1971, 500.
94   See also Geiregat 2022.

However, analogously to smells, even laws can be interpreted as an irradiation adhering to the environment; that is, as a presence that cannot be dissociated from the space where it is passed and enforced. Philippopoulos-Mihalopoulos (2015, 4) has coined the term *lawscape*, indicating *"the way the ontological tautology between law and space unfolds as difference"*. He maintains that every lawscape aspires to become an *atmosphere*; this gradual shift takes place when the lawscape, disguising itself, pretends to be a non-lawscape (ibid, 107). Indeed, the "aesthesic turn" of law is not without consequences in osmospheric terms.[95] As far as smells are concerned, different dimensions of individual and collective life are affected, from trade marks to urban plans, from food safety to air quality. An odour can display a breach, as in the case of spoiled food stench in a shop. In other cases, the smell itself constitutes the offence. In 2012, Colorado legalised the recreational use of marijuana; however, because of residents' complaints, in the city of Denver its odour can result in sanction when exceeding a specific level measured by a field olfactometer called the "nasal ranger".[96] For as much as odours mark the presence of substances and persons, they can be seen as sensory cues of the *lawscape*, often signalling its inconsistencies and, even more interestingly, the porous borders between public and private spheres which mingle encroaching on each other. In this sense, food flavours are particularly problematic.

An industry can be deemed a "public nuisance" when emitting strong odours which affect the air and life quality of the neighbourhood, as in the case of a sriracha (Thai hot sauce) manufacturer in California, criticised because of its irritating emissions.[97] Domestic cooking smells, while expressing the aesthetic quality of a private dimension, often intrude on other ones or invade the public space. In case of annoyance, their regulation or restriction is nonetheless likely, in turn, to infringe upon human rights. In 2018, an Australian vegan woman sued her neighbours because of the constant smell of fish and meat grilling, which limited her right of enjoying her courtyard. For revenge, once the court dismissed her case in 2019, the neighbours planned to organise a massive barbecue outside her house in Perth, transforming an olfactory dispute into a food-related conflict between "traditional meat-eaters" and vegans.[98] As previously discussed,

---

95 See also Philippopoulos-Mihalopoulos 2013, 2019.
96 Meyer 2013. As testified by a wealth of technical literature, Denver is surely a "bad-smelling" city.
97 Marusek 2018, 38.
98 See https://www.theguardian.com/australia-news/2019/sep/03/vegan-takes-neighbours-to-court-in-western-australia-over-smell-from-barbecues and https://www.foxnews.

food and its osmosphere express social and ethnic identities. Whereas reporting them may be determined by chauvinism or intolerance, their banishment may constitute a discriminating policy.[99]

However, there are still sneaky ways to prohibit a food osmosphere, thereby exerting control and repressing a minority. One is to make people feel ashamed of it, thus preventing its cooking. Returning to the case of Hong Kong, it is symptomatic that, most of the time, Chinese employers do not allow Filipino domestic workers to cook their typical dishes in their homes, claiming that they smell awful. Food is indeed an emblematic soft power tool through which social, ethnic and international relations are organised. Political harmony or clash imply the acceptance or rejection (at times, appropriation) of the other's food osmosphere, even undermining its replication, experience and memory.

Cases involving the forbidding of specific foods in public spaces cannot go unmentioned. The durian, an Asiatic fruit particularly polarising for its strong odour, is not allowed in hotels, public transport and airlines in many countries such as Thailand, Japan and China. A proposed ban for the consumption of hot and "smelly" food in the New York subway and London Underground has instead been assessed but then dismissed; in any case, it is discouraged both by the companies and by travel etiquette. However, those who opposed these public bills referred to both class and ethnic issues, in that those who have to commute long distances by public transport and have only this time of the day to eat a hot meal, are mainly low-income and multi-job earners. In general, strategies to manage odours depend on the collective olfactory sensitivity which varies according to diverse factors. Such measures, stabilised over time but always likely to change, in turn mould common sensibilities, determining the aesthetic value and symbolic dimension of smells. The intertwining between law and smell, the latter being both the pretext and the effect of a juridical scene, clearly emerges in the case of the U.S. Prohibition and its preparatory events. The osmosphere took on particularly interesting nuances, exemplifying a conflict rooted in social instances and food habits.

From 1920 to 1933, the "Volstead Act" (the 18th Amendment) prohibited the manufacture, sale, consumption, transportation, importation and exportation of alcoholic beverages with more than 0,5% ABV, with the exception of sacramental wine, industrial alcohol, fruit juice, cider and

---

com/world/bbq-protest-near-home-of-australian-vegan-who-complained-about-neighbors-grilling-fish-canned-of-legal-threats.

99   For some verdicts, Zarychta 2022.

medicines. Nonetheless, the smell of alcohol stood out not only as a sensory salience around which judicial writs, social identities, aesthetic responses and political dynamics were established, but also as a peculiar osmosphere. Interestingly, the osmosphere of Prohibition seems to have systematically disobeyed its very lawscape. Instead of dissimulating, the lawscape of Prohibition took over the atmosphere of that time, becoming its flavour and name. Let us look at the background.

Between the 19th and the 20th century, in conjunction with mass immigration, the U.S. witnessed a rise in alcohol consumption and in the number of drinking venues, especially saloons: in 1914 some New York districts had a saloon every six dwellers (Lerner 2007, 14). Saloons were ethno-class identifying and socialising places, "club rooms of the neighborhood" (Hoke 1931, 314) mostly patronised by immigrants or labourers who were served alcohol and typical food. Whether German, Irish, Italian, Spanish, Eastern European, Chinese, Greek or Puerto Rican, each saloon had its peculiar osmosphere. The patrons were almost exclusively male; this is why saloons used to host politically-oriented gatherings, too. The pulsating, excited and often dirty atmosphere of uninhibited masculinity,[100] thick with cigar smoke and alcohol vapours, was chaotic due to the animosity of discussion and popular songs. However, although apparently unregulated, the lawscape of the saloon prescribed rigid ethical and behavioural codes: toasts, drink-buying and respectability were precise conventions to be complied with.[101] The overlapping between the saloon alcoholic osmosphere and the aura of the forbidden comes up in many childhood memories: the mystery of the saloon was condensed in the aroma of "drying blood and dead men's bones" (Stevens 1927, 266-267).[102] Indeed, the brutality connected to places soaked with alcohol is a recurrent aspect in narrations of the cross section of the pre-Prohibition period. In *The Great Gatsby*, the protagonist's habit of abstaining from drinking depends on its deleterious effects he directly observed while spending time with a pioneer debauchee who "brought back to the Eastern seaboard the savage violence of the frontier brothel and saloon" (Fitzgerald 2001, 64).

---

100 London 1989, 24-25.

101 Powers 1998, 93-118.

102 Although representing a later period, the artwork *The Beanery* (1965) by Edward Kienholz recreates such an ambience. It is a life-size installation reproducing the interior of a bar in a homophobic Los Angeles district. Here, odours are artistically used to convey social conflicts, poverty and bigotry; the osmosphere is saturated with the smell of alcohol, cigarette smoke, grease and urine.

The massive presence of saloons was gradually counterbalanced by the consolidation of the Temperance Movements, predominantly Anglo-Saxon, bourgeois and Protestant associations guided by the dictates of sobriety and control. The main one was the Anti-Saloon League which denounced, rather than alcohol itself, the "saloon problem". However, even if teetotalism (promoting total abstinence) was a minority position, it eventually became the adopted line. The saloon became the scapegoat for the problems of a nation that was turning into a world industrial power. Thus, the ethnic and class osmosphere of the saloons, like the smell of alcohol, lost its captivating connection with the myth of the *out*law, and converted into racial, social and economic issues to be formally regulated.[103] "As an institution", Herbert Asbury (1950, 114) writes, "the saloon was a blight and a public stench. It was dingy and dirty, a place of battered furniture, offensive smells, flyblown mirrors and glassware, and appaling sanitary facilities". When interracial, saloons were blamed for exhaling the stench of promiscuity: "[b]oth blacks and whites mix and mingle as a mass of degraded humanity in this cesspool of iniquity" (Timberlake 2014, 30). Comparable descriptions are plentiful. Drawing a parallel with *Blindness*, bestiality finds its osmospheric transliteration in the reek of the sewer; indeed, as Sloterdijk (2014, 325) argues, "the suspicious emanations of the latrines always result in a form of olfactory cave effect and the exclusion of more remote persons from the established totality of odors". The African American suffered more than other groups from the association with saloons and, in general, with bad smells. The rhetoric of white suprematism used to describe them as depraved, a reputation that had radicalised in the Atlantic slave trade; Weber (1924, 460) contends that "the smell of the Negro is an invention by the Northern States to explain their recent move of 'outdistancing' from the Negroes".[104]

Following the idea of *engineered atmospherics* in which preordained results are pursued through a jurisdictional excess,[105] the osmosphere of "Negro dives", said to be miserable for the scent of cheap liquor but also for the patrons' natural predisposition to immorality, seems to be the result of a deliberate *osmospheric construction*. The osmosphere absorbs the aesthetic qualities of its components, which are modelled from the outside through marginalisation and persecution. A similar case is that of slums, which can be seen as "atmospheric constructions where 'surplus

---

103 On the intersection between alcohol and racism in British Columbia, Mawani 2000.

104 Kettler 2020. For Ku Klux Klan, McGirr 2016, 121-155; see also Horsley 2022.

105 Philippopoulos-Mihalopoulos 2015, 139-145.

humanity' is piled up and kept inside through atmospheric techniques of accumulation through dispossession and primitive accumulation" (Philippopoulos-Mihalopoulos 2019, 169). As human society by-products, their osmospheric discrimination has at least two strategic purposes: containment and decontamination. Restricting and segregating a group through smell means to give out a negative caricature of its osmospheric identity, confining its exhalation because it is deemed infectious; not incidentally, olfactory racism was pivotal in *apartheid,* too. Ultimately, this allows the rest of society to be purged and immunised from aesthetic and moral contagion.

At this point another aspect is worth considering. Air is the public good *par excellence*; it is impossible to be parcelled out and privatised, belonging "to the so-called *commons*, in which all participate, for good or ill" (Diaconu 2021, 61). Spreading and revealing the atmosphere, smells ceaselessly trespass the barriers social groups raise as their *Lebensraum*, the living space one claims. In socio-aesthetic terms, an olfactory imposition in the aerial dimension means colonising the political space and the common imaginary. Odours act as a widening of authority and dominion, that is, a *prosthetic extension of a presence*; in other words, they are claims of jurisdiction. In ancient times, powerful individuals such as emperors and nobles used to radiate intrusive fragrances in order to *master* more volume than that occupied by their body.[106] Warhol (1975, 150), who was obsessed with fragrances, seems to have had precisely this in mind when stating that "[a]nother way to take up more space is with perfume". Conversely, systematically confined smell is the symbol of abuse, the denial of an existence that demands its own dimension in the public world. A targeted deodorisation can be equated to the silencing of a community. To put it differently, the attenuation of individual scent is not without political repercussions: de-odorising a person or, conversely, dissolving their emanation by having it overpowered by another smell, constitute strategies of control, sometimes employed by forms of alienating government and institutions such as dictatorships, armies, asylums, hospitals, prisons and concentration camps. Together with their osmosphere, the person loses the power to manifest their presence as an entity that emerges perceptually and actively in the world, disappearing into the anonymity of a designed and manipulated osmosphere. These effects are exemplarily described in dystopian literature. The domination of the osmosphere therefore translates into real social control: when someone's aura is converted into a "mass

---

106 Potter 1999.

exhalation", political subjugation proliferates. Smell is, in fact, always linked to the overall affective nuance of the atmosphere; the osmosphere condenses the *essence* of a political climate.

Back to Prohibition, in the face of the eventuality of restrictive measures, the U.S. split into *dries*, in favour, and *wets*, against. The latter were largely represented by the working classes who organised protests, strikes, and riots, claiming individual freedom while spotlighting the importance of meeting their needs and attaining their political support as the labour force of the nation. Dries focused instead on medical, religious, gender and, most of all, economical argumentations,[107] ascribing mass poverty to alcohol consumption. A common contention was that, once banned, savings would be funnelled through other consumer goods supporting the U.S. market, solving absenteeism, low productivity and workplace injuries due to hungover and alcoholism. Clearly, Prohibition embodied the externality and premise of a socio-political system aspiring to a consumerist-Fordist paradigm — not by chance, John D. Rockfeller and Henry Ford were dries. So much so that, Weberianly speaking, capitalism is rooted in the Protestant ethics, and assuming that middle-class and Protestant Prohibition was a prelude to the rise of the U.S. as a capitalistic *and* penal state,[108] the link between bourgeoisie and deodorisation suggests further insights. Deodorising policies practised by the middle class conform to its moralising, rationalising, monetising and privatising model.[109] The ethics combining the faith in God to that in money aspires to neutralising smells to the same extent as it aspires to nullifying pleasure and wastefulness in accordance with a profit mindset. Straightforwardly, a deodorised society embodies the ideal prototype of a cost-effective mechanism. In support of this, note that some Temperance Movements even recommended the avoidance of spicy and strongly aromatic foods because they were deemed to inflame alcohol cravings.[110] Control of the osmosphere requires tackling its sources. Hence the political reform gradually implemented since 1917, affecting, through alcohol, the "mispleading" osmospheres of the lower classes and the ethnic minorities.

---

107 Jones 1975.
108 This thesis is supported, among others, by Lisa McGirr (2016, 189-229).
109 Privatisation has of course many aesthetic and environmental consequences, including a sense of privacy and the concealment of everyday activities usually performed in the public space. One, which is interesting in osmospheric terms, concerns the ban on hanging laundry outside in many places; Saito 2017a, esp. 126-134.
110 Murdock 1998, 21.

Prohibition was enforced on January 17, 1920, aesthetically changing all American environments. Banks, offices, shops and temperance bars replaced clubs and saloons which now were concealed, shaping new hidden boroughs. Speakeasies sprang up like mushrooms: during the 1920s, in New York there were more than 30,000 of them as well as night clubs (Lerner 2007, 3). Emblem of the Roaring Twenties, the speakeasy was usually a dark space, often located in basements, attics or inner courtyards where alcohol was illegally served and consumed; crowded and smelly, it was also attended by women. For those who felt nostalgic of the saloon, the secret osmosphere of the speakeasy was quite friendly also thanks to the "faintly sweet aroma of gin" (Markey 1926, 14), which was often the result of industrial alcohol blended with glycerol and juniper oil. The drastic decline in the quality of alcoholic drinks during Prohibition is well-known. Average and modest liquors were rare, expensive and exclusive, not to mention fine ones. The heartbeat of Gatsby's villa is a bar "stocked with gins and liquors and with cordials so long forgotten that most of his female guests were too young to know one from another" (Fitzgerald 2001, 26). Most of the smuggled alcoholic drinks, also called "bathtube" for the makeshift means used for distilling, were cut with denatured alcohol and harmful substances, often to increase the alcoholic content or improve the flavour, which caused several casualties and psycho-physical disorders such as the "Jake leg".[111] The concurrent rise of mixology should not be surprising, also considering the widespread *feminising* of drinking culture.[112] Most of all, cocktails were ideal to perform mimetic tactics. On the one hand, combining an alcoholic base with soft drinks helped to mitigate the bad flavours of the former: "a split of ginger ale, or a small glass of orange juice [...] were generally used to kill the taste and smell of bootleg hooch" (Asbury 1950, 198). Furthermore, mixology partially camouflaged illegality, much like the typical suggestive names. Not unexpectedly, flavourings, especially towards the end of Prohibition, were largely advertised; some companies even gave recipe books for "aromatic cocktails" (e.g. *Peeko*) for free. On the other hand, dries got used to mixed drinks (today called *mocktails*), that is, aromatic and visual non-alcoholic imitations served in bars and restaurants.

Although kept out of sight, alcohol consumption was betrayed by its large presence in the air. The private production in houses or manufacturing laboratories located in run-down industrial or outlying areas contributed

---

111 Lerner 2007, 59.
112 Murdock 1998.

to the alcoholic osmosphere, together with the practice of setting fire to bottles and barrels or pour their content on the streets and sewers, both by moonshiners or consumers when a raid was suspected, as well as by federal agents after seizures. Whether wine, beer or spirits, the making of alcoholic beverages was risky especially because of the strong odours emanating from fermentation. Entire districts exhaled the tang of alcohol; the more pungent the smell, the lower the quality: "in New York, Chicago, Detroit, Pittsburgh, and other cities with large foreign populations, the pungent odor of fermenting mash and alcoholic distillate hung over whole sections twenty-four hours a day" (Asbury 1950, 227). Interestingly enough, the air served as a field to dissimulate its osmosphere through olfactory tricks to overlap with the lawscape. For instance, alcoholic emissions were frequently disguised by smoking meat.[113]

Wets denounced that Prohibition changed nothing but moved the saloon into the private household.[114] Indeed, the bourgeois élite, who largely supported the so-called "Noble Experiment", kept on drinking — and tolerably well — in *private* spaces, often protected by agents who, conversely, broke into the houses of the poor classes and immigrants. Within the same lawscape and osmosphere, the notions of private and public acquired a fluid, socially discriminating meaning. The lawscape and the osmosphere were *compartmentalised*, giving rise to a sort of atmospheric schizophrenia, osmologically characterised by what it explicitly prohibited. Then, the smell of alcohol fluctuated between the lowest vulgarity and the highest *expertise*, a cultural and economic asset codified by the wealthy. An article published in *The New Yorker* dated February 28, 1925, reads:

> Have you observed, of late, how fastidious everyone has become in the matter of liquor? Not only a particular brand, but a definitive vintage and especially-shaped bottle are now almost always demanded. We sniff and scrutinize with the utmost care. What a change from the first year of the Eighteenth Amendment, when cocktails were manufactured out of anything liquid, and whatever had a kick passed muster. But we have become quite as particular today as we ever were in those distant times prior to July, 1920 (Van Bibber III 1925, 3).

Within the current trend of mythologising and commodifying past ages, which also includes design evoking historical osmospheres,[115] Prohibition

---

113 McGirr 2016, 80.
114 Murdock 1998, 95.
115 Also in this regard, Diptyque offers a notable variety; the company sells mono-scented candles suggesting different matches. For instance, fig tree combined with

is not omitted from an idealised olfactory construction. Different brands pledge to recreate the speakeasy osmosphere through scented candles and aroma diffusers. As an example, I quote the description of *Harlem Candle Company*:

> People would slip into hidden clubs, tucked behind storefronts. The thrill of the forbidden was unmatched — embodied by sensual flavors of vanilla and dark chocolate. The simple nod of a doorman would whisk you away to an unfamiliar world: dark, loud, pulsing with excitement.
>
> Auras of palo santo and tobacco swirled the gambling tables where men rotated between cocktails and cigars. On the dance floor, perfumes of swaying women infused the air, creating a sweet elixir of licorice and plum blossom.[116]

Instead of worse-than-mediocre alcohol to be aromatically concealed, and the scent of sexual and ethnic promiscuity (which actually legitimised *and* encouraged the lawscape of that time), Prohibition is osmospherically sweetened and condensed in the redolence of the most privileged and influential social groups. The sweet concoction of vanilla, chocolate, liquorice (not surprisingly, almost all food aromas, except tobacco for a "masculine touch") osmospherically sugar-coat an historical climate characterised by serious social tension where air itself was the contested territory. This case offers a preview of the *extended osmospherification* proclivities of food, commodities and environments we are immersed in today. As serial reproductions that design osmospheric experiences, such a hyperesthesia risks resulting in an olfactory atrophy. *Osmospheric foodification* is part of the question.

---

opopanax would recall the osmosphere of Ancient Rome; iris and waxed wood, "the magnificence of the Italian court during the Renaissance".

116 https://www.harlemcandlecompany.com/products/speakeasy-luxury-candle?_pos=1&_sid=9e246b7dd&_ss=r.

4
OSMOSPHERIC FOOD DESIGN

> The milk smells weird.
> Global weirding.
> Timothy Morton

4.1 *(Food) Flavours*

> It smelled like someone in the room was flipping burgers
> on a hot grill. But when I opened my eyes,
> there was just a narrow strip of white paper
> and a smiling flavorist.
> Eric Schlosser

Food labels sporting nutrition claims such as "no (artificial) flavours added" or "just (organic) natural flavourings" are increasingly common nowadays.[1] This is indicative of the widespread use of flavours and, at the same time, of their different reputation among consumers.[2] The history of flavourings dates back to the first decades of the 19th century, when chemistry succeeded in identifying, isolating and studying molecules from odorous compounds. The first synthetic molecule, coumarin, which is naturally present in the Tonka bean, was created in 1868 by chemist William Henry Perkin thanks to the development of the condensation process. This paved the way for further discoveries: among others, the synthesis of vanillin in 1874 by chemists Ferdinand Tiemann and Wilhelm Haarmann, later improved by Karl Reimer, and various technological refinements. The

---

1   I will not go into the details of the various regulations in force, which vary from country to country and are constantly changing.
2   See Murley, Chambers IV 2019.

gas chromatograph, still used today to separate and detect the components of a mixture, was invented in the 20th century.[3]

The addition of flavourings to food and beverages goes hand in hand with the developments in food chemistry, gradually playing a decisive role in the food industry worldwide. This is due, among many other reasons, to the aromatic impoverishment resulting from intensive production and soil depletion, and to the need to make ultra-processed foods more appealing. Indeed, the food industry is largely based on highly profitable farming and animal husbandry practices. The flavour of food has usually been overlooked in the selection and growing or breeding stages, becoming instead a key factor during processing and packaging. Moreover, the global marketing network itself, with its stages of storage, transport and sale, has detrimental effects on the volatile compounds of food: aromas fade over time, dissolving in the time span between preparation and consumption. Such a production system, apart from causing various problematic effects that seem to outweigh its benefits, has made it necessary to resort to expedients to "fix" bland products that, concurrently, need to appeal to consumers who have a huge variety of choices and brands at their disposal. Flavourings are in general more persistent, ensuring the long-term uniformity of products. This provides industrial foodstuffs with standardisation and recognisability, which are essential to keep customer loyalty; no less importantly, it also allows undesired flavours to be corrected or masked.[4] In short, at least since the 1950s, but especially the 1960s, food itself has been massively food-scented, as shown by the large volume of long-life, pre-packaged and ultra-processed foodstuffs occupying supermarket shelves and the pantries of private households.

Flavourings fall into three categories according to the production method: natural, artificial, and nature-identical. Natural flavourings are aromatic compounds found in nature and extracted through non-chemical technology, i.e. physical, enzymatic or microbiological processes. Artificial ones, on the contrary, are not found in nature and are chemically

---

3   For a detailed and exhaustive research: Barwich 2020, esp. 31-33, 48-49. See also
     Schlosser 2001, 124-129. However, the connection between odour molecules and
     sensory qualities remains obscure to this day. In Gibson's (1969, 150) words, the
     "chemist cannot predict what the smell or taste of a chemical will be until he tries
     it, for no theory is available. Conversely the psychologist cannot explain a smell
     or taste in chemical terms for [...] he does not know what the stimulus is". This
     is why even the most refined analytical instruments always have to be combined
     with a human nose, given that perception does not deterministically correspond to
     the chemical properties of the thing perceived.
4   Classen, Howes, Synnott 1994, 181, 197-200.

synthesised. Nature-identical molecules (which is often the case with truffle flavours) are something in-between: they are created by the same process as the artificial ones but are chemically analogous to their natural counterparts. Although natural flavourings are commonly perceived as better than artificial ones in several respects (aesthetically, ethically, ecologically, from a health perspective, etc.), this discrimination is quite misleading in that the two usually contain exactly the same substances, but derived differently. Flavourings can be either extremely complex or quite simple: if a plausible apple flavour can be synthetically recreated only by mixing at least twenty-six different compounds, a combination of three odorous molecules is enough to suggest the idea of pineapple.[5]

Within this framework, the technician, and specifically the *flavourist* — "a chemist with a trained nose and a poetic sensibility" (Schlosser 2001, 127) —, has become a pivotal professional figure in the food industry. The task of the flavourists is not only to create mimetic olfactory formulations, but also to design new ones, as is often the case with energy drinks. Like perfumers, their skill lies in mixing and balancing chemical compounds properly and with a certain amount of creativity and ingenuity, in order to evoke, in our terms, a plausible food osmosphere. In his investigative book *Fast Food Nation*, journalist Eric Schlosser recounts the anecdote of when the senior flavourist of *International Flavors and Fragrances* (IFF), one of the leading companies in the chemical industry, got him to sample different flavours:

> I inhaled deeply, and one food after another was conjured from the glass bottles. I smelled fresh cherries, black olives, sautéed onions, and shrimp. Grainger's most remarkable creation took me by surprise. After closing my eyes, I suddenly smelled a grilled hamburger. The aroma was uncanny, almost miraculous (ibid, 129).

The possible blends cover an endless olfactory palette, and the slightest variation gives rise to a completely different result. An interesting ethical-aesthetic point is that, in most cases, flavourings have nothing to do with the ingredient or dish they reproduce. Hence, the food osmosphere ends up becoming alienated from its tangible element, detached from its very referent. In 1986, the head flavourist of IFF exclaimed about one of his formulas: "I think it's the best blueberry flavor that's ever been made. And there's not a scrap of blueberry in it" (Shell 1986, 79; cit. in Classen, Howes, Synnott 1994, 197).

---

5   Holmes 2017 is full of such information.

In the food sphere, the idea of "free from" takes on different meanings and has various causes and consequences. First of all, the exponential growth of the *-free* foods — without allergens, or ingredients deemed unhealthy or eco-unfriendly — discloses an aspect seemingly at odds with the dogmas of consumerism, namely the *privative*. But what is osmospherically compelling is that the decrease in ingredients corresponds to an aromatic increase. Added flavourings are thus not limited to enhancing the impoverished olfactory quality of food, but they substitute part of it, replacing the absent ingredients. Not incidentally, the fashionable trend of meal replacements and low-calorie diets coincides with the growing offer of flavourings for scenting tasteless shakes, drinks and powders. Flavour drops, which usually have the aroma of highly caloric foods like cookies, chocolate and caramel, are commonly advertised as zero-calorie, and recommended to be added to healthy ingredients and balanced dishes such as yoghurt and porridge. Effervescent aromatic tablets or flasks with scented pods follow a similar logic, namely to increase the water intake and concurrently restrict caloric consumption by substituting soft drinks.[6] Something similar is *AromaFork*, launched on to the market in 2014 by *Molecule-R:* it consists of a fork designed to contain a blotting paper soaked with essences. So, not only is every bite enriched with further scents, but one can also eat one thing while perceiving another: hence, one can ingest a low-fat food while enjoying the flavour of a highly calorie-dense one. Just think of the previously mentioned flavourings that, during Prohibition, were aimed at mimicking alcoholic beverages, or of the current success of vegan plant-based products that imitate, visually and especially through flavours, non-vegan foods such as cheese, bacon and salmon. In these latter cases, liquid smoke is widely used. Made by condensing wood smoke, this flavouring replaces not just its peculiar aroma but the entire smoking process.

Within this framework, fast-food chains have largely exploited the power of flavourings, even as a counterbalance to changes enforced by new regulations or collective sensitivities. A case in point is McDonald's French fries. Fried in an oil composed of 7% soy oil and 93% beef tallow until 1990, later on McDonald's had to replace the cooking oil with a vegetable one, given the criticism and pressure to reduce the amount of cholesterol in its products. The problem then became the osmospheric profile of its

---

6   An example is *air up*, with variously scented pods: https://uk.air-up.com/. Artist
     Peter de Cupere (2016, 377) was a pioneer in this field: in 1996 he invented the
     Smelldrinks, which he then realised in 2003.

fries: by changing the oil, they would lose the characteristic meaty aroma people were so fond of. To have it both ways, McDonald's had the clever idea of designing a meat flavouring to be added to the frozen potatoes and the vegetable oil, thereby meeting both the demands of the public and the taste of its loyal customers.[7]

Noticeably, research has highlighted not only a correlation between the use of added aromas, smell dullness and eating disorders, but also a relevant affective aspect, namely the coincidence between childhood memories and flavourings in industrial products. One of the longest-term studies on this subject was conducted by neurologist and psychiatrist Alan R. Hirsch in 1991 on people born between the 1920s and the 1970s. Almost one thousand English-speaking people were randomly selected and interviewed in the Water Tower Place shopping mall in Chicago. The purpose was to investigate the relationship between nostalgia, smell, childhood, memory and artificial flavours. The study reveals a clear contrast as regards smell-evoked nostalgia among people born before and after the 1930s. Whereas the former mostly mention nature smells such as pine trees, sea air and meadows, the latter are more likely to feel nostalgic about food flavours, especially branded sweet tarts, treats, candies and breakfast cereals.[8] Flavourings of industrial commodities have thus become the osmospheric references of childhood, invading the emotional sphere of a large part of the population. In turn, nostalgia *sells*; hence the flourishing research on smell in consumer science applied to the new frontiers of technology such as virtual reality.[9]

When dealing with flavours and flavourings, wine is certainly a case to be considered. As an alchemical juice humans obtain from the vine — the king of the vegetable realm, as Bachelard puts it[10] —, its bouquet is one of the most symbolic. Wine is the result of the cooperation between chthonic and atmospheric forces; according to the French philosopher, its aroma preserves the sun's course throughout the seasons and the weather that soaked the grapes. During winemaking period, fermentation vapours constitute an osmosphere that envelops the countryside and the villages where wine is a source of wealth and conviviality. Some lines from the poem *Saint Martin* by Giosué Carducci (1913, 155) point this out: "But through the suburb's alleys/A pungent scent from seething/Vats is wafted, breathing/Of wine and festal mirth". Serres, too, devotes many insights on

---

7   Schlosser 2001, 120.
8   Hirsch 1992.
9   Green *et al.* 2023.
10   Bachelard 2011, 239-241.

the bouquet of great wines, highlighting their ability to awaken the mouth or even to create a new one. Unlike ancient times, when wine was commonly mixed with spices, fruit and flowers, today wine must be the aromatic result exclusively of grapes. More than other foods and beverages, the aroma of wine is linked to the *terroir*, conveying the unpredictability and complexity of an entire ecology. Whereas, on the one hand, unpredictability is a valuable merit, on the other hand it poses quite a few challenges, especially for a market that encourages homologated products and a resulting taste that pursues recognisable and repeatable standards.

In the wine industry, this issue has been the core of copious frauds, with a considerable turnover, where adulterated wines were charged with flavourings and other substances to "correct" their aromatic profile, or to mock and emulate fine wines. In the former sense, a recent Italian scandal, the "doped" Sauvignon, dates back to 2015. The adulteration was made by Ramon Persello, a consultant oenologist at some Friulian wineries, who developed and used a mixture of molecules including cysteine, an amino acid that intensifies the primary aromas of the fruit and "rectifies" any defects, in the vinification process of Sauvignon. This fraud brings to light the close and controversial relationship between aromatic authenticity and inauthenticity; even more interestingly, many adulterated wines have been awarded and appreciated by experts. It could be said that, when the judgement of taste is based on sensory criteria that are independent of what they entail, the *osmosphere* and the *lawscape* are opposed or, at least, have an ambiguous relationship.[11] Similar issues emerge from the case of Rudy Kurniawan, called Dr. Conti due to his partiality to the rare wines produced in Burgundy. The Indonesian wine expert and collector is the most famous wine counterfeiter ever sentenced to prison. By blending nondescript wines, he was able to reproduce the drinking experience of the finest ones, selling fakes for millions of dollars, some of which are probably still found in private collections.[12]

In addition to wine, the relationships between food, smells and social status also partake in osmospheric and ecopolitical structures. The examples are manifold. Coffee and cocoa, initially luxurious colonial goods, have then become mass-products. In the 19th and 20th centuries, as a result of scientific and technological industrial development, coffee and cocoa flavourings have been artificially synthesised and massively associated

---

11   Perullo 2020b, 168.
12   *Sour Grapes* (2016, directed by Jerry Rothwell and Reuben Atlas) is an American documentary about him.

with consumeristic places and commodities. The same happened with other precious foods such as truffles. As anticipated, the synthetisation of their aroma made them apparently more democratic, concurrently gentrifying the ingredients they are added to.

4.2 *Excursus 2: Truffle Aroma Design*

> Put a large truffle on top,
> as if to crown your starter,
> and serve.
> Alexandre Dumas

Prior to the 19th century, truffles were commonly treated as ingredients to be cooked and accompanied with spices. In *De re coquinaria*, a Roman cookbook probably written in the first century AD by Apicius, recipes with truffles are included in the chapter on gourmet delicacies. Here, they are paired with various ingredients such as pepper, coriander, honey and mint, and often grilled, simmered or boiled in wine to create a sauce, together with vegetables and olive oil.[13] In the 15th-century treatise *De honesta voluptate et valetudine* by Italian humanist and gastronomist Bartolomeo Sacchi, also known as Il Platina, recipes with truffles are not too dissimilar from Apicius's ones. He recommends rinsing the truffles in wine, cooking them in hot ash and, once re-washed, seasoning them with pepper and serving them preferably after a meat course (Platina 1999, 185 ff.).

It was only at the turn of the 19th century, when bourgeois taste established itself as systematised in Artusi's cookbook, that truffles began to serve as garnish and toppings, constituting the only fundamental aromatic component of the dish. Alexandre Dumas (1873, 1037) writes that white truffle "does not need to be cooked" — something that is still believed today. Nowadays, truffles are consumed almost exclusively raw to keep their scent as pure as possible, and they are paired with delicate ingredients. Think of the habit of grating truffles into thin slices and serving them on fried eggs, pasta or risotto seasoned with butter or oil, or on beef tartare, a gastronomic vogue originated in the province of Alba (in the Italian region of Piedmont, renowned for its truffles) and then spread everywhere. In restaurants, the place for prized truffles is not so much the kitchen but rather the dining room, where they are displayed and protected in glass bells like

---

13   Apicius 1867, 155; see also Apicius 1984, 180-183.

jewels. Indeed, Brillat-Savarin (1994, 91) compares them to diamonds, as they are the jewels of cookery. Truffles have thus become a seasoning, an adornment, the finishing touch that, paradoxically, alone qualifies a dish. This *gastronomic solo* has contributed to the osmospheric extremism we are witnessing today, namely the design of truffle as a synthetic flavouring, so detached from its origin and so widespread as to have replaced its actual, "natural" counterpart. A brief overview of truffle odours might be of use to describe how they bear a meaningful message as part of an ecological environment.[14]

The truffle is a mushroom that grows underground (hence its characterisation as *hypogeous*) through mutual exchanges called mycorrhizae[15] in symbiosis with a bush or a tree. The imagination and symbolism around truffles often have to do with the various relationships they have with different entities.[16] Delving deeper into the vastness of this topic would exceed the scope of my analysis;[17] suffice it to say that even the names for truffles are etymologically linked to weather phenomena or to the animals who eat them.[18] The chthonic nature of the truffle — literally "callosity of the earth" from the Latin expression *terrae tuber* — makes it osmospherically substantial. Worthy of glory, the heady scent of black truffle symbolises, according to Serres (2008, 162), a progression which runs

> from light to dark, from trivial to serious and dense, from puerile to trained expertise. The order or series keeps descending, towards the decomposing earth where animal and vegetable remains in the undergrowth mix with the humus. All these bouquets are wedded to decay: the vegetable realm discovers sublime aromas when it merges with the inert.

The truffle synthesises its peculiar aroma to lure fungivores: wild boars, flies, dogs, pigs, bears, rodents, and humans. Its smell indicates that it is ripe and ready to reproduce. Certainly, this is not something exclusive to truffles. Plants and mushrooms rely heavily on the emission of odours to drive the movements of other organisms. Flowers attract pollinating insects thanks to their scent, whereas some vegetables give off irritating compounds to deter animals from eating them. However, for a hypogeous mushroom,

---

14 Zambonelli *et al.* 2016.
15 Composed of μύκης, "mushroom", and □ίζα, "root".
16 For an ecological and relational understanding of mushrooms (and specifically truffles) — following Tsing (2015) — see Sheldrake 2020.
17 One of the first modern studies is de Borch 1780.
18 Beekes 2010, 1526; Helttula 1996. Truffles are believed to emit a pheromone that attracts fungivores; in relation to pigs, Claus *et al.* 1981; Le Guérer 1994, 9.

the importance of the aroma is even more central and evident: it must be localised and unearthed. Since it is not visible, it has to be *smellable*. Its smell is then a survival strategy meant to propagate its spores. In order to germinate, truffles need to be freed from the fruiting body; to spread and propagate, they need to be transported elsewhere. For that, the role of the animals comes into play. Intrigued by the scent of the truffle, animals dig it up, eat it and, in doing so, crush it. Some spores are deposited on the same area, ensuring its formation the following year; other spores, once expelled somewhere else, recreate the mycelia and mycorrhizae, increasing the likelihood of dissemination of the truffle itself. Plants and fungi grow and spread but they do not move; still, through olfactory signals, they acquire a kind of proxy walking ability. The different kingdoms — animal, plant, fungi — cooperate. The need for propagation of one meets the need for nourishment or the gastronomic pleasure of the other. Therefore, the different abilities of locomotion and movement complement each other; to express it with an alliterative *calembour*: *the hypostasis of the hypogeous consists of stasis after metastasis by means of ecstasy.* That is to say, the truffle emerges as a temporarily static entity, albeit constantly in relation, following a change of location — a shift that occurs thanks to the propagation of its cells. This transmission is carried out by animals that are able to smell the ecstasy of the truffle, effusing its osmosphere into the environment.

As a metabolic signal of a living entity in relation to others, the smell of truffle, despite its intensity, is extremely faint. It depends on the relationships the truffle has with its surroundings, the soil and, of course, the ripening period.[19] Its odour is the sensory result of an incessant process of transformations, calls and answers among organisms. In turn, humans, and specifically truffle hunters, rely on the sense of smell of other animals that sniff the environment and follow the aerial traces that radiate from the ground. During the search for truffles, which usually involves the interspecific cooperation between humans and other mammals (today mostly dogs,[20] but a long-lasting tradition involved the use of truffle hogs),[21] the ground becomes a porous surface: the connection between what is below and what is above draws a liminal dimension, an interstitial olfactory fabric that reveals the convergent phenomena between high and low. Hence a proper *milieu*, as Serres would maintain, which is an in-

---

19 Strojnik *et al.* 2020.
20 In a kind of metonymic relationship, a nickname for the dogs nose is "truffle", although mostly due to similarity of shape and colour.
21 On trained dogs for truffle hunting, Čejka *et al.* 2022; for the connection between *dimethyl-sulphide* and truffle detection by animals, Talou *et al.* 1990.

between crisscrossed by messages and messengers, namely odours and noses able to smell them.

I have succinctly alluded to the repercussions on the truffle imaginary due to the synthetic recreation of its aroma. By abstracting it from the interweaving of ecological relationships, the flavour of truffle has been freed from the constraints that determine its very existence. Along with many other organisms that are part of our diet, truffles are today *disembodied*, detached from the material sublayers that determine their scent. Like other ingredients, the aroma of which is commonly experienced in the form of added flavouring (strawberry, banana, etc.), confusion may occur between the fake and the original. Indeed, many people believe that the odour of truffled food *is* the aroma of truffles themselves. Of course, the expensiveness of truffles plays a non-negligible role. It is generally easier and more affordable to experience truffle in its artificial rather than in its natural version. Noticeably, when people who are used to its synthetic flavour have the opportunity to sample a real truffle, it may even happen that the latter tastes "wrong". Such an aspect, which opens up important issues about aesthetic-ethical education,[22] can be read as a peculiar trait of many contemporary food osmospheres, falling into the more general topic of *air design*.

4.3 *Air Design*

> The underlying subtrend toward an "odor-hedonistic society" joins up at this point with the primary consumer society trend that consists in developing "experience markets" and "scenes" in which atmospheres are dispensed as part of the general situation of attractions, signs, and contact opportunities.
> Peter Sloterdijk

Air design can roughly be taken as synonymous with *air conditioning*, a concept to which Sloterdijk dedicates interesting meditations, and which is increasingly entering the philosophical discourse. A broad definition of air design/conditioning may be that it comprises the all-encompassing set

---

22   Today, the ability to identify food through its flavour has to be understood not so much as an "epicure prerogative", but as a political task to be carried out by everyone. In this sense, the cooking performance *Sound Kitchen* (2021) by Mari Lena Rapprich, based on everyday synaesthetics involving sounds and smells, discloses interesting aspects. See Lähnemann 2021, 44; Reinarz 2021, 191.

of aerial strategies, including scent marketing.[23] The latter is outlined by Sloterdijk (2002, 94) according to its objectives, namely to modify "the mood of airspace users". More in detail, "it serves the indirectly manifest purpose of enticing a space's passers-by with pleasant, smell-induced impressions of a situation, contributing to heightened product acceptance and willingness to buy" (ibid). Specifically, this would be achieved by opting for "complex 'olfactory offers' [which] are preferable to 'mono-fragrances'" (ibid, 95).[24]

As we are persistently subjected to the conditioning of scent marketing, namely the staging of osmospheres as auratic adherences to places and commodities,[25] comprehending the influence of air design becomes a philosophical necessity. In this sense, when Tonino Griffero (2022a, 87) argues that olfactive atmospheres are "only marginally intentionally producible", several objections could be raised, especially taking into account not only their actual creation, but also their effectiveness and operativeness in the contemporary age. Commodities are aimed at drawing the attention of potential consumers through invasive stimuli. Traditionally conveyed through sight and hearing, such enticements have gradually crept into the olfactory sphere.[26] Precisely for this reason, the new frontier is air design, which implies the transformation of the air into an advertising milieu through fragrances created *ad hoc* to trigger affective responses. As already seen, occupying the air coincides with colonising the common imagination and, in general, the vital space *par excellence.*

Once flavours are designed from synthesised, isolated and controlled chemical compounds, commodifying them is a rather effortless operation. This makes it possible to exploit their pervasiveness and affective power, using them as osmospheres permeating spaces or in association with a potentially unlimited variety of goods. In the case of food scents, their superimposition on non-edible commodities has the positive effect of gaining stability as well as durability. Detached from perishable goods whose experience only lasts for the time corresponding to their ingestion, aromas take on a persistent character that is independent of consumption. Whereas studies on ambient and food scenting are gaining ground, the specific issue of osmospheric foodification still remains unexplored. Yet, I advance the claim that it constitutes a key aesthetic aspect of our age.

---

23 Rempel 2006, Stöhr 1998.
24 On the contraposition between simple and complex scents, Leimgruber 2010.
25 Anderson 2014, 25-37; Becher, Feldman 2016; Medway, Warnaby 2018.
26 On sensory marketing, Krishna 2010.

Air design surrounds an element, enveloping it. If the smell of bread hovers in a supermarket, it will be assumed that it comes from bread itself. It is precisely this *qui pro quo* that scent marketing is based on, constituting a range of promotion strategies based on aromatic propagation through air. The aroma industry is, of course, not only a relevant part of the food industry; commercial environments are often saturated with specific fragrances. Diffusing given perfumes in shops, offices, recreation areas, streets and various private or public facilities (airports, hotels, stations, banks, etc.) is nowadays a common strategy, in that the use of odours has many advantages. Scent marketing includes all the ways in which smells may be exploited for economic purposes. For instance, olfactory branding is a strategy of scent marketing based on the creation of an "olfactory signature" for the benefit of a brand identity. Smells are fairly cheap but powerful.[27] Without the need for posters, billboards, digital or physical advertising campaigns, odours spread through space occupying the aerial dimension and attracting passers-by. Moreover, their mnestic and affective power has a profound influence on consumer and buying behaviour. Some research shows that smells can increase not only the percentage of sales, but also the perceived quality of commodities and services and the price one is willing to pay for them.[28] In the presence of a good scent, people tend to stay longer in a shop and to have a greater propensity to purchase.

Beyond the direct rise in turnover and sales volume, the use of fragrances provides further indirect pros, improving the performance of employees and optimising working time. Studies demonstrate that certain smells can increase efficiency and productivity (speed, concentration, reduction of errors, etc.), concurrently acting as mood boosters. There is evidence that certain aromas can help induce or deter behavioural attitudes, thereby facilitating discipline, control or social care. This is why they are used in clinics, public transport or waiting rooms, where they have been proven to facilitate cooperation with staff, and to reduce irritability and fights. Although not exclusively, many of the most effective smells are food-related: coffee, herbs, citrus fruits and bread.[29] Ruwen Ogien reflects on ethics by referring to the case of aromas as mood modifiers and, specifically, to an experiment on the correlation between the scent of warm croissants and induced prosocial behaviours. It follows that kindness and altruistic actions are not so much guided by decontextualised ideological

---

27   On neuromarketing, Lindstrøm 2005, 2008.
28   Costa *et al.* 2021.
29   Damian, Damian 2006; Shiner 2020, 278-295.

or moral instances; rather, they seem to depend on the factual situation and especially on the person's mood. In turn, one's emotional attitude is easily determined by external stimuli, noticeably olfactory ones: "it is a good mood linked to the perception of the agreeable smell that is decisive. And what is striking is the trivial, insignificant character of the factor that serves as a trigger. A pleasing smell of warm croissants suffices!" (Ogien 2015, 115). Leaving aside the ethical value of an act set out by an odour, I deem it useful to spend a few words on the use of food aromas as such — an issue that raises further ethical questions regarding their effects.

When dealing with scent marketing, ethical concerns are manifold, especially because smells evoke responses and are even more effective when they are below the consumer's absolute threshold of consciousness.[30] In general, studies agree in detecting a correlation between prolonged exposure to synthetic odours and increased hypersensitivity to chemical compounds or allergies. More and more activists are adhering to movements fighting to ban perfumes and scents in public spaces.[31] With regards to food-related aromas, their massive spread leads to various problems that affect eating habits. By inducing food cravings and whetting appetite, they make people more inclined to eat even if they are not hungry. In this respect, a connection can be drawn between the ubiquity of food flavours and the increase of obesity and other malnutrition-related disorders, as well as the general tendency to eat too much, too often, or to opt for unhealthy foods.[32] This is not only because food smells encourage consumption regardless of actual hunger, but also because the inconsistency between the ingredients perceived and those actually ingested causes a short-circuit in the organism, which can eventually lose its ability to trigger the biophysical and psychological processes determining the sensations of satiety and hunger. Obesity is followed by a decreased olfactory capacity; vice versa, a low body mass index usually coincides with a heightened olfactory sensitivity. Some research shows a close link between hyperlipidic diets and a weakening of olfaction.[33] This is a vicious circle, given that processed foods contain flavourings and high levels of fat, sugar and salt, all ingredients that seem to cause even severe forms of addiction. Furthermore, the sense of smell gets fatigued and desensitised; this is why it demands more and more intense flavours. This paradigm ends up being the shared olfactory paradigm of a whole society, shaping its taste, food preferences and

---

30   Bradford, Desrochers 2009; Borch 2014.
31   Shiner 2020, 290-292.
32   Riera *et al.* 2017.
33   Thiebaud *et al.* 2014.

choices. The "artificial" model then replaces the "natural" one which, in the end, becomes unfamiliar. Hence the paradoxicality of the contemporary phenomenon of aestheticisation: the increasing intensification of stimuli leads to an olfactory habituation that weakens the ability to perceive more delicate tones, causing a generalised hypoesthesia and the consequent need for stronger aromas. In turn, intensification produces anaesthetisation, with a subsequent injection of further enhanced stimuli in a seemingly endless perceptual bombardment.

KFC was one of the first fast-food chains to systematically exploit the technique of ambient flavouring, spreading the smell of its fried chicken through pipes and ducts on the street, so as to pervade the restaurant premises.[34] Similar cases highlight the power of food odours as triggers for consumption.[35] To promote the purchase of snacks, many movie theatres spray their auditoria with the aroma of popcorn. Since the early decades of the 20th century, first in the U.S. and then worldwide, popcorn scent has become the iconic osmosphere of cinemas and home film occasions.[36] For the same purpose, while Dunkin' Donuts and Starbucks use the scent of coffee, in fast-food restaurants serving hamburgers, a specific odorous compound from spray canisters often permeates the air — RTX9338PJS is the name for "just-cooked-bacon-cheeseburger-like-fragrance" (Lindstrøm 2008, 148). A further common strategy consists in vaporising the flavouring of bread around cafes and bakeries or inside supermarkets. A tactic in-between ambient and commodity osmospherification is the direct use of foodstuffs (often with added flavourings) in order to osmospherically saturate a space. Hence the positioning of ovens for baking bread and pastries at the entrance of shops, so that the smell of baking welcomes customers and wafts through the merchandise display space. Cinnabon does the same with its rolls, and the aroma they give off hovers about the streets of the pedestrian traffic areas where the shops are generally located. In addition to building and boosting brand identity through smell marks, one of the purposes of air design is to make osmospherically attractive places that have little appeal, but also to enrich a banal experience with an emotional aura promising aesthetic gratification.

More and more multinational brands and fast-food chains are selling merchandising flavoured with the peculiar smells of their iconic products. This trend began in the 2000s. In 2008 and 2012, for example, Burger King

---

34   Drobnick 2006a, 345.
35   See, in general, Hultén, Broweus, van Dijk 2009, ch. 3; Hultén 2020, ch. 5.
36   Smith 1999, 35-36, 102; Geiling 2013.

and Pizza Hut launched two body sprays (smelling, respectively, of grilled meat and freshly baked, hand-tossed dough). Several and similar cases followed. Since 2016, KFC has also started to commodify its signature spicy chicken fragrance by designing various scented items: a sunscreen (U.S., 2016), nail polishes (Hong Kong, 2016), a bath bomb (Japan, 2017), a surf wax (Australia, 2018), a firelog (U.S., 2018-2021), footwear (collaboration with Crocs, 2020), and scratch and sniff Valentine's Day cards (in collaboration with Moonpig, 2020). One of the recurring motifs in the advertising slogans of such gimmicks is to boast of the accuracy between the real food and its disembodied and decontextualised aroma. Hence the frequent admonition not to eat the objects from which the smell emanates. The osmospheric standardisation of food implies a caricaturised homologation of its odours which, by emphasising and accentuating the features of the foods they refer to, end up replacing them. Being surrogates, flavours are divorced from the edible and perishable substances, fulfilling their functions even when effused from inorganic matters. The increasing design of scented merchandising has several causes and advantages. If visual and auditory advertising can enter the intimate space of the home through technological devices (including television and the Internet), olfactory ones need a scented material support. At least that has been the case so far, as work is being done on digital platforms, websites and bits that transmit odours online or via texting.[37]

Yet, instead of being economically driven, contemporary air conditioning has its origins in war strategies. This is what Sloterdijk (2022, 9-46) calls "terror from the air" or *atmoterrorism*, referring to offensive technologies adopted in the gas warfare. Here it is worth recalling a dramatically crucial episode. In the late afternoon of 22 April 1915, on the Ypres front (Belgium), a huge yellowish cloud of about one hundred and fifty tons of chlorine, six kilometres wide and six to nine hundred metres high, was released from more than five thousand containers. This was the first massive use of lethal gas by the German army against the French-Canadian troops, thus inaugurating modern chemical warfare. Since that day, the very nature of warfare has changed: attacks are no longer aimed at directly, physically eliminating the enemy, but rather at rendering their milieu uninhabitable and, especially, unbreathable. Sloterdijk recurs to that event to discuss the new awareness of the environment's role as a life-sustaining ecology. This awareness can be said to be the Zeitgeist of the 20th century and even more so of the 21st. Indeed, a connection may be ventured

---

37   Edwards 2018, 242-253.

between *atmoterrorism* and the miasmatic theory, by interpreting the latter as the archetype of the former. From this standpoint, it is interesting to note how the use of chemical weapons was — and unfortunately still is — counterbalanced, on the one hand, by a meticulous study of weather phenomena and especially of the wind, since its deviation would cause a boomerang effect; on the other hand, by an olfactory education to teach soldiers and civilians to recognise the danger. For instance, chlorine gas has a peculiar colour but above all a distinctive smell, hence its nickname "mustard gas" or "sulphur mustard". In a way, the nose fully carries out its function as guardian and custodian when dealing with the toxicity of the air as a vehicle of contagion and death. Many reports highlight the salvific role of olfactory training to detect deadly substances. However, the most used gases are particularly insidious because they have apparently harmless scents: in addition to new-mown hay, many smell like common edible ingredients such as garlic, horseradish and onion.[38] To a certain extent, an even more terrifying *osmoterrorist* strategy would consist in making toxic air undetectable or, even worse, reassuring through the osmospheres of particularly comforting food.

I have previously drawn a parallel between osmospheric foodification and the perils we perceive in the air: climate crisis and air pollution, war conflicts and viruses — not least, nuclear threats and food sophistication. The massive use of ambient fragrances therefore comes as no surprise. Candles evoking the aromas of grandmothers' kitchens, or the many food-themed home aroma diffusers can be interpreted as the implementation of a palliative strategy to remedy a hostile and uncanny perception of the air. Taming the osmosphere meets the need to inhabit it aesthetically by replacing it with a vital and welcoming space. In other words, the *utopia of an odourless city*, as Illich (1985, 51-54) calls it, seems to coexist with a tension towards a foodified osmosphere or, better, an *osmospheric foodification*. Hence, the old saying "no smell is good smell" is no longer valid, let alone the socio-aesthetic variant "good smell is bad smell". Today a third option appears to be more fitting: *good smell is no smell*. Interestingly, in a study on Romantic literature, Morton (2000) wittily puts forward the idea of the *poetics of spice*, indicating, through a tribute to Bachelard, the convergence between capitalism, consumerism, alienating commodities, imperialism, environmental awareness and globalisation. In his words, in this "early form of advertising language, global flows of trade are represented as flow of spicy odor toward the nose of the consumer, in

---

38   Plunkett 2014.

a form of ekphrasis (vivid description) that is often very deeply ambient" (Morton 2007, 93). Moreover, the poetics of spice creates a space dense with potentials: it is an "atmosphere, a realm in which events have room to happen, a thick, embodied, heightened atmosphere" (ibid). Nevertheless, given the subsequent developments, we no longer seek the *exotic*. Rather, a *poetics of staples* might be suggested to describe the current osmospheric foodification we dwell in: comfort, home-cooked and often sweet food. Not incidentally, dark ecology, as Morton (2016, 5) puts it, implies an ecological awareness that is not only dark-uncanny, but also dark-sweet, like chocolate. The designed air we dwell in perfectly osmospherises it.[39] Before further discussing osmospheric foodification, I deem it useful to present and comment briefly on a performative dystopian installation based on a peculiar air design dealing with flavours, food and ecological issues.

4.4 *Excursus 3: Ghost Food*

> You know, I know this steak doesn't exist.
> I know that when I put it in my mouth,
> the Matrix is telling my brain that
> it is juicy and delicious.
> Cypher Reagan

Artists Miriam Simun and Miriam Songster designed the performative installation *Ghost Food Truck Project* in order to think about the impact of climate change on everyday life. Through the use of synthetic flavours of foods at risk of extinction, it aims at making people aware of their possible impending disappearance. Believing that people have a mostly indirect engagement with climate change, which is filtered through an intellectual rather than affective and aesthetic understanding, the artists conceived this project to make the repercussions of the environmental crisis tangible and emotional.[40] Hence the use of food osmospheres.

---

39 Serres (2014), too, defines the era we are living in as *l'âge du doux*, "the sweet age" (even if not in olfactory terms), namely the time of fluidity, virtuality, potentiality; see Borsato 2023, esp. 212-213.

40 At the same time, they were willing to adopt creative strategies that do not necessarily entail a denialist attitude or, vice versa, a detached sense of duty towards undetermined future generations. This insight comes from a personal communication with Miriam Songster, whom I thank for her kindness in answering my questions and providing me with further materials.

Staged in 2013 and 2015 in various cities in the U.S. and in 2019 in Moscow, the *Ghost Food Truck* consists of a food truck with a futuristic and minimal design, and waiters wearing uniforms that contribute to giving the whole ambiance a sci-fi and hi-tech atmosphere. Same as with ordinary food trucks, passers-by and participants can order food from a displayed menu, which includes three options whose main ingredients are species threatened by the ecological crisis and environmentally harmful practices. All dishes are made of sustainable and climate-resistant plant-based proteins such as algae, while their specific ingredients are evoked through osmospheric stimuli. The food is indeed served together with a DOSD, a direct olfactory stimulation device to be worn so as to have the scented pod under the nose. Once the customers are properly equipped thanks to the help of the trained waiters, the eating experience begins.[41]

For this purpose, it was not enough to offer just any kind of food, but it had to be a *familiar* one that could, on the one hand, create expectations, surprise or disappointment; on the other hand, condense an emotional value spoiled by the sense of loss in the face of its future unavailability. Thus, Simun and Songster adapted the menu to the place the performance was set in each time. In the U.S., it offered "PB&J" (the popular peanut butter and grape jelly sandwich), drinking chocolate, and beer-battered, deep-fried cod, a traditional Lusitanian recipe that was specifically chosen for the inhabitants of Newark, where the *Ghost Food Truck* was first conceptualised and staged, given its large Portuguese community. In Russia, the options consisted of buttered bread with salmon caviar, cranberry "mors" (a fruit drink), and "kartoshka" chocolate cake, a Soviet potato-shaped dessert. Peanuts/cranberries, chocolate, cod/caviar represent three different biomes (grassland, rainforest and oceans) with their respective species at risk.

The dystopian aspect relies on the short circuit between what is actually ingested and what is suggested through olfactory and visual clues. We might say that the ghost food is summoned through its *osmospheric hologram*, in a gap where aesthetic qualities do not coincide with the edible substances. The entire performance relies on osmospheres in order to recreate ordinary eating habits in atypical circumstances. In essence, this eating experience implies the alternation and contrast between known and perceived, present and absent elements. The synthetic smell is the only perceptual link, together with verbal labelling, through which the relationship with the food it evokes and represents can be reconstructed. Furthermore, as ingredients, they become osmospheric tools through which it is possible

---

41   Songster 2018; Spence 2017, 37-38.

to experience global environmental dynamics and biodiversity disasters. It is also interesting to note that, as the menus read, the products' origin is explicitly indicated; the selected foods are therefore associated with a local and circumscribed area, further stressed by the specific gastronomic preparations and combinations, conveying a sense of place. Nonetheless, the synthetic aromas are all but local.[42] Not secondarily, the *Ghost Food Truck* is visually but especially osmospherically different if compared to regular food trucks, which are quite common in the U.S. Having no kitchen, it does not emit cooking smells. The atmosphere it evokes is perceivable; I have already discussed the extent to which vendors contribute to the osmosphere of a city, as well as the perturbing character of the absence of food osmosphere.

The *Ghost Food Truck* plays precisely on the spectral nature of food, whose presence/absence is rendered through its osmosphere. The aesthetic gap is filled by a cognitive understanding, while memory helps stimulate a coherent experience. On the one hand, flavours are vectors of ethical and aesthetic issues; on the other hand, they are themselves the result of political, ecological and economic strategies. This provocative and somehow premonitory performance also contributes to testifying in concrete ways the role smell plays in eating, while giving it artistic dignity. The *Ghost Food Truck* highlights the ambiguous nature of odours which, as easily identifiable and alterable elements, alternate between fiction and reality. And yet, issues such as global warming and the desalination of the oceans can be conveyed through the sense of smell, thus becoming a strong educational tool.

Something similar can be found in *Salmo_NO_Way* (2001) by Norwegian researcher and artist Sissel Tolaas. This installation consists of a pink neon-lit room with 30 neon tubes representing as many chemical nutrients used in salmon farming. The gallery space is saturated with a nauseating stink simulating that of salmon farms, making visitors think about the salmon industry in Norway and, more in general, about food production, the loss of ocean biodiversity, pollution and exploitation. Whereas, in this case, smell is intended to raise awareness on environmental issues and sustainability by making aesthetically detectable what is usually not, the *Ghost Food Truck* pursues the same objective adopting an opposite strategy. By osmospherising familiar food, it presentifies its future absence. Air design

---

42 Specifically, the flavours are from the Takasago International Corporation, based in Japan.

and food flavours ensure the feasibility of an aesthetic experience while illuminating its shadow sides.

4.5 *Osmospheric Foodification*

> This presents the question as to how tasting is connected
> with "taste," and how smelling is related to atmosphere.
> Hubertus Tellenbach

Nidoricupius is a humorous formation coined by Plautus indicating a person who loves the smell or, better, the stink of cooking.[43] Differently translated with insults that often overshadow the original olfactory meaning of the Latin term, it appears in the first act of *The Haunted House* (*Mostellaria*) as an epithet uttered by Grumio, a slave, to his peer Traio in the kitchen.[44] As an object of ridicule in the Roman world, the idea underlying this offence shows that the enjoyment of food odours is all but long-standing. Hedonic values attributed to cooking smells and food aromas have remarkably changed throughout history. As already mentioned, the collocation of kitchens within the domestic spaces has been modified accordingly: in the houses of wealthy Roman families, they were located next to the lavatories.[45] Furthermore, dining rooms were scented with garlands and flowers, balms and perfumes; food itself, like wine, was garnished and flavoured with the same substances. Today, the situation is reversed. Food smells are among the most appreciated, so much so that they are used to perfume commodities and environments not necessarily related to eating. The same applies to bodily fragrances: *gourmand* perfumes, characterised by edible notes such as vanilla, caramel, cocoa and liquorice, are quite popular.[46] In osmospheric terms, our age represents a paradigm reversal with respect to the past, being marked by a pronounced *nidoricupiditas*.

In the mediaeval calendar, as Han (2017a) observes, the days, rather than being counted, were inscribed in a homogeneous timeframe punctuated by

---

43   *Nidor* means "strong smell, fumes" (De Vaan 2016, 408).
44   Fontaine 2010, 171-172.
45   Rybczynski 1986, esp. 132-133.
46   As an example, *DO NOT DRINK* by Sephora is a collection of "tasty fragrances" whose ingredients are within the food domain: salt and vanilla, sage and tonka, tangerine and matcha.

festivities, which acted as narrative elements and marked the passing of time. Food smells played a fundamental role, in that they constituted the key elements of rites, celebrations and seasons, giving them their recurring *flavour*. A trace of this model remains in the collective imagination. Despite the fact that every food is now available all year round or replaced by flavourings, scented candles show how each seasonal osmosphere is always intertwined with its typical ingredients, in that their fragrances are adapted to the time of the year, especially with regards to food scents. Spiced cookies at Christmas, chocolate at Easter, chestnuts in autumn months are just some possible examples.[47] The success of these osmospheric products is perhaps also linked to the desire of discovering a sense of duration and rhythm in the domestic sphere, through the osmosphere of different meals. As an example, the Stinky Candle Company sells a *Sausage Candle*, whose description reads: "One of the most welcoming smells to waft out of any kitchen on a Saturday morning. Pair our Sausage Candle with our Bacon Candle to create an irresistible aroma that will have the entire household demanding breakfast no matter what time of day".[48] Artificial food smells act as surrogates for the overall experience, even saving time in the kitchen. Analogous cases are manifold; sold by the same company, the *Pumpkin Pie Candle* emphasises the aforementioned aspect: "The delicious scent of homemade pumpkin pie is brought to life with this aptly named candle. Light it whenever you want to experience the aroma of Thanksgiving desserts without the 6 hours of preparation".[49] What I call *osmospheric foodification* may also be symptomatic of a discomfort towards a loss of ties which are embedded in gastronomy. Rituals, practices and the affective dimension of food are then made up for by their designed osmospheres. Instead of wafting from food being actually prepared and cooked, shared and consumed, the osmosphere is synthetic, standardised, detached from its environmental and affective ecology, coming from a non-edible object. Food flavours parody circumstances, contexts and relationships that are in reality broader, more complex, nuanced and participatory. In this osmospheric paradigm, which is concurrently intimist and depersonalising, the standardisation of food odours seems to symbolise, conceal and at the same time soothe the loss of its aura.

Food-scented candles are also part of the merchandising of several fast-food chains. In 2015, Greggs, a UK baking company, designed a candle with

---

47   Among many companies, see Yankee Candle: https://www.yankeecandle.com/yankee-candle/candles/.
48   https://stinkycandlecompany.com/products/sausage-candle.
49   https://stinkycandlecompany.com/products/pumpkin-pie.

the aroma of its bacon sandwich. In 2016, KFC designed a fried chicken candle for New Zealand and, in 2019, a gravy candle for the UK. In 2020, McDonald's launched a set of six candles, each featuring one ingredient of the famous burger "Quarter Pounder": sesame seeds bun, 100% fresh beef, cheese, onion, pickles and ketchup. With a burn time of twenty-five hours, they should be preferably lit together "for maximum deliciousness". Where food consumption is fast, smell strategically calls for slowing down, so as to fix the food experience in the sphere of memory and duration. Moreover, the same flavours are no longer confined to the sale points or to the actual eating of food, but are always potentially available everywhere.

Whereas, according to Benjamin's well-known explanation, the aestheticising of political life through technological reproduction is the key feature of fascism, one of the self-empowering mechanisms of capitalism is the artification of its commodities and their aestheticising exacerbation.[50] Starting from the idea of an *odour-hedonistic society*, Sloterdijk (2002, 95-96) links osmospheres, social space and marketing strategies:

> Let us not forget that today's so-called consumer society was invented in a greenhouse — in the very same glass-canopied, nineteenth-century arcades in which the first generation of "experience customers" learned to breathe the intoxicating scent of an enclosed, interior-world full of commodities.

I assume there will be no objections to my questioning the idea that we are living in an age characterised by olfactory silence. Nonetheless, late capitalism implies a general aesthetic overstimulation, or *hyperesthesia*,[51] which turns into a perceptual congestion with anesthetising results — the typically urban and modern aesthesiological dynamic Simmel (1950, 414-415) calls *die Steigerung des Nervenlebens*, the "intensification of nervous stimulation".

As will be clear by now, the perceptual intensification occurring today seems increasingly oriented towards and characterised by a focus on the sense of smell. For all these reasons, Han's analysis appears to overlook some pragmatic aspects we are facing. According to him, smell is characterised by a certain slowness and, "as a medium, it is not adapted to the age of haste" (Han 2017a, 46). Contemporaneity would be a scentless age, since a "society dominated by scents would probably also not develop any inclinations towards change or acceleration. It would live off its recollections and its memory, off those things that are slow and long-

---

50   Lipovetsky, Serroy 2013.
51   Howes 2005.

lasting" (ibid). Instead, I believe that our society seems to emphasise the fleeting nature of smells, while also exasperating their emotional values as replacements for what they stand for. Moreover, while Han sets the visual or "cinematographic" against the olfactory, I would suggest that what is taking place is precisely the cinematographisation of smell. As variously proposed in connection with the birth of sensory marketing, targeting alternative perceptual channels to that of sight, the sense most burdened with conventional advertising methods, has become a good way to bypass the overload of optical images. Odours thus offer the possibility of eluding a sense saturated by a hyper-density of stimuli and messages, concurrently exploiting the affective charge inherent in the sense of smell. It should then come as no surprise that the most evident contemporary phenomenon is not so much deodorisation but, instead, *diffused hyper-odorisation*. This phenomenon is still little investigated, especially in terms of its aetiology and effects. And whereas *food porn* and *foodstagramming* have attracted the attention of food studies, sociology and semiotics,[52] noticing and addressing the typical gargantuan display of food through visual representation, a *gastrosmomania*[53] has yet to undergo a systematic inquiry.

If buying commodities means achieving or preserving a certain status, their osmosphere plays a considerable role. Indeed, smell marketing is designed to meet class peculiarities. As Warhol (1975, 237) observes when considering the smell of "fried chicken frying" that lingers in some Woolworth's shops, in "high-class stores they sell through 'display,' in low-class ones they sell through 'smell'". This implies that the reaction to a given odour is not only symptomatic of the social class of the smeller, but that odour is, or was, in itself, a class-specific stimulus. Böhme (2017b, 77-78) suggests adding to the Marxian categories of use-value and exchange-value that of stage-value, corresponding to the aura of goods which opens up to the possibility of new forms of life and properties. In this sense, the specific osmospheric emanation acts both as a label and as a prescriptive element in the context of a collective existence and coexistence, establishing what is or is not socially appropriate.

Although in a marginal way, there is now also an interest in unpleasant smells as a sort of compensation and counterbalance to a long-neglected existential dimension. Instead of speaking of a purely "odour-hedonistic society", we can thus propose the idea of an *odour-heuristic* one. Olfactory

---

52 Contributions dedicated to these topics are several. For instance: Rousseau 2012; Dawkins 2020; Allard, David 2022.

53 I borrow "gastromania", a term coined by Marrone (2014), reworking it in an osmospheric key.

arts can provide us with several examples of how we are increasingly curious about diving into disturbing osmospheres in order to push the aesthetic limit of the olfactory unbearable, which turns out to be a useful means to reflect on perception, social issues, and shared imaginaries. Commodities are not only scented with conventionally pleasant aromas, but also with what are commonly considered as reeks. The Stinky Candle Company, along with more common and positive smells, sells candles wafting the most diverse pongs: body odour, farts, urine, vomit and, among the food-themed ones, garlic and rotting flesh. The same company has created a candle that osmospherically reproduces the year 2020, the period coinciding with the covid-19 pandemic. The aroma is foul and its description reads:

> Don't miss out on your chance to own this once-in-a-lifetime keepsake from this horrible year. — Smells just like the year — Every horrifying new development that 2020 has thrown at us has inspired the smell of this candle, which we guarantee will shut down your nostrils until 2021. — Own a piece of history — This year will be remembered for generations, and you were there to experience it firsthand. — Relive 2020 anytime, anywhere — Simply open the lid and feel the desperation and fear that accompanied every single day of this awful year. — Unlike the rest of our products, this candle contains paraffin in order to smell as strong as possible.[54]

Apparently, the pervasive osmosphere of homemade bread and baked goods during lockdown periods seems not to have prevailed over the general atmosphere of malaise that permeated the air in 2020.

This kind of osmospheric design, now an integral part of the aesthetic economy, modulates and mirrors affective responses towards, one might say, the (òikos)nomia — a consumerist system that, absurdly, aims precisely at alienating itself from the very atmosphere by which it is supported. Nonetheless, the opposite might be legitimately argued as well: food smells succeed in restoring and providing it a specific context and feeling — its osmosphere.

---

54   https://stinkycandlecompany.com/products/2020-candle.

5
Osmospheric Arts

> [W]hat Strattis said in deriding
> Euripides is true, "When you make pea-soup
> don't put perfume in it".
>
> Aristotle

5.1 *Anosmic Aesthetics*

> The smell of thyme may symbolize a Mediterranean hillside
> at daybreak, but that is due to the little that the human sense of
> smell still has to do with spatiotemporal reference.
>
> André Leroi-Gourhan

In April 1940, Albert Camus (1963, 179) entered a short annotation in his *Notebooks*, "'I,' he said, 'am an olfactive type. And there is no art that addresses itself to the sense of smell. Only life'". We do not know who this olfactive person is, whether someone whose thoughts he was merely reporting, or the writer himself.[1] In any case, we know that, as early as 1940, at least a modicum of explicit attention to smell as an artistic medium was (re-)emerging, although it was certainly niche if compared to the role played by the other senses. Camus' observation offers us the possibility of

---

[1] Indeed, this does not sound too implausible, considering the several pages dedicated to the sense of smell in his autobiographical final novel *The First Man*. Consider this passage: "Ernest had a very well-developed sense of smell [...]. This privileged condition brought him great delights, as when he inhaled the odor of split-pea soup or those dishes he loved above all others, squid in its ink, sausage omelet, or the stew of innards made with beef heart and lung, the bourguignon of the poor [...]. But his sensitivity in this regard also caused him trouble. [...] For example, he had gotten in the habit of sniffing his plate before beginning the meal, and he would turn red with anger when he discovered what he claimed was the smell of egg" (Camus 1995, 113-114).

going over some of the main cruxes of the whole gamut of issues raised by smell within the aesthetic discipline.[2] The situation basically presents itself as a vicious circle: there are no arts addressing smell insofar as aesthetics does not recognise them as arts.

As a preliminary remark, it should be noted that the denial of the olfactory dimension in philosophy and aesthetics can be traced back to the earliest days of Western thought, but this path is far from linear, unambiguous and univocal. If philosophical positions excluding smell from the aesthetic domain have certainly been in the majority as a well-entrenched legacy of Western modern philosophy, the alleged long-standing and still current neglection of olfaction in the arts can be seen as more of a platitude to be reconsidered. Let us not forget that scents were fundamental in ancient Greek dramas, where the burning of incense and even the smell of food used to inundate theatres.[3] What today goes by the name of "olfactory arts" has always existed, although with seesawing destinies. They have advanced mostly since the end of the 20th century.[4]

Hence, by the locution *anosmic aesthetics*,[5] I refer, more than to "deodorised" arts, to those philosophical stripes that, holding their noses at the whiffs hovering in the artworld, have explicitly refused to grant an aesthetic status to smell (as well as to taste and food), mostly drawing on Kant's and Hegel's arguments.[6] Indeed, the topic is a lively one at present. On the one hand, interdisciplinary research is flourishing, speculating on the current widespread use of odours and fragrances by disparate artists; on the other hand, aesthetics itself has undergone a shift, becoming not only more inclusive of all sensory domains, but also particularly interested in the everyday horizon and in ordinary perceptual experiences. Claiming the need to include the *prosaics* within the aesthetic field, Katya Mandoki (2007, 13) disapproves of the mainstream position by sarcastically underlying that "[a]estheticians continue to work alone in the museums, libraries and art galleries with their coffee table books and academic journals so as not to be disturbed by the smell, heat, and sweat of everyday life".

As many scholars have pointed out, aesthetics reveals a paradoxical contradiction whereby the meaning of its name has mostly not coincided with the content of its thematisation. Derived from the ancient Greek

---

2   For a more detailed inquiry, Mancioppi 2022a, ch. 1. See also Berleant 2004.
3   Banes 2001, Kjellmer 2021b.
4   Wicky 2018, Nicklaus-Maurer 2021.
5   See also Tafalla 2013a.
6   Winterbourne (1981) provides an interesting case, criticising Harris's (1979) account.

α☐σθάνομαι, "to perceive, to feel through the senses", and α☐σθησις, "sensation", aesthetics was founded by Alexander Gottlieb Baumgarten in the mid-18th century as a philosophical discipline dealing with the "science of sensible knowledge". It was precisely meant to give scope and dignity to all the experiences that, albeit central to human life, were excluded from the hard sciences because they were difficult to measure analytically. However, such a program was not in keeping with the prerequisites of its own foundation. Rather than a philosophy of perceiving and experiencing, aesthetics became, at least in its major expressions, a reflection on certain perceptions in the context of extraordinary experiences; specifically, those related to fine arts. In short, aesthetics ended up being limited to just those senses directly involved in the perception of some artworks, namely sight and hearing. One of the recurrent criticisms is that aesthetics has programmatically turned its gaze away from life to focus only on what was apparently detached from it.[7] Camus' quote makes this contrast clear: *there is no art that addresses itself to the sense of smell. Only life.* As anticipated, smell was categorically excluded by Kantian and Hegelian aesthetics, together with taste. Once disembodied and purified of its sensual matrix and gastronomic determination, the latter became the metaphor for the faculty of judgement.

Considering that modern aesthetics rests its foundations on an eminently oculocentric structure, it is no surprise that smell poses multiple problems. Questions such as: can smells exceed the biological sphere? can odours be considered beautiful? is it possible to have a universally valid judgement on them?, are just a few among many queries that get philosophers to assess smell as a thorny sense. Further questions follow when trying to define what art is and what it is not, with perfumery always occupying an ambiguous and borderline position often relegated to the dimension of craftsmanship.[8]

---

7   This is the urgency highlighted by John Dewey and underpinning his entire oeuvre, which has since found numerous continuators. For example, Arnold Berleant (1970, 191), proposing an empirical approach, maintains that "[f]reed from the restrictions of being confined to an art object or to the spiritual flexings of an esthete, aesthetic experience will be recognized as having a primary place in the life of man as its original source and final culmination".

8   Many perfumers (e.g. Ellena 1994, 2015), as well as scholars (Shiner, Kriskovets 2007; Le Guérer 2015; Brozzo 2020), have expressed their view on this issue. French master perfumer and author Edmond Roudnitska spearheaded the battle for the recognition of perfumery among the fine or major arts (Roudnitska 1977). As a practice as old as humanity, in which religious, medical, culinary, spiritual and cosmetic purposes intertwine, I will not embark on the history of perfumery and its aesthetic relevance. The latter is already clear in Theophrastus's *De Odoribus*,

Things become even more complicated with regard to food flavours, since they imply the cross-cutting issue of whether cooking, cuisine and food can be considered art.[9] All this is then compounded with practical aspects that challenge or limit the effectiveness of smells: the inherent difficulty to control them is a concern for many artists to this day.[10]

The lack of coincidence with many mainstream aesthetic codes, along with copious others that here will be intentionally overlooked or tackled later, has been commonly brought to bear on the already sketched hierarchy of the senses, where olfaction has often been regarded as a lower sense, and odours as inferior stimuli. This thesis is rooted in ethical, ontological and epistemological assumptions. Therefore, since these issues often recur and overlap throughout history, I will neither follow a chronological order nor over-schematise them, so as to connect the different thematic nodes as much as possible, even juxtaposing historically distant thinkers.

A starting point for a dissertation on the anosmic paradigm of aesthetics can be stability, a deliberately general idea that includes a range of specifications such as durability and structure. Hegel's categorical rejection of odours in aesthetics rests on their transience. According to him, smell should not be considered an organ of artistic enjoyment in that "things are only available to smell in so far as they are in process and [their aroma is] dissipated through the air and its practical influence" (Hegel 1975, 622). Acknowledging in this respect a similarity between smells and sounds, Hegel clarifies that their difference, which is decisive in aesthetic terms, lies in the fact that, whereas the former has to do with a "process of dissolution" of the thing, the latter is the "vibration of the body" (ibid). Although both are transient, sound waves leave the object they are emitted from intact. The same is argued by Kant (2006, §22, 51), who stresses the fleeting and transient nature of olfactory stimuli. The ontological ambiguity of smells emerges clearly in Plato's *Timaeus*, where he defines them as "half-breed: no single figure, as it turns out, has the proportions that would give it a scent" (*Tim.*, 66d). He insists on their hybrid nature and constant becoming in the intermediate stage of occurring elemental processes, something paraphrased by Serres (2008, 170) when stating that "a highly complex compound, a blend of a thousand proximities, unstable knot of capricious currents, an aroma comes about like an intersection, or confusion, we

---

where he describes in detail the techniques of the Hellenistic age, together with the perceptual and curative properties of the raw materials (Squillace 2012). For a comprehensive cultural overview on perfumery: Munier 2003, Turin 2006.

9   See Perullo 2013.

10   Drobnick 2014.

do not smell simple, pure odours". Smell would thus be the opposite of sight,[11] where the latter allows for the grasping of ideas as fixed and eternal forms and of the "extended 'present' of enduring objects", to use Jonas's (2001, 145) words. On the contrary, instead of registering the persistent essence of things, smell, perhaps more than the other senses, operates by detecting changes, differentials, subtle variations. Furthermore, since smells do not persist, it follows that they cannot be contemplated. Arguing that in "tasting and smelling I contemplate not the object but the experience derived from it", Roger Scruton (1979, 114) belongs to the philosophical strand that, at most, places odours and tastes on the fringes of aesthetics.[12] The extreme transience of olfactory perception also plays a role in what is generally interpreted as an impossibility of symbolisation. This occurs in both an intransitive and transitive meaning. Intransitively, the difficulty in labelling odours as well as in formalising them in "phonemes" are the most illustrative circumstances. By considering the formal peculiarity of smells, Tellenbach (1968, 29) denies the existence of odour "figures" or "images" because, among other things, they do not stand out against an amorphous background. Transitively, as put by Leroi-Gourhan (1993, 292), "the sense of smell, being purely receptive, has no complementary organ for the emission of symbols of odors". This is precisely the reason why, according to him, "gastronomy and olfactory aesthetics in general do not fall within the category of the fine arts" (ibid).

Another main reason for the marginality of smells in aesthetics concerns their problematic relationship with the idea of beauty in its various definitions. Here, the central reasons are their subjectivity and the lack of disinterestedness. Again, the complexity of the issue requires extreme simplification. Despite the semantic extension that beauty has enjoyed in ancient times, smells certainly did not stand out among the qualities deemed by Greek and Roman philosophers as possible gateways to beauty. Whereas the latter generally had a metaphysical, spiritual and immaterial meaning, odours were commonly associated to carnal and sensual pleasures; this

---

11   While stressing the role of the use of the gaze for vision, Merleau-Ponty (2012, 232) maintains that each sense organ has its own way of exploring and synthetising by quoting Dr. Marius von Senden (1960, 129). Reviewing numerous cases of cataract patients who recovered from blindness after surgery, he cites a remark by Dr. Grafé who notices that these patients "see colours much as we smell an odour of peat or varnish, which enfolds and intrudes upon us, but without occupying any specific form of extension in a more exactly definable way".

12   On Aquinas' account on tastes and smells together with a comparison with Scruton's view, see McQueen 1993.

difference persists to this day.[13] It is in the context of the debate on beauty according to sophists that Plato, in the *Hippias Major*, writes that "anyone in the world would laugh at us if we called it not *pleasant to eat* but *fine*, or if we called a pleasant smell not *pleasant* but *fine*" (*Hipp. M.*, 299a).[14] Nonetheless, in the *Philebus*, Plato includes a great deal of smells among the *pure pleasures* because, although of "a more earthy set" (*Phil.*, 51e) if compared to sight and hearing, they are not mixed with any distress.[15]

As justly pointed out by Jaquet (2010, 256-257), Plato opens up to a sort of olfactory aesthetics, admitting to the legitimacy of certain smells. That said, the situation seems divergent for food odours and flavours, which tend to be excluded. Whereas the question remains quite implicit and only inferable in Plato's works, Aristotle discusses it explicitly. Put very succinctly, Aristotle, too, asserts that there exist smells that are pleasant in themselves, singling out the fragrance of flowers. Food smells are instead in his view analogous to tastes, that is, always pleasant or unpleasant *incidentally*. Moreover, they would please because they are heralds of the pleasures of eating, so they refer to *something else*. According to Aristotle, humans would thus be endowed with two senses of smell. One, which is peculiar to them, is mainly connected to health. The other, common to all animals, is linked to nourishment. The latter, contrary to the former, is not always reliable and beneficial, since "sweet food, whether dry or moist, is often unhealthy, whereas that which has a smell which is in itself pleasant is nearly always beneficial to persons in any state of health" (*De Sensu*, v., 444a). By arguing that "what Strattis said in deriding Euripides is true, 'When you make pea-soup don't put perfume in it'" (ibid, 443b), Aristotle

---

13   The myth of Adonis is emblematic: Detienne 1972. Mazzeo (2022) partially dismisses this interpretation by analysing the myth of Aphrodite. Along these lines, Diderot (1916, 165) argues that smell is "the most voluptuous" of the senses, whereas sight is the most superficial, hearing the proudest, taste the profoundest.

14   Leopardi (2013, 807) agrees, adding that smells, "which no one calls beautiful, but simply pleasurable", are pleasant or unpleasant neither in themselves nor essentially, but accidentally.

15   More details can be found in the *Timaeus*, which reads that "[a]ny body that undergoes a gradual departure from its normal state, a gradual depletion, but an overwhelming and sudden replenishment, has no perception of the depletion but only of the replenishment, and therefore gives the most intense pleasure to the mortal part of the soul, without any perception of pain. This is easy to see in the case of pleasant scents" (*Tim.*, 64a). Shortly afterwards he integrates the distinction between pleasant and unpleasant smells discerning them according to their somatic effects: "unpleasant scents roughen and assault the whole of the trunk between the head and the navel, and that pleasant scents mollify the trunk and restore it, with a feeling of contentment, to its normal state" (ibid, 67a).

warns against mixing two distinct pleasures that correspond to different, if not opposite, functions. Indeed, he states that fragrances do not entice consumption and are totally disconnected from eating.

Within this framework, Aristotle also observes that the aesthetic quality of food flavours varies with the perceiver's condition: "smells are pleasant when we are hungry, but to those who are sated and require nothing they are not pleasant; nor is the smell pleasant to those to whom the food having the smell is unpleasant" (ibid). This phenomenon, also known as *alliesthesia*,[16] has been put forward by numerous philosophers after Aristotle as proof of the subjectivity, idiosyncrasy and variability of smell perception, especially when dealing with edible substances. Olfactory reactions are contextual, and they depend on the overall situation. Kant (2006, §22, 51) takes it as evidence to demonstrate the total absence of disinterestedness in smell, which is mostly driven by physiological needs: "by means of the smell of his favorite food the hungry person is invited to pleasure, just as the satiated person is repelled by the same smell". However, differently from Plato and Aristotle, Kant categorically rejects the idea that there are pleasant smells *per se*. As he exemplifies, even the scent of flowers is problematic in view of a universal agreement on its aesthetic value, since "[o]ne person revels in it, but it gives another a headache" (Kant 2007, §32, 111). Olfactory perception embraces such variability and interest that, ultimately, odours cannot be considered beautiful but belong to the realm of the agreeable. The reason is that smell and taste acquire "more a representation of *enjoyment* than of cognition of the external object"; therefore, "the way that the subject feels affected by it can be entirely different" (Kant 2006, §16, 46). This point leads to further problems when taking into account that, whereas visual arts permit to choose whether to be exposed to their stimuli or not, scented objects such as perfumed handkerchiefs waft olfactory impressions which compel to perceive them, regardless of their pleasantness (Kant 2007, §53, 158).

This coercive and voluptuous nature of smell would not only distance humans from beauty, but also relegate them to a condition of immorality. Aromas have never universally benefited from a good reputation. According to some, they symbolise corruption, over-indulgence and slackness of morals, as in Plato's *Republic*. The East, the motherland

---

16 Named by French physiologist Michel Cabanac, it shows the variation of the sensory qualities of a stimulus according to the internal state of the perceiver. Pleasure and displeasure are not invariable and unchangeable but contingent and relational values. Although it is not limited to taste and smell, this mechanism is commonly triggered by food.

of fragrances, was often taken as the emblem of decadence.[17] Similarly, Pliny the Elder (1945, XIII, 99) draws a parallel between moral decline and the spread of the oriental habit of using redolent substances. He traces their invention to the Persians, who would use fragrances to mask their "dirtiness". Moreover, differently from other expensive objects that can be inherited and last over time, perfumes are the most superficial of luxuries since "unguents lose their scent at once, and die in the very hour when they are used" (ibid, 111). The theme of transience here takes on an ethical-political connotation which would also mark the following centuries.[18] It is worth noting, however, that in a mirror-image manner Christian literature abounds with redolent balms and perfumes as metaphors for the encounter with God and religious faith; as an example, Augustine's *Confessions* are replenished with perfumes even if, as he admits, he is not strongly affected by their allurement: "[w]hen they are absent, I do not look for them. When they are present, I do not reject them" (*Confess.*, X, xxxii, 48). According to others, instead of constituting sensual and ephemeral epiphanies, smells are connected to a sense of dissatisfaction. To use Nogué's (1936, 231) words, "something eternally unfinished, a promise never fulfilled, and an indefinite solicitation reside in smell". This is all the more so in food, the scent of which is often better than its taste, as Theophrastus (1916, 331) notes about some types of fruit.

Having ascertained that Plato and Aristotle did the groundwork for a kind of olfactory aesthetics, we can see that from its most embryonic form it already excluded anything food-related. It is no coincidence that the philosophical role attributed to smell often coincides with that of food. Only recently, since the 1980s, has the possibility emerged of a path that appraises the philosophical value of food, discrediting the contrast between the head and the belly. In parallel, a gradual acceptance of the chemical senses has spread, liberating them after centuries of isolation. Indeed, aesthetics has long turned up its nose to avoid the whiffs of perfume and food flavour, and even the stench that has begun to exhale from the margins of the art world itself.

---

17   Squillace 2014.
18   Jaquet 2010, 58-59.

5.2 *Redolent Arts*

> Good art theory must smell of the studio,
> although its language should differ from
> the household talk of painters and sculptors.
> Rudolf Arnheim

Aestheticians who have openly stood up for smell are not few. Starting off by assuming that "art is a sensuous phenomenon" and building his argumentation on a series of objections to some faults ascribed to the oral senses, John Harris (1979) endorses the idea that smells and tastes can be art forms. In the wake of Harold Osborne (1977) — while noting the latter's reticence on some points — Harris tries to illustrate that the distinction in aesthetic delights drawn between those inherent to sight and hearing on the one side, and to the other senses on the other, is nothing but prejudice. Placing much of the blame on mind/body dualism, Emily Brady shares the same opinion, stressing the complexity of smells and their importance in appreciating the environment.[19] These perspectives and many others owe much to Dewey's theory, which paved the way for a renewed aesthetics where the emphasis is not placed on *what* is perceived but on *how* it is perceived. What is at stake here is the acceptance of the proposal to transfer aesthetic value from the object or content of perception to the relationship or modality of perceiving as a knot immersed in an ecological milieu. In Deweyan terms, it means foregrounding the notion of *experience* as a flowing event with its unique flavour. By nullifying the chasm between aesthetic and non-aesthetic senses, and between art and everyday life, the hierarchy of the sensible is dismissed, concurrently calling for an aesthetic education.[20] Of course, this does not mean that smells *always* give rise to

---

19 Brady 2003, 126; 2005; 2012.
20 Education, especially with respect to smell, is a pivotal aspect I have discussed elsewhere (Mancioppi 2022a, 126-131; Mancioppi, Perullo 2020) but cannot be further expanded on here. For an ecological perspective on perception and education: Perullo 2020a. Some hints have been suggested by Brady (2012, 83) especially with regards to attention and consciousness in smelling (on this, see also Keller 2011). Notoriously, Dewey (1980, 49) provides the example of the epicure to argue that "[e]ven the pleasures of the palate are different in quality" for those who are conscious of more food-related aspects. Indeed, "seeing, hearing, tasting, become esthetic when relation to a distinct manner of activity qualifies what is perceived" (ibid). Dewey's insight can be supplemented by a passage by Pessoa (2003, 453) about *sentimental education* which is quite telling. It reads: "to be able to achieve in the vision of a sunset or in the contemplation of a decorative

aesthetic experiences; but they do so in the occurrence of smell becoming salient and valuable in itself, scenting an event while turning it into *an* experience.

In addition to proposing the *aesthetic* as a perceptual *field*,[21] Berleant clarifies an aspect that is crucial for our analysis. According to him, the task of aesthetics is to elaborate a system only after collecting and examining a significant set of artistic phenomena on the basis of a pattern of inquiry which is not dissimilar from other disciplines. Hence, aesthetics should *follow* and explain art and what is associated with it instead of determining aprioristically what can be considered as such. Given the current vivacity of olfactory art,[22] this alone should be reason enough for aestheticians to consider it an area within the confines of their expertise, which demands being investigated and comprehended. This way of proceeding also requires an *intimate knowledge* of the arts — Rudolf Arnheim (1974, 4) exemplified this by arguing that "[g]ood art theory must smell of the studio, although its language should differ from the household talk of painters and sculptors". In view of our premises, Arnheim's utterance should be accepted almost literally.

The appreciation of the aesthetic power of fragrances is anything but a recent acquisition. Carmen XIII by Catullus, *Cenabis bene, mi Fabulle, apud me*, is a mock-invitation addressed to Fabullus, who is asked to bring food, wine, company, salt and cheerfulness to the home of the penniless Latin poet. In return, Catullus will present him with such a good perfume that he will pray to the gods to make him *totum nasum*, "all nose" (vv. 9-14). Jumping forward in time, far from playful is instead the attitude towards smells and fragrances adopted by the famous protagonist of *À rebours* by Joris-Karl Huysmans.[23] Des Esseintes, a sharp nose able to detect the slightest nuance, "believed that the sense of smell could

---

detail that intensity of feeling which generally can't occur through sight or hearing but only by way of the carnal senses — touch, taste and smell — when they sculpt the object of sensation on our consciousness".

21   This field is influenced by several factors including biological ones: as he exemplifies through the case of certain odours as well as sounds and textures, the "exposure to steady stimulation at some fixed level will ultimately deaden perception" (Berleant 1970, 75). This applies to all the senses, questioning their hierarchy in aesthetic terms.

22   For instance, *Olfactory Art Keller* is a gallery in Manhattan entirely dedicated to artistic experimentations with odours (see https://www.olfactoryartkeller.com/). It was founded in 2021 by scholar Andreas Keller, whose works on olfactory perception have already been mentioned in this book.

23   Jaquet 2010, 257-274.

experience pleasures equal to those of hearing and sight" (Huysmans 1998, 92). Something similar is advocated by Gabriele D'Annunzio, whose correspondence with his perfumer aptly shows the central role smells played in his life as genuine aesthetic pleasures.[24]

As already mentioned, artistic experimentation with smells, and not just perfumes, reached its zenith from the 20th century onwards. Within this framework, Arte Povera, Land Art, Fluxus, Junk Art, Performance Art, Body Art and Eat Art are among the most prolific movements or groups, before "olfactory art" was labelled and formalised into a specific, although rather fluid branch. As artistic movements driven by an innovative, experimental or openly subversive spirit, their appeal and attention to odours are fully consistent not only with their underlying intents, but also with their tools, materials and modus operandi. On the one hand, as Jaquet (2015, 10-11) explains, the use of smells encourages "the deconstruction of the traditional conception of the work of art, which ceases to be a solid and imperishable object, and its reconfiguration to integrate the dimension of passage, of flux, of becoming". Happenings are emblematic cases, sharing with smells a fleeting and evenemential nature as well as a stronger bodily engagement. Indeed, by employing unconventional substances, aggregations and things that are often smelly and part of everyday life (such as waste, food and countless other materials), these arts naturally result in a stress on the olfactory dimension.[25] As such, new art forms also challenge the limits within which mainstream ones operate, both in emotional and perceptual terms. Hence the deliberate triggering of feelings such as annoyance, shock and pain. In olfactory terms, this translates into the "display" of stenches as a specific trait.[26] In short, the sense of smell becomes a prominent artistic medium as art changes its theoretical and poetic orientation, concurrently expanding its medial field. Osmospheres are now in the spotlight.[27]

A systematisation of what is presented under the name of "olfactory art" is Peter de Cupere's *Olfactory Art Manifest* (2014). Here he draws

---

24 Fabbian 2012, 77-107; Gibellini 2017.
25 Examples are endless: from engine oil in Richard Wilson's *20:50* (1987) and decaying roses in Anya Gallaccio's *Red and Green* (2012), to soiled mattresses and decomposing frosting in Nancy Rubins's *Mattresses and Cakes* (1993) and earth in Walter de Maria's *Earth Room* (1968), as well as in Delcy Morelos's *Inner Earth* (2018). Of course, it is impossible to provide a comprehensive list of all artists engaged in olfaction. However, I would like to mention at least Klara Ravat and Clara Ursitti.
26 Shiner 2020, 182-200.
27 It is also interesting to note the coining of neologisms to name new concepts and art forms involving the sense of smell: https://www.odorbet.com/.

four terminological distinctions proposing different (and in many cases overlapping) -*isms* (*olfactism*, *olfactionism*, *olfactorism* and *olfactourism*) according to the role played by smells in the diverse artistic practices in which they are involved.[28] Further alternative subdivisions have been proposed by aestheticians. For instance, Diaconu (2022a) identifies four major fields: perfumery, olfactory design, olfactory art and the production of smellscapes. Differently, Jaquet (2022) distinguishes more generally between *integrated* and *integral* olfactory art. For my part, I propose to subdivide olfactory arts into three areas which are based on the executive function taken on by odours: *evocation*; *amplification*; *essence*. The first is not strictly olfactory in that smells are not *materially* present; it includes all the works where osmospheres are evoked through diverse perceptual channels. In the second, odours are used as extras in combination with other stimuli in a non-discordant but reinforcing, somehow overstating, manner. The third comprises artworks in which the olfactory dimension is an integral part.

I will now proceed to briefly outline the three different groups. Nevertheless, in the remaining pages my attention will be mostly devoted to the third category, *essence*. This choice is motivated by the fact that, in order to understand how osmospheres are perceived and used artistically, I consider it necessary to focus on cases in which they are essential to the artworks themselves. By paying specific attention to food, essential osmospheric artworks will be further investigated, firstly through the case of Futurism, secondly through a miscellany of artistic cases so as to outline the state of the art of food osmospheres.

Evocation

By endorsing an ecological understanding of perception, I agree with Drobnick (2015) when, in attempting a definition of what "olfactory art" is, he comes to the conclusion that it is inherently a *hybrid art*. Certainly, the same applies to all other art forms since, under normal conditions, we experience them while immersed in an environment criss-crossed by stimuli that affect all the senses. Possibly, even a work of art that does not directly target the sense of smell can turn out to be osmospheric for the cross-sensory nature of atmospheres.[29] However, given the difficulty

---

28   de Cupere 2016, 101-108.
29   Something similar is stressed by Cézanne, who argued that, like the mysteriously perfumed compositions by Baudelaire and Zola, a painting should convey "a movement sensed equally by our eyes, our ears, our mouth and our nose, each

in defining this kind of experience, I am referring here to artistic works that *explicitly* evoke or represent an osmosphere without an actual smell being present.[30] It is the case with poems, novels, movies, music, videos, sculptures, etc. which make explicit reference to an odour or its effect.

Olfactory titles (in all kinds of art) provide the work with a peculiar osmosphere. In the figurative arts, smells can be illustrated through the representation of smelly objects and places, of smoke or visible trails, or of their effects on the perceiver.[31] Figures sniffing with ecstasy and voluptuousness evoke different osmospheres if compared with faces wrinkled by an expression of disgust.[32] In movies and theatre plays, smells can be recalled both visually and verbally. The role of osmospheres in literature has been dealt with extensively in the previous chapters: odours can give specific episodes a certain tone, acting as narrative tools or even as protagonists.

Indeed, an *essential* olfactory artwork can be *evoked*, as is the case with an osmospheric performance described in À *rebours*. Believing that "the flavour of each cordial corresponded [...] to the sound of an instrument" (Huysmans 1998, 39-41), Des Esseintes imagines an orchestra in which the savouring turns into the performance of interior symphonies, "providing his gullet with sensations analogous to those which music affords the ear" (ibid, 39). Dry curaçao corresponds to the clarinet, penetrating and velvety; crème de menthe and anisette to the flute, honeyed and pungent, whining

---

with a special kind of poetry" (Gasquet 1990, 151). As he puts it, a canvas lacking overall harmony is a canvas without smell. Merleau-Ponty (2012, 333) sums up Cézanne's idea stating that "the thing is the absolute plenitude that projects my undivided existence in front of itself". This suggests an osmospheric modality of seeing and, as Han (2015, 14) argues drawing from these very observations, the "visualization of fragrances requires profound attention. In the contemplative state, one steps outside oneself, so to speak, and immerses *oneself* in the surroundings". This is why, resorting to Cézanne's intuitions, smelling the odour of pine trees while observing the Monte Sainte-Victoire paintings means that the colours do not achieve the effect desired by the artist; instead, "the pure blue smell of pine, which is sharp in the sun, ought to blend with the fresh green smell of meadows in the morning, and with the smell of stones and the distant marble smell of Saint-Victoire" (Gasquet 1990, 151).

30 For different cases, Jaquet 2010, 138-222.

31 Kinne 2021.

32 Apart from the various allegories of the senses, mention may be made of *The Resurrection of Lazarus* (c. 1545, Church of San Giovanni Evangelista, Brescia) by Il Romanino, where a character plugs his nose, and of Edvard Munch's *The Smell of Death* (1895, Munch Museum, Oslo) where, in addition to the olfactory title, two persons appear to cover their mouths and noses.

and sweet; gin and whisky to cornets and trombones, explosively strident, and so on.[33] Such an osmospheric-musical experience,[34] in which melodies are played on the tongue,[35] can take place in reverse. A parallel can be drawn with the experience had by Josef Knecht in *The Glass Bead Game* by Hermann Hesse (1969, 70), according to whom the chords of Schubert's *Die linden Lüfte sind erwacht* have "exactly the same fragrance as the sap of the young elder, just as bittersweet, just as strong and compressed, just as full of the forthcoming spring".

Amplification

As a kind of spin-off of the above-mentioned area, this category includes artworks with which supplementary odours are *combined* and *matched*, whose purpose is essentially to endow them with "a feeling of intensity, of volume" (Studio Ólafur Elíasson 2016, 31).[36] Smells are therefore present. Odours are then optional for an iterative amplification. Examples include buildings and architectures, sculptural and pictorial exhibitions in which each work is enveloped in an osmosphere specifically created to enhance its impact. Often, the intention is to recreate the evoked osmosphere of a masterpiece. The smell acts as a reverberation and strengthening of the content or meaning conveyed by the work itself.

Many attempts have been made to create or improve technological devices or mechanisms capable of dispersing scents in theatres, cinemas or concert halls so as to match and accompany scenes or melodies with their respective osmospheres. In any case, smell acts as an ancillary and additional element helping to create a more "immersive" experience. To

---

33 In *Under the Jaguar Sun*, Calvino (1988, 5) makes a comparison between the cuisine of Mexican nuns and a musicality of flavours, where "the thought of nuns called up the flavours of an elaborate and bold cuisine, bent on making the flavours' highest note vibrate, juxtaposing them in modulations, in chords, and especially in dissonances that would assert themselves as an incomparable experience — an absolute possession exercised on the receptivity of all the senses".

34 It ends with a recollection à la Proust: "his thoughts followed the impression that had been on his palate, closely pursuing the taste of the whiskey and awakening, by a fatal conjunction of odours, memories that had long since vanished" (Huysmans 1998, 40).

35 On fragrance and music in Shelley, Boyson 2013. On music and atmospheres, Scassillo 2020.

36 The same is maintained by Tuan (1977, 13), according to whom odour "is capable of suggesting mass and volume"; he also insists on the importance of exercising and educating the sense of smell.

put it differently, smells do not bring about any change or enrichment at a semantic level, adding nothing but intensity or a sort of three-dimensionality to what the work already possesses in itself. In this respect, theatre is perhaps the most prolific artistic terrain.[37] In this regard, it is worth mentioning the works by Paul-Napoléon Roinard who, aspiring to a form of total theatre, in 1981 staged the *Cantique des cantiques*, a pièce saturated with the vaporisation of odours. However, the work was not reviewed favourably.[38] A very positive reception, on the contrary, was given to *The Governor's Lady* (1912), a play written by Alice Bradley and directed by David Belasco, which was performed more than a hundred times. In a scene set in a Childs Restaurant (one of the first dining chains in the U.S. and Canada), pancakes were cooked on stage precisely to recreate the osmosphere of the popular restaurants and to envelop the audience with their aroma.[39] Recently, there has been no shortage of similar cases of *mise-en-scène*.[40]

The incorporation of smells in movie theatres dates back to the mid-20th century. *AromaRama*, *Scentovision*, *Smell-O-Vision* and *Odorama* are just some of the most famous olfactory systems that, since the late 1950s, have been designed to enrich cinematographic experiences with odours corresponding to the images projected on the big screen. However, no technique so far has proved fully satisfactory, due to the difficulty in directing and controlling scents. Olfactory overlaps or excessive saturation are difficult to avoid. This is why, for one reason or another, these experiments have almost always ended in failure.

Virtual reality is one of the most recent artistic phenomena that is entering the aesthetic investigation and the olfactory arts.[41] Rather than immersiveness, the use of scents is motivated by the need to arouse a *sense of presence* in the users.[42] This is why odours mostly take on an accompanying function in support of audiovisual stimuli because, especially when *congruent*,[43] they can improve task performances and

---

37 Banes 2001, Paquet 2004, De Carné 2015.
38 Bruschi 2017; Di Stefano, Murari, Spence 2022, 164-165.
39 Banes 2001, 69.
40 The numerous contributions on the topic include: D'Errico 2018; McGinley, McGinley 2018; Shiner 2020, 158-165; McPhee 2020.
41 I am very grateful to Lorenzo Manera for sharing many readings and insights with me. His works on digital aesthetics and reality media include: Manera 2022a, 2022b.
42 Persky, Dolwick 2020; Archer *et al.* 2022; Fiala 2022.
43 Flavián *et al.* 2021, Brengman *et al.* 2022.

offer psychophysiological advantages.[44] Nonetheless, similarly to the above-mentioned cases, there are practical complications that restrict the potentials of olfactory experiences in virtual reality. One of the biggest obstacles is the discomfort caused by having to wear bulky devices, intensifying a sense of fictitiousness.[45]

Essence

What I have tautologically designated as "essence" approximately coincides with Peter de Cupere's (2016, 101) very broad notion of *olfactism*, where smell is a "medium that gives context and/or can be the concept of the work". Here, the olfactory dimension is not just subsidiary but a central factor. This does not necessarily mean that odour is the *only* stimulus, but that, in combination with the others, it is a constitutive and integral part of the work of art, giving access to its meaning. Of course, smells *can* be the only elements on condition that perfumes and odours are understood as potential works of art in themselves. Nevertheless, it is interesting to note that one of the olfactory arts *par excellence*, the Japanese incense ceremony called *kōdō*, involves the combination of different perceptual, intellectual, expertise and artistic domains through the exclusive use of smell. Attested since the Middle Ages as an aristocratic game but formalised as an artistic practice in the 15th century, it involves a ceremony where the participants — traditionally of the upper class due to the expensiveness of fragrances — "listen to" and contemplate the incenses that are properly prepared by the kōdō master. Like in a competition, people have to guess the various scents. Furthermore, what each incense "inspires" is expressed by the players in the form of short poetic compositions.[46]

As well as with poetry, the analogy between odours and music recurs from multiple perspectives. Their shared aerial nature makes them interchangeable in the cosmologies of certain populations. The Dogon of Mali "hear" smells: the auditory and verbal sphere overlaps seamlessly with the olfactory one, so much so that, among other practices, they perfume their breath when they want to make sure they give a good speech.[47] This interplay underlies *Riverberi...* (2022) by Bruna Esposito,

---

44 Kaimal *et al.* 2021; Niedenthal *et al.* 2023; Abbott, Diaz-Artiles 2022.
45 Carulli *et al.* 2015.
46 Kōdō is receiving increasing attention from scholars: Jaquet 2018. More information can be found in many of the monographs on smell referenced throughout the book. Shusterman (2011a, 154) also makes references to it.
47 Classen, Howes, Synnott 1994, 119.

an installation consisting in a gong placed on a laurel wreath. Visitors can use the knocker to hit the metal disc, activating the sound together with a greater dispersion of the scent exhaling from the leaves. However, more than everything, smells and sounds become entwined in the jargon of perfumery, which is particularly indebted to musical lexicon.[48] Indeed, not only the olfactory pyramid is made up of base, middle and top *notes*, but a synonym for perfumers is *perfume-composers*, their skill being that of *arranging* aromas by attuning one to the other and, in so doing, providing the whole with a *pitch*, a *rhythm* and a *progression*. This affinity is the basis of the theory set forth by Septimus Piesse (1862, 25), who invented an olfactory categorisation system on a musical cast — "the gamut of odours" — complete with semi-odours. Indeed, the 19th-century chemist and perfumer believed that there exists "an octave of odours like an octave in music; certain odours coincide, like the keys of an instrument".

Since the early 20th century, various artists have experimented with creating scent concerts.[49] From Sadakichi Hartmann's *A Trip to Japan in Sixteen Minutes* (1902), where odours mingle with the reading of a text,[50] to some exhibitions of Aleksandr Skrjabin's *Prometheus*,[51] with far from intuitive associations between perceptual elements. Indeed, the "scent organ" described in 1932 by Aldous Huxley (2005, 153-155), in addition to inspiring the Futurists,[52] appears to be the prototype of all the disparate olfactory technologies developed since the late 1970s. An example is Wolfgang Georgsdorf's *Smeller 1.0* (1979), refined over the years and upgraded to *Smeller 2.0*,[53] an enormous and complex hi-tech machine designed to be very sensitive to the keyboard, and to avoid any mingling of odours by completely changing the air of the room once or twice per minute. In addition to performances that fall into the second domain of "amplification" — patterns of essences to accompany films, poetry, etc. —, the Austrian artist is famous for his smelly solos such as *Autocomplete: Synosmy* (2016), a purely olfactory symphony. Georgsdorf is convinced that odours can convey proper stories and even sentences, which he calls

---

48   See Serra 2019.
49   Jaquet 2019.
50   Hartmann 1913, Meier 2017.
51   Runciman 1915.
52   Verbeek 2021, 126-127.
53   Other examples are de Cupere's smell piano — *Olfactiano* (1997) and *Olfactiano VII* (2014) (de Cupere 2016, 37, 379) — and the scent organ used for Christophe Laudamiel and Stewart Matthew's *Green Aria: A Scent Opera* (2009) (Shiner 2020, 172-174).

scentences.[54] Smells are then treated as narrative elements on a par with words and images.

Performances and installations are not only the most conspicuous expressions of olfactory art, but also they often make use of food flavours. That is why it is necessary to devote a specific inquiry to them. In what follows, my concern is not to conjecture about the relationships between art, food flavours and cooking as a performance. I am not interested in speculating on the acts of eating and smelling as a possible form of art, that is, a performance carried out by the eater,[55] nor will I reflect on dishes and their aromas as possible olfactory installations. What I will do, rather, is try to understand the role played by food osmospheres as the very *substructures* giving rise to an aesthetic experience. This is explicitly at odds with what is argued by Leroi-Gourhan (1993, 291), who defines smell as a *superstructure* of gastronomic aesthetics, supporting his assertion by claiming that "the embellishments of olfactory gastronomy are superimposed" on taste and mouthfeel, which are instead the deeper part of culinary aesthetics. In this respect, Futurism proves to be a fertile source of reflection.

5.3 *Futurist Osmospheres*

> We must destroy the inappropriate mono-odority
> of all environments.
> Ennio Valentinelli

From the very start, Futurism has all but underestimated the power of smells.[56] One might even venture to say that the osmospheric dimension plays a pivotal role in its programmatic renovation of the arts. Before focusing on food and eating, let me first sketch a panoramic overview.

In *The Founding and Manifesto of Futurism* (1909) by Filippo Tommaso Marinetti (1973, 20), the olfactory dimension is celebrated through the praise of the *nose* (in Italian, *fiuto*), in contrast to "the deceitful mathematics of [the] perishing eyes". Furthermore, consistently with the push towards the constant renewal of ideas and society, the Futurists hoped

---

54   Georgsdorf 2021; Shiner 2020, 178-181.
55   Interesting remarks on the topic have been proposed by Shusterman (2016), from whose work numerous scholars have drawn inspiration to theorise the role of taste, food and the body in the realm of art (Koczanowicz 2023).
56   Verbeek 2018.

they would be surpassed and dismissed, in turn, by their successors, who would sniff, like dogs, "at the academy doors the strong odour of [their] decaying minds, which will already have been promised to the literary catacombs" (ibid, 23). The focus on the olfactory sphere recurs in a large number of exhibitions and events held internationally, and also in some of the manifold manifestos devoted to the various arts. In 1909-1910, Luigi Russolo paints *Perfume*, where olfactory perception is rendered through a divisionist use of colours. In August 1913, Carlo Carrà writes *The Painting of Sound, Noises and Smells*, which includes many osmospheric insights. Core issues include the ideas of dynamism, plasticity and atmosphere, through which Carrà develops the concept of the *plastic whole* to be created by triggering enveloping sensations and synesthesia. According to him, smell alone suffices "to determine in our minds arabesques of form and colour which could be said to constitute the motive and justify the necessity of a painting" (Carrà 1973, 114). In fact, if shut in a dark room with flowers, petrol or other smelly things, "our plastic spirit will gradually eliminate the memory sensation and construct a very special plastic whole which corresponds perfectly, in its quality of weight and movement with the smells found in the room" (ibid). Hence, inexplicably, these odours "have become environment-force, determining that state of mind which for us Futurist painters constitutes a pure plastic whole" (ibid).[57]

Such an idea finds specific discussion in *The Art of Odours: A Futurist Manifesto* by Ennio Valentinelli, presumably written in 1914-1915 but published posthumously.[58] After a foreword on the marginalisation of olfaction — "since the Middle Ages we have forgotten the sense of smell" (Valentinelli 1996, 133) — and a few remarks on the history of fragrances, Valentinelli insists on the need to promote an aesthetic education parallel with the development of a new form of art: the art of odours, which is basically "the art of creating atmospheres" (Duranti, Pesola 1996, 17). In order to avoid being romantic and sentimental, this art must include the full spectrum of *olfactory lyricism*, i.e., the whole palette from perfumes

---

57 Similarly, in his manifesto on Futurist sculpture published the previous year, Boccioni (1973, 65) argues that there "can be no renewal unless it is through *environmental sculpture*, since only by this means can plastic art develop and come to *model the atmosphere* which surrounds our objects". Here, however, the atmosphere has nothing to do with smells but mostly with materials, dynamic force-lines, vibrations of lights, interpenetration of planes and the opening of figures, whereas in Carrà's (1973, 115) view on painting, smells, either pleasant or unpleasant, play a pivotal role in rendering it "*a plastic state of mind of the universal*".

58 Daly 2016.

to stenches. The aim is to destroy the *uni-odority* of environments and to strengthen the senses, the will, and the nerves. The programme is therefore to

> educate [the] nostrils to perceive the sensations of perfumes and reeks more acutely, lyrical sensations with varying degrees of tempo, simple composite compenetrating sensations: chords of perfumes and reeks. We will create a new music of odours, the sister of the music of sounds and noises (Valentinelli 1996, 133-134).

Valentinelli proposes the diffusion of smells matching different environments: in places of entertainment, odours have to be light and hilarious; in sex-related places, languid and exhausting. Furthermore, smells have to combine with abstract concepts conveyed by the reciting of poetry. Interestingly enough, food flavours come into play in two out of four peculiar correspondences: the "sharp smells of garlic medlars onions sulphuric acid correspond to rough powerful upsetting concepts" (ibid, 134); and "odours of rotten cabbages of valeric acid hydrogen sulphide of acrid urine of mould of corpses of narcotics correspond to passéist concepts" (ibid). Bruno Munari undertakes something similar in cinema with *The Futurist Movie: Noises...Odours...Colours...* (1928). Introducing smells which are consistent with the visual inputs, the "audience will thus get the whole feeling of the scene and identify with the film, experiencing it to the fullest" (Munari 1928).

Within such an osmospheric revolution, the attempt at substituting spontaneous scents with artificial ones cannot go unmentioned. The theme was elaborated in 1924 by Fedele Azari, who published *The Futurist Flora and Plastic Equivalents of Artificial Smells*. The manifesto encourages the creation of new plants, arguing that the smell of natural flowers — together with their appearance and, in general, the imagery that surrounds them — no longer suited the taste of the period.[59] Somewhat in line with Gustave Flaubert (1910, 245), who wished "for new perfumes, for vaster flowers, for pleasures never felt before", Azari (1924) promotes the need to replace the spontaneous flora with a human-made one, since even "the so-called pleasing scents of flowers are not enough for our nostrils that demand increasingly violent olfactory sensations, so much so that the

---

59 In 1920, Fedele Azari also published *Olfactory Sociology*, which is part of *The Bank Clerk*, where he draws a parallel between banknote denominations and their smells, corresponding to the people owning them (Sharp 1983, 23-25; Verbeek 2020, 259-260).

perfumes extracted from flowers [...] are now completely supplanted by industrially created inebriating synthetic fragrances". Futurist flowers are no longer associated with natural environments but with anthropogenic ones, and they smell of substances such as petrol, carbolic acid, benzene and chloroform. The faith in technology and modernity driving this general osmospheric renewal is also apparent in Futurist gastronomy, where the attention to osmospheres and the application of the art of odours reach their peak.

Since the late 1920s, Futurism had developed a cutting-edge way of designing, cooking and consuming meals, which were deemed as emblematic examples of a synesthetic art form: "[e]ating futuristically, one uses all five senses" (Marinetti 2014, 95). A crucial moment was December 28, 1930, when the *Manifesto of Futurist Cooking* was published in the *Gazzetta del Popolo* of Turin. In it, Marinetti and Fillìa (Luigi Colombo) present some programmatic points. As is known, Fascism banked on the identitarian and social role of food; Futurism resumes this political motif in the artistic and aesthetic sphere, although in different terms. Indeed, such an operation is not meant to preserve and extol culinary customs. Quite to the contrary, its aim is to uproot each and every tradition through a radical and creative gastronomic revolution: the Futurist culinary renewal is systematically outlined on the basis of the ideals of speed, originality and surprise. Since humans "think dream and act according to what they eat and drink" (ibid, 33), old-fashioned food habits necessarily make people *passéist*, nourishing and supporting a nostalgic attitude that corresponds to heavy bodies and lethargic moods. This is why the Futurist social revolution also involves food, and smells are essential means for it to succeed.

If well matched, smells not only foster the aesthetic appreciation of the meal, but they also feed imagination and creativity, offering at the same time physical *and* mental nourishment. Prof. Nicola Pende, a supporter of the Futurist culinary campaign, believed that many of its opponents underestimate the power of perfumes, attributing to them a merely exciting function; instead, they are able to influence one's mood, appetite and digestive processes.[60] In *simultaneous dinner*, designed for businessmen who do not have time to enjoy a meal by putting their work activities on hold, some perfumed letters and invoices are used to waft more or less intense perfumes "to calm, satisfy or excite the appetite" according to

---

60   For a Bachelardian distinction between a superficial and a deep epicureanism, where flavours play a pivotal role also in digestive terms, Bachelard 2000, 141-142.

need (ibid, 185). Scents can cause astonishment, contrast and harmony as well, providing the meal with a peculiar atmosphere. According to the Futurists, the olfactory dimension must be reorganised, from the fragrance that lingers in restaurants to that of dish soap, in order to bring about the revolution in everyday life too. The importance attributed to synthetic aromas and to the most diverse devices (electric fans, ozonisers, etc.) is consistent with the general drive for innovation and chemistry that characterises Futurism. Interestingly enough, this is an aspect that can still be found today in modernist cooking,[61] with osmospheric repercussions that will be addressed shortly. Given that the "use of the art of perfume to enhance tasting" (ibid, 38) is fundamental in Futurist cuisine, it constitutes a constant in the various dinner-performances designed by the artists who subscribed to this project. In such gastronomic happenings, different ways of matching food and smells can be detected.

Futurism is not particularly fond of the linear equivalence between food and its "natural" odour. Denoted by accumulation, synthesis and confusion, Futurist gastronomy aims at disorienting and deconstructing what is conventional and comfortable. In light of this, we understand why a report of *the futurist aerobanquet in bologna* (1931), published in *Il Resto del Carlino*, reads that one diner was accused by Marinetti of conservatism and pusillanimity when surprised in the act of sniffing the meat before eating it. The cowardice would consist in a sense of suspicion before ingestion, whereas passéism would lie in the equivalence between an ingredient and its smell. From here we can advance the hypothesis that Futurism also aspires to subvert the automatic evolutionary gestures linked to the function of olfaction as a guardian sense thanks to its pre-established associations.

On the contrary, Futurists fully exploit the suggestive power of smells, even making them protagonists in many "provocative and evocative" dinners. The fragrances, sprinkled in the air or added to food, are not directly connected to the ingredients of the dishes but have the purpose of evoking landscapes, whether a local countryside or a distant exotic paradise, or of arousing specific affective inclinations. In *the synthesis of italy dinner*, the smells are meant to express aerial geographies: each course is combined with and immersed in its own osmosphere, which is artificially recreated thanks to technological devices. The room temperature is adapted according to the season each food recalls; the same goes for scents. For instance, "Civilized Rusticity" (a cake of rice, rose leaves, frog meat and cherries)

---

61   Helstosky 2017.

is coupled with geranium fragrance; "Colonial Instinct" (mullet, Marsala, various exotic fruits) with a "violent perfume of carnations, broom and acacia" (ibid, 173).[62] The roles are reversed in the *dinner of white desire*, which is designed for ten black people, in accordance with the idea that the "Negroes' state of mind is almost unconsciously influenced by the paleness and whiteness of all the foods" (ibid, 186 [slightly modified]). For this reason, "from the ceiling an incandescent globe of milky glass descends towards the table and a smell of jasmine fills the room" (ibid, 187).

In the *aerofood* devised by Fillìa, while people enjoy a minimal tactile dish,[63] the orchestra plays deafening jazz pieces and the waiters, armed with sprinklers, drench the heads of the diners with a carnation-scented solution. Something similar can be found in the *tactile dinner party*: whenever the diners lift their heads from the plate to chew, "the waiters spray their faces with perfumes of lavender and eau de Cologne" (ibid, 171). It might be said that Futurism systematically contradicts the Aristotelian principle that pea-soup must not be complemented with perfume, concurrently showing that smell is also capable of inducing a political orientation, a central aspect of this avant-garde movement. This is theatrically staged in *heroic winter dinner*. Typically decadent and nostalgic sweet scents (rose, jasmine, honeysuckle and acacia) are outpoured; the diners — brave and heroic soldiers, as the title suggests — must defend themselves by wearing gas masks (Marinetti 2014, 138). Likewise, a course served in the *official dinner* called "the solid treaty" consists in "a multi-coloured castle

---

62   Looking at the legacy that Futurism has left to the so-called "molecular cuisine", we can think of dry ice, which is used to release a dense and theatrical cloud of aromatic vapour to provide a dish with a particular osmosphere. Examples are manifold; suffice it to mention "Oak Moss" by Heston Blumenthal, British celebrity chef owner of the fine-dining restaurant The Fat Duck in Bray, Berkshire. The dish is made of quail and black truffle, the permanent ingredients of a preparation with several variations over the years, depending on where it is served. In any occasion, the consumption is preceded by an oak film that the diners have to melt in the mouth, then accompanied by a tray covered with moss and dry ice from which, once water is poured over, a dense fragrant mist rises, evoking the osmospheric places where food originated (Spence 2017, 24-25). Here, the environmental scent enriches the gastronomic experience acting as an ecological background.

63   A slice of fennel, an olive and a chinotto orange accompanied with a strip of cardboard with different materials to be touched (velvet, silk and sandpaper). It is not recommended for hungry people.

of nougat with, inside, very tiny nitroglycerine bombs which explode now and then, perfuming the room with the typical smell of battle" (ibid, 146).[64]

Even more interesting and gastronomically unorthodox is the idea that the actual ingestion of food is not necessary for its enjoyment. As a matter of fact, some dishes are just to be prepared, displayed, watched and sniffed, *not* eaten, to "increase [guests'] curiosity, surprise and imagination" (ibid, 39). In *autumn musical dinner* one course is "a roast quail for each of the guests to look at and inhale the smell deeply without eating" (ibid, 142). *The extremist banquet* — one of the most original and complex Futurist performative formulas — exasperates this aspect, being based entirely on such a logic: only perfumes are served instead of food, and the guests, who must have fasted for two days, have to satisfy their hunger only by smelling. This olfactory meal alternates environmental essences (lake, barn, sea and greenhouse) with just as many smelly courses.[65] The torture of the "diners" on an empty stomach involves being tormented by food aromas to the point of "feverishly chewing the emptiness" (ibid, 157),[66] and subsides only at the end of the meal, when

> [a] fragrance wafts by — the very delicate, strong, sweet, putrid, hothouse smell of cultivated irises which, coming from the greenhouse, meets an identical perfume, but wild, coming from the lake. The two perfumes of life, flesh, luxury, death combine and thus gratify all [...] starving palates (ibid, 157-158).

The replacement of food with olfactory courses can be connected to the exaltation of agile, light and thin bodies, which are not burdened by full stomachs struggling with the arduous digestion of large volumes of

---

64 In the supplement of the *Technical Manifesto of Futurist Literature* published in 1912, where, among other things, Marinetti encourages the abolition of articles, adjectives, adverbs, prepositions and punctuation, he writes "BATTLE: WEIGHT + ODOUR", a long list of evocative smells, together with disparate nouns and verbs; for instance: "atmosphere = lead + lava + 300 stenches + 50 perfumes" (Marinetti 2005, 13 for an excerpt).

65 For instance, a food sculpture looking and smelling like a ship composed of fried aubergines sprinkled with vanilla, acacia flowers and red pepper.

66 We can venture to draw a parallel with the prisoners in Nazi concentration camps described by Levi, who often flail their jaws in hunger while sleeping. Indeed, the most common dream is that of eating, a tantalic and collective dream where "[y]ou not only see the food, you feel it in your hands, distinct and concrete, you are aware of its rich and striking smell; someone in the dream even holds it up to your lips, but every time a different circumstance, intervenes to prevent the consumption of the act" (Levi 1959, 65).

heavy food. The right smells forge fervent and energetic souls suitable for the glorified high-speed modernity. Moreover, to economise and facilitate the spiritual as well as intellectual ascent of humans, the attention to odours seems to also act as a perceptual counterweight to nourishment in powder or pills which, according to the Futurists, would make life easier, relieving humanity of the most tiring and time-consuming tasks. At the same time, Futurism questions the results of biological evolution, namely the depository of psychophysical adaptations, passed on and sedimented in the primitive and natural mechanisms that regulate hunger, craving, the impulse to satisfy them, and satiety. In this model, smell fully becomes a positive *act of consumption* which aspires to improve the humans of the future in medical, psychological, emotional and ideological terms. In this sense, when Gibson (1969, 137) considers the common use of the verbs "to taste" and "to smell" arguing that the difference between the two has to be found in sampling or detecting a substance *inside* or *outside* one's mouth, he is somehow corroborating the Futurist thesis, which seeks to destabilise their ordinary meaning. In order to create a short circuit in the usual way the experience of eating unfolds, Futurism attempts an overturning of the material/immaterial dualism: on the one hand, by disembodying ingestion and, on the other, by fully materialising the act of smelling. The nose is regarded as a *true digestive organ*.

Differently from the aforementioned *Ghost Food Truck Project*, where food flavours are meant to recreate usual and comforting eating habits in atypical circumstances serving as holograms, the *osmoclastic* character of Futurism seeks to renew eating, although, it has to be said, it does not go as far as to fully dissolve the edible/non-edible dualism in terms of olfactory values. As an example, the exciting smell of fossil fuel is never directly related to the pleasures of food; a partial exception can be found in Marinetti's comment on *Flowers of Italy* by Bruno G. Sanzin, where he acknowledges that the author has perfectly rendered the peculiar odours of Italy, including those of "the motorways fed with eccentric speed and the good smell of warm bread from the tyres for cars" (Marinetti 1977, 260).

Considering the use of food flavours in terms of health benefits and aesthetic satisfaction endorsed by Futurism, innovations in the same vein can be found not only in commodities which promote an *osmospheric foodification*, but also in the very field of gastronomy.[67] For the former, some scented items serve the specific purpose of exploiting the hedonic value of food, concurrently bypassing the cons of its consumption. This

---

67   In general, Shiner 2020, 296-306.

aspect can be exemplified by the Stinky Candle Company's *Burrito Candle*, that "wraps you up in the smell of ground beef, spices, and all the extra, *minus the stomach ache*".[68] An interesting example is the "aerosol cuisine" conceived by David Edwards, professor of Biomedical Engineering at Harvard University who, for several decades, has been working on food at the intersection between art and science.[69] All his inventions are based on a fundamental, and markedly Futuristic, question: "Might we breathe food?" (Edwards 2018, 61). Among many devices, in 2009 he launched *Le Whif*, an inhaler similar to an electronic cigarette designed to enjoy chocolate and coffee by savouring the aroma without intaking calories and harmful compounds such as caffeine, fats and sugar.[70] In 2012, in joint effort with Philippe Starck, Edwards designed *Wah Quantum Sensations*, a small vaporiser that triggers an instant and brief sensation of intoxication without the need to drink alcohol. Also from the same year is *Le Whaf*, an ultrasonic pitcher/decanter that nebulises all kinds of liquids transforming them into a dense aromatic cloud. Again, the olfactory experience is intensified while ingestion is minimised.[71]

All these examples concern technologies aimed at eliminating the harmful materiality of food, while preserving its hedonic potential through the olfactory dimension. Are we going in the direction of a "disembodiment" of food, consuming it through the nose? Difficult to predict. Nevertheless, it seems undeniable that we are moving towards an *osmospheric gastronomy* that, by emphasising the aerial dimension of foods, abstracts them from their effective metabolisation and aspires to eliminate any possible side-effects. While the actual viability of such a move in gastronomy remains doubtful, in other avant-garde movements this has taken hold to an increasing extent.

---

68   https://stinkycandlecompany.com/products/burrito-candle (my italics).
69   See Edwards 2008a. His particular focus on smell and breathing can be traced back to his first research, namely the development of inhaled insulin for diabetics and inhaled dopamine for Parkinson's disease (Edwards 2018, 39-45). During the Covid-19 pandemic, Edwards devoted his work to respiratory tracts and airborne pathogens, designing a nasal sanitising device called FEND (https:// www. hellofend.com/).
70   Edwards 2018, 240. See also Edwards 2008b.
71   Edwards 2018, 232, 241.

5.4 *State Of The Art Of Food Osmospheres*

Avant-garde is a grocer's art:
mixed smell of cheese and detergent.
Luciano Fabro

The 1938 *Exposition internationale du Surréalisme* at the Gallerie des Beaux-arts in Paris can be regarded as the prototype and precursor of the future development of (food) olfactory arts that, since then, have progressively expanded. André Breton commissioned Marcel Duchamp to design a multi-sensory exhibition, challenging the rules of the museum. Semi-dark to provocatively disempower sight, and filled with objects, materials and sounds unusual for an art display, the space was pervaded by a strong smell of coffee because the poet Benjamin Péret installed a roasting machine.[72] The "whole place smelled of Brazilian coffee", recalls de Beauvoir (1962, 258-259) who joined the exhibition, commenting: "I don't think surrealism had any direct influence on us, but it has impregnated the very air we breathed" (ibid, 259).

For its part, food art is grafted onto such art movements that include odours among their artistic media. This is evident when considering Daniel Spoerri's work that, as early as the 1960s, incorporated edible ingredients, cooking performances and even food leftovers. A good example is his famous "snare-pictures of eaten meals" (*tableaux-pièges*): a series of Neo-Dadaist canvas seeking to capture and immortalise the time spent eating with friends or family. Food leftovers, dirty dishes, cutlery, bottles, used napkins and disparate items such as ashtrays filled with cigarette butts are assembled and fixed as they are on the support the meal was consumed on, to be affixed on the wall like a picture. The first is *Kichka's Breakfast* (1960), which was followed by several others, including the tableau-piège *Eaten by Marcel Duchamp* (1964). Although smell is not the key point of these works, food osmospheres are certainly important to the artist. In *The Mythological Travels of a modern Sir John Manderville,* insights on meals and food flavours abound. As soon as he left the Greek island of Symi, where most of the gastronomic experiences reported in the book occurred, his interest in cooking also led him to open his *Restaurant Spoerri* in 1968, and the *Eat Art Gallery* in 1970, both in the city of Düsseldorf.[73] While believing that "the flavor of a dish depends upon the taste habits of the one

---

72 Jaquet 2015, 9-11; Verbeek 2016.
73 Novero 2017.

who eats it, and that it is just as difficult to overcome a taste prejudice as an artistic prejudice" (Spoerri 1970, 123-124), Spoerri's sketches usually revolve around the difficulty in repressing the repugnance aroused by food odours, as when he cooked a *fressure vendéene* made of goat that gave off a strong reek of ram (ibid, 214), or when he was served a vegetable stew spoiled by the last-minute addition of a can of mackerels. In this episode, his disgust depended on the *brand* of the fish, the same used to prepare cat food, because he "associated the dish automatically with the smell of old fish, which can last four days for the cats" (ibid, 190). He also lists various scenting strategies that can be achieved through a food osmosphere, including the shepherd Kosta's habit of cooking "branches of rosemary in a tin can in the middle of his fire to make the house smell good" (ibid, 155 n. 3). An anecdote on the omnipresence of food osmospheres in Spoerri's life and art can be found in the introduction artist Allan Kaprow wrote to *Daniel Spoerri's Room No. 631 at the Chelsea Hotel* (1965): "Spoerri's philosophical works were made in a hotel room, where he slept, made love, cooked marvelous meals, and defecated. His constructions crowded the space, mingling with the bed, the clothes, the odor of lasagne" (Spoerri 1966, 76).[74]

Given the current flurry of activity in olfactory and food art, often in combination, I have opted to focus these last pages on more or less recent artworks, especially installations, where food smells are essential to convey and grasp the meaning of the work. I have grouped them within two wide thematic families that seem to be the most widely addressed: *decay* and *identity*.

Decay

Many examples of decaying osmospheres are provided by Swiss-Icelandic Fluxus artist Dieter Roth who, already in the 1960s, used biodegradable and edible materials such as meat, chocolate and cheese for self-portraits and pictures characterised by unpleasant smells, leading to several interesting vicissitudes.[75] A good example is *Staple Cheese (A Race)*, exhibited in 1970 in the U.S. Thirty-seven suitcases filled with cheese were installed on the floor, to be opened one a day and to be left to

---

74   Similarly, in *Jailbird: A Novel* by Kurt Vonnegut (1979, 136), the protagonist
     comments on the small flat of Mrs. Sutton by saying to her: "It is a nice place you
     have here [...]", and she replies "You're the only person who think so [...]. It's
     crowded. Everything that goes on in the kitchen you can smell out here".
75   Vischer, Walter 2003, 96, 114, 120.

rot in the summer; some pieces of ripe cheese were pressed on the wall, gradually sliding downwards.[76] In a few days, the room became saturated with an unbearable stench, along with a lot of maggots, flies and larvae. Two inspectors of the local health authority visited the exhibition; although they pointed out to the gallerist that she was contravening some public health regulations, they allowed her to keep the installation until the end of the month, when it was packed in special containers created by Roth and stored in the gallerist's garage. After several years, the suitcases were thrown into the desert by the gallerist's husband because of their smell,[77] echoing the epilogue of the comic episode of *Three Men in a Boat*.

Along the same lines, Belgian multidisciplinary artist and choreographer Jan Fabre is not alien to "stink art", as some have nicknamed his practice. *De lente komt eraan* (Spring Is Approaching, 1979) is an installation made of condoms filled with sprouting onions and potatoes hanging from the ceiling. While progressively rotting, the vegetables start to emit foul odours and make the osmosphere of the room intolerable for visitors. On the occasion of a further display of this installation in 2008, besides the usual stench, some buds burst through the condoms, breaking them, and a few smashed to the ground. Despite visitors and staff's complaints, decomposed vegetables were not removed, except for those that had fallen. Another example of Fabre's foetid art is *The Legs of Reason Skinned* (2000): it consists of eight large pillars at the entrance to the exhibition at Ghent University (Belgium) covered with 8,000 ham slices wrapped in plastic. The artist opted for cured meat and its fat not only to achieve a marble-like effect, but also to create a living sculpture. Over time, the food would spoil, giving off whiffs of odours and attracting flies and worms. A metamorphosis would transform the building from inorganic, scentless and static to dynamic, strong-smelling and teeming with organisms.

The display of life is the concept at the basis of the famous *A Thousand Years* (1990) by Damien Hirst, considered by the artist his most successful work.[78] In a large double-chambered vitrine are placed a bloody cow's head together with an electric insect killer ("insect-o-cutor"), and a cube-incubator of larvae with sugar and water. The two parts are separated by a perforated glass sheet that allows the passage of maggots and flies. Once the insects are born, they are attracted by the smell of the cow's head; they migrate to the other room, where they feed, grow and are eventually

---

electrocuted. The smell of rotting flesh, albeit faint thanks to the glass showcase, infects the air, concurrently acting as the invisible driver of the life and death cycle, where the main activities are being born, eating, reproducing and dying.

Decaying food osmospheres are the artistic traits of the installations by French artist Michel Blazy, who since the late 1990s has incorporated organic materials and especially food in his artworks. A famous case is *Mur de poils de carotte* (Carrot Hair Wall, 2000),[79] which results in sumptuous marbled orange walls on the surfaces of which fluffy and colourful mould develops, emitting pungent odours. The artwork is made by coating the walls with mashed carrots and potatoes, and by covering the walls immediately after the core coating is applied, in such a way that humidity and temperature foster the development of micro-organisms. It is displayed once the process is in its stage of degeneration, as the edible plaster starts retracting and cracking, falling in pieces to the ground until its complete disintegration. As an actual "recipe", each reformulation of this autopoietic work is at the same time unique and unvaried. The work encourages reflection on the latent energies of living bacteria, and also sheds light on the conflict between the wild and the domestic. Indeed, the artist specifically uses processed foods. Here, the osmosphere retains a somewhat opposing relationship with the visual aspects of the work. On the one hand, the variegated walls invite prolonged observation and lead to a contemplative attitude; on the other hand, the unpleasant smell of rottenness causes the impulse to leave quickly. Rotten food, osmospheres of putrefaction and the idea of inter-species conviviality return in his *Le Grand Restaurant* (The Great Restaurant, 2012), Blazy's solo exhibition at Le Plateau. The installations include snails that paint a beer-soaked carpet with their slime, and rotten orange peels that attract flies and spiders; human visitors thus realise the inextricable relativity of smell judgements in a non-anthropocentric perspective: what for them is a revolting food osmosphere, for other species is the scent of an irresistible feast.[80]

Within this genre, it is worth considering *24-Hour Food Degeneration Process* (1997) by Wang Guangyi, one of the most prominent contemporary Chinese artists known for his explicitly philosophical poetics where food plays a significant role.[81] The installation consists of four plexiglass boxes

---

79   A variation is *Murs de double concentré de tomates* (Walls of double tomato paste, 2007).

80   Bonacorsi 2012.

81   Food is used by Guangyi both indirectly (food sketches, pictures, names, symbols and brands) and directly (food concretely displayed in installations), expressing

hanging from the wall, open at their ends and filled with vegetables, fruit, plastic bags, bottles, jars and other materials. Between the two boxes ten posters are placed with pictures related to food safety regulation. As the title anticipates, Guangyi's aim is to let food undergo its inexorable process of decomposition; this would create a short circuit between organic and inorganic matter, as well as between reality and representation, regulation and degeneration. The artwork is thus a ready-made *sui generis*, since it calls for a reflection on how things change once left to themselves. However, on one occasion, as the rotting process proceeded and the space became more and more saturated with nauseating food smells, visitors increasingly complained, demanding that tainted foods be replaced with fresh ones.

In many examples of "decay art", the osmospheric disgust ends up obscuring the very idea behind the works. Indeed, the osmosphere is meant to change in conjunction with the transformation undertaken by the organic material, thus providing the apparently immutable visible elements with a further meaning. To put it differently, the osmosphere acts as a marker of their latent becoming; the museum, instead of an aseptic and odourless space, would become an expressive dimension in itself. The common annoyed reactions testify to the stubborn ideology of the art gallery understood as what Brian O'Doherty calls the "white cube", namely an ideal and clean space without interferences and intrusions. Indeed, a space where art exists "in a sort of eternity of exposure" (O'Doherty 1976, 15) is, as Drobnick (2005) maintains, an anosmic space as well.[82] The smell of decay and death subverts and is inconsistent with the space-time order that such a traditionally oculocentric environment implies. However, the use of smells and food flavours in museums is a growing phenomenon, which suggests that, in the future, these spaces will be increasingly saturated with osmospheres.[83]

---

political and social issues. His main works revolve around the human condition, not so much in historical but in metaphysical terms, despite what some of his works of art might lead to believe by depicting political figures (e.g. Mao) or icons of capitalism (among others, Coca-Cola and Gucci). See Paparoni 2013; Andina, Onnis 2019. On food in Guangyi's artworks: Wiseman 2019, Perullo 2019.

82 See also Philippopoulos-Mihalopoulos 2013.

83 For different contributions on the topic, from olfactory heritage to the odour of buildings and the multisensory museum: Drobnick 2006b; Levent, Pascual-Leone 2014; Castel 2019; Spence 2020; Bembibre, Strlič 2022; Verbeek, Leemans, Fleming 2022.

Identity

The first example I want to set forth is *Things-in-Themselves* (2012), another work by Guangyi which has to do with identity in a metaphysical sense. The installation consists of a majestic work composed of thousands of jute sacks filled with rice and rice bran, stacked on top of each other to completely cover the walls of the exhibition space up to the ceiling. Visitors are inebriated by the smell of rice, which corresponds to and is emitted from the solemn structure. The osmospheric dimension is central because, while recreating the atmosphere of a granary, it gives significance to what can be seen. In other words, smell is the manifestation of what is hidden, concurrently questioning the dualism between container and content, outside and inside. The osmosphere serves to reflect on the visible and the invisible, evoking the Kantian reference to the "thing in itself". Rice, *the* staple food in the history of humanity, is the emblem of materiality, the flesh of humans from generation to generation. In *Things-in-Themselves*, the "immateriality" of smell turns out to be inherently material, capturing and restoring the essence of the visually absent food. It is its osmosphere, precisely the "thing-in-itself", that remains and incarnates the idea.

In most cases, food osmospheres convey socio-political issues, playing on the identity value of food and the dimension of memory.[84] Two famous examples are *Spice Chess* and *Smell Chess* by Japanese Fluxus artist Takako Saito, manufactured in 1964-1965 and launched in 1965. The rules are the same as in classic chess, but the pieces are substituted with visually identical vials filled with aromatic substances or liquids. Each piece is distinguished by a smell (ginger, cinnamon, nutmeg, cumin, etc.); odours are different for the white and the black sets. The game is based on a perceptual overturn: chess moves depend on the olfactory ability of players. In an interweaving of olfactory and personal identities, Saito's chess "links odors to the status and movements of the individuals in society generally, and also proposes them as a sensory counterpoint to social boundaries and mobility" (Higgins 2002, 43). Spices are also the stylistic hallmark of Brazilian artist Ernesto Neto as symbols of his homeland.[85] In 2001, he made his debut on the international art scene at the Venice Biennale with *O Bicho!* (The Animal!), an exhibition space occupied by large lycra bags full of spices (turmeric, black pepper, cloves) hanging from the ceiling. The majestic shapes are

---

84   Verbeek, van Campen 2013.
85   Spices were used by Roth too, as in the 1970s he moved from rotten food smells to a more pleasant osmospheric poetics; Vischer, Walter 2003, 132.

reminiscent of weird beasts or insects, while the enveloping osmosphere recalls Brazil and its indigenous people. The installation has had several variants over the years, adapting colours, spices and shapes to different concepts.[86]

Peter de Cupere, too, has resorted to the food dimension for his olfactory artistic practice.[87] Amongst his many works, the question of socio-political identity is addressed in *Stay Awake* (2021). It is a simply furnished room totally covered with 660 kilograms of coffee beans and ground coffee emanating an inebriating smell. The reference to colonialism and coffee slavery becomes clear when visitors smell the invisible olfactory monument placed in front of the work. By pressing a foot pump, a mix of coffee, fear sweat and smoke strikes the nose and makes the pleasant aroma of coffee controversial.[88] The disputable nature of the hedonic value of food in connection to social identity emerges in his *Una Pasta Per Giulietta* (2001), a room-installation covered with spaghetti, tomato sauce, vegetables, etc., and *Spaghetti House* (2007) as well, the latter being a small house made of 900 kilograms of boiled and dried spaghetti seasoned with typical Italian ingredients such as garlic, oregano, basil, tomatoes and shallots. Gastro-stereotypical osmospheres embedding the idea of comfort and "good" clash with the different tastes and food identities of people, even possibly turning good into "bad".

The recreation of a national osmospheric identity is the project behind *Scents of Holland* (2008) by Dutch-Japanese artist Maki Ueda.[89] "Osmospheric Dutchness" is rendered through five essences, three of which are gastronomic: Dutch cheese, Speculaas spices[90] and overboiled Brussels sprouts.[91] More than emphasising geographical and inter-ethnical aspects,

---

86 For Neto's work, Wilson 2010; Vv. Aa. 2022, 112-115. As an emblem of olfactory sculptures, Shiner (2020, 184) mentions his *Mother Body Emotional Densities*.

87 Like in *G-Perfume* (1996), a perfume made of scraps of food, and in *The Collector's House* (2003), with Herve cheese, wine, etc.; Renders 2016, 53.

88 Lähnemann 2021, 36; Diaconu 2022c. On de Cupere's engagement with the environmental crisis, Hsu 2020, 106-111. We can draw parallels with *Imperium* (2014) by Luca Vitone, in collaboration with Maria Candida Gentile, an "olfactory sculpture" aimed at making the invisible perceptible; specifically, the exercise of power. The fragrance is designed in such a way that it pleases at first, gradually turning nauseating and suffocating, hence revealing the entire range of modulations authority can take on.

89 Ishii-Fôret 2015 for an inquiry on her art.

90 Shortcrust biscuits baked with specific spices and traditionally consumed during winter festivities.

91 See https://www.ueda.nl/index.php?option=com_content&view=category&layout=blog&id=106&Itemid=791&lang=en.

the work brings out inter-generational osmospheric shifts. Overcooked vegetables are "only familiar to people over a certain age" (Verbeek, van Campen 2013, 138) due to the constant change of culinary habits and tastes; this not only proves the time-specific feature of collective memories, but also the inherent difficulty in homogenising a national identity which is, in itself, porous, differentiated and composite.

Identity and colonialism are explored by multi-ethnic interdisciplinary artist Sita Kuratomi Bhaumik, whose olfactory installations, like those of Ernesto Neto, are mainly spice-scented. In *Home and Away* (2008), a set of framed prints, each made of a single spice (cumin, coriander, turmeric, garam masala, chilli powder), combine to evoke the osmosphere of curry that, as the title suggests, can trigger either a sense of home or, on the contrary, of exoticism and otherness. Curry as a cultural marker is exploited in further artworks, such as *MCDXCII* (2010) and *To Curry Favor* (2015). The former, alluding to the discovery of the Americas in 1492, is a room full of objects (a low table, plates on the walls, goblets, chocolate coins, etc.) wrapped in golden chocolate foils; sugar and curry powder are sprinkled on the floor creating a flowery lace pattern. The combination of ingredients, both visual and olfactory, stresses how a cultural identity, exemplified by its food osmosphere and culinary products, is the result of exchanges, hybridisation and migrations. Such topics recur in *To Curry Favor*, exhibited in the conservatory of Kilkenny Castle, Ireland. By painting the building walls with curry geometries, the artist invites viewers to draw parallels between Irish history and that of other nations through their cuisine as the result of imperial powers, trade, emigration, social disparities and even genocides, like the 19th-century Irish Potato Famine. As the artist explains,

> what we, in the West, recognize today as "curry" is also associated with immigration, working class peoples, and neighborhoods. [...] I was surprised to find that the small town of Kilkenny had two Asian grocery stores [...and] to discover that the nearest restaurant to the castle was a curry takeaway catering to Irish residents. [...] Before I had arrived with my bags of spices, the family used the conservatory to enjoy curry takeaway on rare, sunny Irish evenings.[92]

Identity, migration and socio-political dynamics are the core issues of many food osmospheric installations.[93] I would like to conclude by

---

92   http://www.sitabhaumik.com/mamasitas-tea-house.
93   Not to mention all the copious artworks expressing the social, aesthetic and psychological repercussions of exodus through bodily odours and memories,

mentioning Goeltzenleuchter's ongoing project *Scents of Exile*, staged in New York (2019) and in Bremen (2021).[94] By interviewing immigrants and asking them to associate home to a smell, the artist creatively manufactures their osmospheric memories. The fragrances are added to hand sanitiser in dispensers at the disposal of the gallery visitors and flanked by conversation extracts. In contrast to the rather ordinary appearance of the work, the unusual smells strike those who use the liquid, making them aware of the affective reverberations that a smell can reflect. Some disinfectants make explicit reference to food. Notes of "sugary sweet pastry" are the osmospheric transposition of the history of Pedram, aged 48, from Iran. His reminiscence is the following:

> As a kid in Iran, I was a picky eater. My daily meal was rice and ketchup. Literally, that's all I ate. But in Turkey I started eating other things. And one of the things I really liked was Baklava. It had this smell that came out of the bakeries and filled the streets of Aksaray neighborhood in Istanbul.[95]

Interestingly enough, he associates "home" not to the smell of rice and ketchup consumed during his childhood spent in Iran, but to the aroma of sweets he particularly enjoyed after moving to Turkey. The osmospheric home, as seen previously, is likely to smell good, and sweet pastries are the emblem of such a feeling. "Buttery milk and stone fruit" are instead the tones the artist used for the recollection recounted by Azira, aged 52, from Bosnia, an immigrant working in a refugee centre:

> When we fled Bosnia my cousins took their cow and hid it in the woods. Every morning they gave me a bowl of boiled milk, straight from the cow. Even now, if someone says, "I am refugee" I smell boiled milk.[96]

---

for instance *Migratory sense* (2017) by Helga Griffiths and *Immigrant Caucus* (2017) by Anicka Yi. With respect to food flavours, the latter writes: "Growing up in a Korean-American household, I was immersed in pungent kitchen aromas. The smell of fermenting kimchi and *doenjang* seemed to sink into our furniture, clothing, and hair. As a child, I often felt ashamed of my family's olfactory world. I wanted to smell American, which I imagined would involve becoming perfectly odorless. But shame works in mysterious ways: the strongest odors disgusted but also excited me, eliciting a tingling response" (Yi 2017).

94 https://www.scentsofexile.com/. It has been exhibited in a few other places that are not yet documented. See also Lähnemann 2021, 35.

95 https://www.scentsofexile.com/pedram/.

96 https://www.scentsofexile.com/azira/.

The word has absorbed the osmosphere, radiating its smell whenever its sound is heard and revealing the "state of being (*Befinden*) of man as a category which comprises and characterizes a certain human condition" (Tellenbach 1981, 221). These food "osmobiographies" (Diaconu 2021, 62) function as the perfect epilogue, epitomising the cross-sensory affective condensations I have called by the name of *osmospheres*.

Osmospheres can be taken as telltales of the way we live and feel. More than that, they show *the way we live how we are feeling*, and *the way we feel how we are living*. Böhme provides a fitting example of this. In his hometown, Darmstadt, people used to complain about a bad smell lingering in the air. As the city was the headquarters of a big pharmaceutical company, scientists carried out some research. Eventually, they established the absence of any chemical substance in the air of the city. Nevertheless, the problem persisted: "the inhabitants of Darmstadt 'did not feel well'" (Böhme 2017a, 1). A hovering sense of disquiet took on osmospheric qualities. Indeed, "when there is a foul odour, one does not merely smell a stench, but feels bad" (Böhme 1989, 47).

Osmospheres manifest the *way we feel* as beings-in-the-air rooted in the relational pattern making up the intricate environment we dwell in. As such, they gravitate towards a social aesthetics. This proves particularly useful today, in that "sensescapes" are the aesthetic outcomes of economic disparities, ghettoisation and social frictions. More specifically, food osmospheres can shed light on environmental injustice, marginalisation and racism, becoming a fertile field to develop a new ethics and politics. For this to be made true, aesthetics must not only fully include smells, but also the perceptual experiences that fall within the realm of *negative aesthetics*. Indeed, the disadvantaged segments of society often have to deal with perceptual annoyances including air pollution, littered streets, industrial fumes, crowded and poorly ventilated buildings, not to mention limited food choice, which often falls on junk food. As Saito (2022, 181) observes commenting on Berleant's view on negative aesthetics, all these "are aesthetic matters insofar as senses are assaulted by eyesores, stenches, untoward noises, as well as dulled and enfeebled by the lack of stimulation".

Although philosophers are divided on the issue of whether it is possible to intentionally create an atmosphere, the relationship between smell, affective spaces and even "emotional marketing" has attracted the attention of many *aesthetic works*, as Böhme (2017a) calls them, in recent years.

Design, retail, and more and more businesses in the service sector are using odours, and especially food ones, to stage, evoke and enhance the desired feelings. To put it differently, osmospheres are increasingly designed and intended to serve practical and commercial ends, *mood-managing* being the ultimate goal.

Back in the 1970s, Warhol (1975, 159) claimed that New York restaurants serve bad food but have a *good atmosphere*, venturing that "when food prices go really up, they'll be selling only atmosphere". Instead of going out to dinner, people will *go out to atmosphere*. All in all, time has proven him quite right. Although Warhol does not refer specifically to aromas, today's phenomenon of osmospheric foodification, which can also be found in the artistic world, further problematises this issue, prompting aesthetics to investigate the affective role of smells in general, and food flavours in particular. This urgency finally requires bridging the gap between art and life in the aesthetic domain. After all, as Camus suggests, we are all olfactive types, for better or worse, so long as we breathe.

Bibliography[1]

The bibliography only includes works that have been directly referenced throughout the text.

Abbott, R.W., Diaz-Artiles, A. (2022). *The Impact of Digital Scents on Behavioral Health in a Restorative Virtual Reality Environment*, "Acta Astronautica" 197, 145-153.

Aciman, A. (1994). *Out of Egypt: A Memoir*. New York: Farrar Straus Giroux.

Ackerman, D. (1990). *A Natural History of Senses*. New York: Random House.

Agrest, D. (2000). *Architecture from Without: Body, Logic and Sex* (1993). In J. Rendell, B. Penner, I. Borden (eds). *Gender Space Architecture: An Interdisciplinary Introduction*. London & New York: Routledge, 358-370.

Ahmed, S. (2006). *Queer Phenomenology: Orientations, Objects, Others*. Durham & London: Duke University Press.

Alač, M. (2017). *We Like to Talk About Smell: A Worldly Take on Language, Sensory Experience, and the Internet*, "Semiotica" 215, 143-192.

—— (2020). *Beyond Intersubjectivity in Olfactory Psychophysics II: Troubles with the Object*, "Social Studies of Science" 50(3), 474-502.

Alison, A. (2020). *Atmospheres and Environments: Prolegomena to Inhabit Sensitively*, "Aesthetica Preprint" 115, 97-121.

Allard, L., David, G. (2022) (ed.). "Communication & Langages — #Foodporn. Les 'mobiles' du désir" 213(3).

---

1   Divided into chapters and sub-chapters, here is the list of the references of the epigraphs. Preface: Ingold 2020, 27 [modified]. Chapter 1: Pessoa 2003, 233; 1.1: Minkowski 1999, 115 [slightly modified]; 1.2: Nogué 1936, 236; 1.3: Bachelard 1988a, 136; 1.4: Nietzsche 2007, 88; 1.5: Benjamin 1968, 214. Chapter 2: Tuan 1995, 64; 2.1: Serres 2008, 165; 2.2: Pallasmaa 2012, 59; 2.3: Calvino 1981, 25; 2.4: Cisneros 1988, 6-7. Chapter 3: Simmel 2009, 577; 3.1: Horkheimer, Adorno 2002, 151; 3.2: Corbin 1986, 39; 3.3: Aciman 1994, 105; 3.4: Ellison 2014, 296; 3.5: Renowden 2005, 21 [slightly modified]; 3.6 Asbury 1950, 227. Chapter 4: Morton 2016, 5; 4.1: Schlosser 2001, 129; 4.2: Dumas 1873, 888; 4.3: Sloterdijk 2002, 95; 4.4: Cypher Reagan in Matrix (1999, directed by Lana and Lilly Wachowski); 4.5: Tellenbach 1981, 225. Chapter 5: Aristotle, *De Sensu*, v., 443b; 5.1: Leroi-Gourhan 1993, 292; 5.2: Arnheim 1974, 4; 5.3: Valentinelli 1996, 134; 5.4: Fabro 1978, 82.

Allen, L. (2022). *We Are What We Smell: The Smell of Dis-ease During Lock-down*, "Subjectivity" 15(4), 264-281.

Almagor, U. (1987). *The Cycle and Stagnation of Smells: Pastoralists-Fisher-men Relationships in an East African Society*, "Anthropology and Aesthetics" 13, 106-121.

Amis, M. (2007). *House of Meetings* (2006). New York & Toronto: Alfred A. Knopf.

Anderson, B. (2014). *Encountering Affect: Capacities, Apparatuses, Conditions*. Farnham: Ashgate.

Andina, T., Onnis, E. (2019) (eds). *The Philosophy and Art of Wang Guangyi*. London & New York: Bloomsbury.

Apicius (1867). *De re coquinaria libri decem*. Heidelbergae: Caroli Winter.

—— (1984). *The Roman Cookery of Apicius: A Treasury of Gourmet Recipes & Herbal Cookery*. Translated and Adapted for the Modern Kitchen by J. Edwards. Point Roberts: Hartley & Marks.

Archer, N.S., Bluff, A., Eddy, A., Nikhil, C.K., Hazell, N., Frank, D., Johnston, A. (2022). *Odour Enhances the Sense of Presence in a Virtual Reality Environ-ment*, "Plos One" 17(3), 1-20.

Arendt, H. (1992). *Lectures on Kant's Political Philosophy* (1982). Edited by R. Beiner. Chicago: The University of Chicago Press.

Aristotle (1964). *On the Soul — Parva Naturalia — On Breath*. Translated by W.S. Hett. London: William Heinemann; Cambridge: Harvard University Press.

Arnheim, R. (1974). *Art and Visual Perception: A Psychology of the Creative Eye* (1954). Berkeley, Los Angeles & London: University of California Press.

Artusi, P. (2003). *Science in the Kitchen and the Art of Eating Well* (1891). Edited by M. Baca, S. Sartarelli. Toronto, Buffalo & London: University of Toronto Press.

Asbury, H. (1950). *The Great Illusion: An Informal History of Prohibition*. New York: Doubleday.

Augustine of Hippo (Saint) (2008). *Confessions*. Translated by H. Chadwick. Oxford: Oxford University Press.

Azari, F. (1924). *La flora futurista ed equivalenti plastici di odori artificiali*. Roma: Direzione del Movimento Futurista.

Bachelard, G. (1964). *The Psychoanalysis of Fire* (1938). Translated by A.C.M. Ross. London: Routledge & Kegan Paul.

—— (1969). *The Poetics of Reverie: Childhood, Language, and the Cosmos* (1960). Translated by D. Russel. Boston: Beacon Press.

—— (1983). *Water and Dreams: An Essay on the Imagination of Matter* (1942). Translated by E.R. Farrell. Dallas: The Pegasus Foundation.

—— (1988a). *Air and Dreams: An Essay on the Imagination of Movement* (1943). Translated by E.R. Farrell, C.F. Farrell. Dallas: The Dallas Institute Publications.

—— (1988b). *The Flame of a Candle* (1961). Translated by J. Caldwell. Dallas: The Dallas Institute Publications.

—— (2000). *The Dialectic of Duration* (1936). Translated by M. McAllester Jones. Manchester: Clinamen Press.

—— (2002). *Earth and Reveries of Will: An Essay on the Imagination of Matter* (1947). Translated by K. Haltman. Dallas: The Dallas Institute Publications.

—— (2011). *Earth and Reveries of Repose: An Essay on Images of Interiority* (1948). Translated by M.C. Jones. Dallas: The Dallas Institute Publications.

—— (2014). *The Poetics of Space* (1957). Translated by M. Jolas. New York: Penguin.

Baldi, E.A. (2019). *Art and Science in Calvino's* Palomar*: Techniques of Observation and Their History*, "Italian Studies" 74(1), 71-86.

Ballerini, L. (2003). *Introduction:* A *as in Artusi,* G *as in Gentleman and Gastronome*. Introduction to P. Artusi, *Science in the Kitchen and the Art of Eating Well* (1891). Edited by M. Baca, S. Sartarelli. Toronto, Buffalo & London: University of Toronto Press, xv-lxxiv.

Baltussen, H. (2015). *Ancient Philosophers on the Sense of Smell*. In M. Bradley (ed.). *Smell and the Ancient Senses*. London & New York: Routledge, 30-45.

Balzac, H. de (1951). *Old Goriot* (1835). Translated by M.A. Crawford. London & New York: Penguin.

Banes, S. (2001). *Olfactory Performances*, "The Drama Review" 45(1), 68-76.

Barbara, A., Perliss, A. (2006). *Invisible Architecture: Experiencing Places Through the Sense of Smell*. Milano: Skira.

Barkat-Defradas, M., Motte-Florac, E. (2016) (eds). *Words for Odours: Language Skills and Cultural Insights*. Newcastle upon Tyne: Cambridge Scholars Publishing.

Barthes, R. (1989). *Sade, Fourier, Loyola* (1971). Translated by R. Miller. Berkeley & Los Angeles: University of California Press.

Barwich, A.-S. (2019). *A Critique of Olfactory Objects*, "Frontiers in Psychology" 10, 1-11.

—— (2020). *Smellosophy: What the Nose Tells the Mind*. Cambridge: Harvard University Press.

Batty, C. (2010a). *Olfactory Experience II: Objects and Properties*, "Philosophy Compass" 5(12), 1147-1156.

—— (2010b). *A Representational Account of Olfactory Experience*, "Canadian Journal of Philosophy" 40(4), 511-538.

—— (2014). *Olfactory Objects*. In D. Stokes, M. Matthen, S. Biggs (eds). *Perception and its Modalitites*. Oxford & New York: Oxford University Press, 222-245.

Baudelaire, C. (1993). *The Flowers of Evil* (1857). Translated by J. McGowan. Oxford & New York: Oxford University Press.

Becher, S.I., Feldman, Y. (2016). *Manipulating, Fast and Slow: The Law of Non-Verbal Market Manipulation*, "Cardozo Law Review" 38(2), 459-507.

Bedini, S.A. (1963). *The Scent of Time: A Study of the Use of Fire and Incense for Time Measurement in Oriental Countries*, "Transactions of the American Philosophical Society" 53(5), 1-51.

—— (1994). *The Trail of Time: Time Measurement with Incense in East Asia*. Cambridge: Cambridge University Press.

Beekes, R. (2010). *Etymological Dictionary of Greek*. With the Assistance of L. van Beek. Leiden: Brill.

Beer, B. (2007). *Smell, Person, Space and Memory*. In J. Wassmann, K. Stockhaus (eds). *Experiencing New Worlds*. New York & Oxford: Berghahn Books, 187-200.

Bembibre, C., Strlič, M. (2022). *From Smelly Buildings to the Scented Past: An Overview of Olfactory Heritage*, "Frontiers in Psychology" 12, 1-7.

Benjamin, W. (1968). *The Image of Proust* (1929). In Id. *Illuminations: Essays and Reflections*. Translated by H. Zohn, Edited and with an Introduction by H. Arendt. New York: Schocken Books, 201-215.

—— (1972). *Lob der Puppe. Kritische Glossen zu Max v. Bohens* Puppen und Puppenspiele (1930). In Id. *Gesammelte Schriften*, vol. III. Edited by H. Tiedemann-Bartels. Frankfurt am Main: Suhrkamp, 213-218.

—— (1999). *Fresh Figs* (1930). In Id., *Selected Writings*, vol. II, part I, 1927-1930. Edited by M.W. Jennings, H. Eiland, G. Smith, Translated by R. Livingstone *et al.* Cambridge & London: The Belknap Press of Harvard University Press, 358-359.

—— (2008). *The Work of Art in the Age of Its Technological Reproducibility* (1936, 2nd version). In Id. *The Work of Art in the Age of Its Reproducibility: And Other Writings on Media*. Edited by M.W. Jennings, B. Doherty, T.Y. Levin, Translated by E. Jephcott, R. Livingstone, H. Eiland *et al.* Cambridge & London: The Belknap Press of Harvard University Press, 19-55.

Bentley, A. (2005). *Men on Atkins: Dieting, Meat, and Masculinity*. In L.M. Heldke, K. Mommer, C. Pineo (eds). *The Atkins Diet and Philosophy: Chewing the Fat with Kant and Nietzsche*. Chicago & La Salle: Open Court, 185-195.

Bérillon, E. (1915a). *La bromidrose fétide de la race allemande/Der stinkende deutsche Rassenschweiss — Foetor germanicus*, "Revue de psychothérapie, bulletins et mémoires de la société de médecine de Paris". Paris: Maloine et fils.

—— (1915b). *La polychésie de la race* allemande/*Das übertriebene Darmleerungsbedürfnis der deutschen Rasse — Superlienteria germanica*, "Revue de psychothérapie, bulletins et mémoires de la société de médecine de Paris", Paris: Maloine et fils.

Berleant, A. (1970). *The Aesthetic Field: A Phenomenology of Aesthetic Experience*. Springfield: Charles C. Thomas.

—— (2004). *The Sensuous and the Sensual in Aesthetics*. In Id. *Re-Thinking Aesthetics: Rogue Essays on Aesthetics and the Arts*. London & New York: Routledge, 73-81.

Biasin, G.-P. (1993). *Under Olivia's Teeth: Italo Calvino*, Sotto il sole giaguaro. In Id. *The Flavors of Modernity: Food and the Novel* (1991). Princeton: Princeton University Press, 97-127.

Bischoff, W. (2006). *"Grenzenlose Räume": Überlegungen zum Verhältnis von Architektur und städtischem Geruchsraum*, "Wolkenkuckucksheim" 10(2).

Biscuso, M. (2000). *Il naso dei filosofi e l'aroma del materialismo*. In Vv. Aa. *Le tattiche dei sensi*. Roma: Manifestolibri, 11-28.

Black, R.E. (2012). *Porta Palazzo: The Anthropology of an Italian Market*. Philadelphia: University of Pennsylvania Press.

Bloch, E. (1970). *Politische Messungen, Pestzeit, Vormärz*. Frankfurt am Main: Suhrkamp.

Bloch, O., Wartburg, W. von (1964). *Dictionnaire étymologique de la langue française*. Paris: PUF.

Boccioni, U. (1973). *Technical Manifesto of Futurist Sculpture* (1912). In U. Apollonio (ed.). *Futurist Manifestos*. Translated by R. Brain, R.W. Flint, J.C. Higgitt, C. Tisdal. Boston: MFA Publications, 51-65.

Bochiccio, V. (2019). *Epistemologia dell'oggetto olfattivo. Evidenze psicobiologiche e caratteristiche fenomenologiche a confronto*. In V. Bochicchio, M. Mazzeo, G. Squillace (eds). *A lume di naso. Olfatto, profumo, aromi tra mondo antico e contemporaneo*. Macerata: Quodlibet, 107-119.

Bock, H. (1552). *De Stirpium: maxime earum, quae in Germania nostra nascuntur, usitatis nomenclaturis... facultatibus commentariorum libri tres*. Argentorati: Excudebat Wendelinus Rihelius.

Böhme, G. (1989). *Für eine ökologische Naturästhetik*. Frankfurt am Main: Suhrkamp.

—— (1998). *Anmutungen. Über das Atmosphärische*. Ostfildern vor Stuttgart: Tertium.

—— (2001). *Aisthetik. Vorlesungen über Ästhetik als allgemeine Wahrnehmungslehre*. München: Fink.

—— (2017a). *Atmospheric Architecture* (2013). Edited and Translated by A.-C. Engels-Schwarzpaul. London & New York: Bloomsbury.

—— (2017b). *The Aesthetic of Atmospheres*. Edited by J.-P. Thibaud. London & New York: Routledge.

—— (2019). *Smell and Atmosphere*. In T. Griffero, M. Tedeschini (eds). *Atmosphere and Aesthetics: A Plural Perspective*. London: Palgrave Macmillan, 259-264.

Boisvert, R.D., Heldke, L.M. (2016). *Philosophers at Table: On Food and Being Human*. London: Reaktion Books.

Bonacorsi, I. (2012). *The Great Restaurant*, "Domus" (October 8).

Bonaiuti, G. (2022). *Spherology* (November 30, 2020), "International Lexicon of Aesthetics". Milano & Udine: Mimesis International, 415-420.

Bonasoni, P., Gilardoni, S., Barbieri, P., Moraca, S., De Gennaro, G., Infantino, V. (2022) (eds). *Molestie olfattive. Studi, metodi e strumenti per il controllo*. Pisa: Edizioni ETS.

Borch, C. (2011). *Foamy Business: On the Organizational Politics of Atmospheres*. In W. Schinkel, L. Noordegraaf-Eelens (eds). *In Medias Res: Peter Sloterdijk's Spherological Poetics of Being*. Amsterdam: Amsterdam University Press, 29-42.

—— (2014). *The Politics of Atmospheres: Architecture, Power, and the Senses*. In Id. (ed.). *Architectural Atmospheres: Experience and Politics of Architecture*. Basel: Birkhäuser, 60-89.

Bordo, S. (1993). *Unbearable Weight: Feminism, Western Culture, and the Body*. Berkeley, Los Angeles & London: University of California Press.

Borges, A., Babin, B.J. Spielmann, N. (2013). *Gender Orientation and Retail Atmosphere: Effects on Value Perception*. "International Journal of Retail & Distribution Management" 41(7), 498-511.

Borloz, S.-V. (2019). *Le parfum de l'inverti*, "Littératures" 81, 131-142.

Borsato, M. (2023). *Il dolce. Una relazione estetica.* Pisa: Edizioni ETS.

Bourlessas, P., Loda, M., Puttilli, M. (2022). *Cibo e trasformazioni urbane. Varianti di* foodification, "Rivista geografica italiana" 129(4), 5-12.

Boussingault, J.B., Dumas, J.B. (1842). *Essai de statique chimique des êtres organisés.* Paris: Fortin Masson.

Boyson, R. (2013). *Shelley's Republic of Odours: Aesthetic and Political Dimensions of Scent in "The Sensitive-Plant"*, "The Keats-Shelley Review" 27(2), 105-120.

Bradford, K.D., Desrochers, D.M. (2009). *The Use of Scents to Influence Consumers: The Sense of Using Scents to Make Cents*, "Journal of Business Ethics" 90, 141-153.

Bradley, M. (2015) (ed.). *Smell and the Ancient Senses.* London & New York: Routledge.

Brady, E. (2003). *Aesthetics of the Natural Environment.* Edinburgh: Edinburgh University Press.

—— (2005). *Sniffing and Savoring: The Aesthetics of Smells and Tastes* (2002). In A. Light, J.M. Smith (eds). *The Aesthetics of Everyday Life.* New York: Columbia University Press, 177-193.

—— (2012). *Smells, Tastes, and Everyday Aesthetics.* In D. Kaplan (ed.). *The Philosophy of Food.* Berkeley, Los Angeles & London: University of California Press, 69-86.

Branco, P., Mohr, R. (2018). Odore di Napoli*: What if Jurisprudence Came to us through Smell?.* In D. Mandic, C. Nirta, A. Pavoni, A. Philippopoulos-Mihalopoulos (eds). *Smell: Law and the Senses Series.* London: University of Westminster Press, 58-75.

Brault-Dreux, E. (2021). *Smells and Scents in Lawrence's Poems: Strange Connections to the Environment*, "Études Lawrenciennes" 53, 1-10.

Brengman, M., Willems, K., De Gauquier, L., (2022). *Customer Engagement in Multi-Sensory Virtual Reality Advertising: The Effect of Sound and Scent Congruence*, "Frontiers in Psychology" 13, 1-20.

Brennan, T. (2004). *The Transmission of Affect.* Ithaca & London: Cornell University Press.

Bressani, M. (2019). *Interview with Tonino Griffero*, "Journal of Architectural Education" 73(1), 83-90.

Brill, A.A. (1932). *The Sense of Smell in the Neuroses and Psychoses*, "The Psychoanalytic Quarterly" 1, 7-42.

Brillat-Savarin, J.-A. (1994). *The Physiology of Taste* (1825). Translated by A. Drayton. London: Penguin.

Brozzo, C. (2020). *Are Some Perfumes Works of Art?*, "The Journal of Aesthetics and Art Criticism" 78(1), 21-32.

Bruni, F. (1891). *Tartufi. Loro natura, storia, coltura, conservazione e cucinatura.* Milano: Ulrico Hoepli.

Bruschi, F. (2017). *Synesthesia and Totality in the Theatre of Paul-Napoléon Roinard (1856-1930)*, "Itinera" 13, 126-136.

Buè, F. (2019). *"Tura...sonant et odorant aëra fumis". Incenso e suoni nell'immaginario antico.* In V. Bochicchio, M. Mazzeo, G. Squillace (eds). *A lume di naso. Olfatto, profumo, aromi tra mondo antico e contemporaneo*. Macerata: Quodlibet, 33-52.

Burges Watson, D.L., Campbell, M., Hopkins, C., Smith, B., Kelly, C., Deary, V. (2021). *Altered Smell and Taste: Anosmia, Parosmia and the Impact of Long Covid-19*, "Plos One" 16(9), 1-18.

Burke, E. (1998). *A Philosophical Enquiry into the Origin of our Ideas of the Sublime and Beautiful* (1757). Edited by A. Phillips. Oxford: Oxford University Press.

Calvino, I. (1959). *The Baron in the Trees* (1957). Translated by A. Colquhoun. New York: Random House.

—— (1962). *The Nonexistent Knight & The Cloven Viscount* (1959-1951). Translated by A. Colquhoun. San Diego: Harcourt.

—— (1968). *Cosmicomics* (1965). Translated by W. Weaver. New York: Harcourt Brace Jovanovich.

—— (1969). *T Zero* (1967). Translated by W. Weaver. San Diego: Harcourt.

—— (1971). *The Argentine Ant* (1952). In Id. *The Watcher & Other Stories*. Translated by A. Colquhoun. New York: Harcourt Brace Jovanovich, 139-181.

—— (1974). *Invisible Cities* (1972). Translated by W. Weaver. San Diego: Harcourt.

—— (1980). *Italian Folktales: Selected and Retold by Italo Calvino* (1956). Translated by G. Martin. New York & London: Harcourt Brace Jovanovich.

—— (1981). *If on a Winter's Night a Traveler* (1979). Translated by W. Weaver. San Diego: Harcourt.

—— (1983a). *Marcovaldo: Or, The Seasons in the City* (1963). Translated by W. Weaver. San Diego: Harcourt.

—— (1983b). *Theft in a Cakeshop* (1949). In Id. *Adam, One Afternoon: And Other Stories*. Translated by A. Colquhoun, P. Wright. London: Secker & Warburg, 97-104.

—— (1985). *Mr. Palomar* (1983). Translated by W. Weaver. San Diego: Harcourt.

—— (1988). *Under the Jaguar Sun* (1986). Translated by W. Weaver. San Diego: Harcourt.

—— (2013a). *Stamps from States of Mind* (1981). In Id. *Collection of Sand* (1984). Translated by M. McLaughlin. London: Penguin, 138-142.

—— (2013b). *Light in Our Eyes* (1982). In Id. *Collection of Sand* (1984). Translated by M. McLaughlin. London: Penguin, 114-120.

—— (2023). *The Written World and the Unwritten World* (2002). Translated by A. Goldstein. London: Penguin.

Camus, A. (1963). *Notebooks: 1935-1942*. Translated by P. Thody. New York: Alfred A. Knopf.

—— (1995). *The First Man* (1994). Translated by D. Hapgood. New York: Alfred A. Knopf.

Canepa, E. (2022). *Architecture Is Atmosphere: Notes on Empathy, Emotions, Body, Brain, and Space*. Milano & Udine: Mimesis International.

Cantarin, M.M., Marino, M.C. (2018). *Post-War Ecosophic Intuition: About the (Im)Possibility of Ecological Coexistence in* Marcovaldo, or The Seasons in the City *by Italo Calvino*, "Humanities" 7(3), 64-75.

Carducci, G. (1913). *Carducci*. A Selection of his Poems, with Verse Translations, Notes and Three Introductory Essays by G.L. Bickersteth. London: Longmans, Green & Co.

Carlisle, J. (2001). *The Smell of Class: British Novels of the 1860s*, "Victorian Literature and Culture" 29(1), 1-19.

Carnevali, B. (2006). *"Aura" e "ambiance"*. *Léon Daudet tra Proust e Benjamin*, "Rivista di Estetica" 46(33), 3, 117-141.

—— (2020). *Social Appearances: A Philosophy of Display and Prestige* (2012). Translated by Z. Hanafi. New York: Columbia University Press.

Carrà, C. (1973). *The Painting of Sounds, Noises and Smells* (1913). In U. Apollonio (ed.). *Futurist Manifestos*. Translated by R. Brain, R.W. Flint, J.C. Higgitt, C. Tisdal. Boston: MFA Publications, 111-115.

Carulli, M., Bordegoni, M., Cugini, U. (2015). *Integrating Scents Simulation in Virtual Reality Multisensory Environment for Industrial Products Evaluation*, "Computer-Aided Design and Applications" 13(3), 1-9.

Cashell, K. (2009). *Aftershock: The Ethics of Contemporary Transgressive Art*. London & New York: I.B. Tauris.

Cassirer, E. (1957). *The Philosophy of Symbolic Forms* (1923-1929), vol. III: *The Phenomenology of Knowledge* (1929). Translated by R. Manheim. New Haven & London: Yale University Press.

Castel, M. (2019). *La muséologie olfactive, una actualisation résonante de la muséalité de Stránský par l'odorat*, PhD Dissertation in Héritage culturel et muséologie, Université Sorbonne Paris Cité.

Catullus, G.V. (2005). *The Poems of Catullus*. Translated by P. Green. Berkeley, Los Angeles & London: University of California Press.

Cavallaro, D. (2010). *The Mind of Italo Calvino: A Critical Exploration of His Thought and Writings*. Jefferson & London: McFarland & Company.

Cavedon-Taylor, D. (2018). *Odors, Objects and Olfaction*, "American Philosophical Quarterly" 55(1), 81-94.

Ceccarelli, A. (2018). *L'opuscolo sui tartufi di Alfonso Ceccarelli (XVI secolo)* (1564). Edited and Translated by G. Nonni. Pesaro: Metauro Edizioni.

Čejka, T., Thomas, P.W., Oliach, D., Stobbe, U., Egli, S., Tegel, W., Centenaro, G., Sproll, L., Bagi, I., Trnka, M., Büntgen, U. (2022). *Understanding the Performance of Truffle Dogs*, "Journal of Veterinary Behavior" 52/53, 8-13.

Chantraine, P. (1999). *Dictionnaire étymologique de la langue grecque. Histoire des mots*. Paris: Klincksieck.

Chaumier, S. (2003). *L'odeur du baiser.* In P. Lardellier (ed.). *À fleur de peau. Corps, odeur, parfums*. Paris: Belin, 77-95.

Chekhov, A. (2010). *The Cherry Orchard* (1904). Translated by L. Senelick. New York & London: W.W. Norton & Company.

Chu, S., Downes, J.J. (2000). *Odour-Evoked Autobiographical Memories: Psychological Investigations of Proustian Phenomena*, "Chemical Senses" 25(1), 111-116.

—— (2002). *Proust Nose Best: Odors are Better Cues of Autobiographical Memory*, "Memory & Cognition" 30(4), 511-518.

Cimatti, F., Flumini, A., Vittuari, M., Borghi, A.M. (2016). *Odors, Words and Objects*, "Rivista Italiana di Filosofia del Linguaggio" 1, 78-91.

Cinotto, S. (2013). *The Italian American Table: Food, Family, and Community in New York City*. Urbana, Chicago & Springfield: University of Illinois Press.

Cisneros, S. (1988). *The House on Mango Street* (1984). New York: Vintage.

Claflin, K.W. (2005). *La Villette, la viande – "Enseigne et marchandise" (1867-1914)*, "Food & History" 3(2), 53-78.

Classen, C. (1990a). *La perception sauvage. Étude sur les ordres sensoriels des enfants "sauvages"*, "Anthropologie et Sociétés" 14(2), 47-56.

—— (1990b). *Sweet Colors, Fragrant Songs: Sensory Models of the Andes and the Amazon*, "American Ethnologist" 17(4), 722-735.

—— (1991). *The Sensory Orders of "Wild Children"*. In D. Howes (ed.). *The Varieties of Sensory Experience: A Sourcebook in the Anthropology of the Senses*. Toronto, Buffalo & London: University of Toronto Press, 47-60.

—— (1993). *Worlds of Sense: Exploring the Senses in History and Across Cultures*. London & New York: Routledge.

—— (2005). *McLuhan in the Rainforest: The Sensory Worlds of Oral Cultures*. In D. Howes (ed.). *Empire of the Senses*. Oxford: Berg, 147-163.

Classen, C., Howes, D., Synnott, A. (1994). *Aroma: The Cultural History of Smell*. London & New York: Routledge.

Claus, R., Hoppen, H.O., Karg, H. (1981). *The Secret of Truffles: A Steroidal Pheromone?*, "Experientia" 37, 1178-1179.

Clements, A. (2015). *Divine Scents and Presence*. In M. Bradley (ed.). *Smell and the Ancient Senses*. London & New York: Routledge, 46-59.

Clough, P.T., Halley, J. (2007) (eds). *The Affective Turn: Theorizing the Social*. Durham & London: Duke University Press.

Condillac, É.B. de (1982). *A Treatise on the Sensations* (1754). In Id. *Philosophical Writings of Étienne Bonnot, Abbé de Condillac*. Translated by F. Philip, with the Collaboration of H. Lane. Hillsdale & London: Lawrence Erlbaum Associates, 155-339.

Corbin, A. (1986). *The Foul and the Fragrant: Odor and the French Social Imagination* (1982). Oxford: Berg Publishers.

Costa, C., Carmenates, S., Madeira, L., Stanghellini, G. (2014). *Phenomenology of Atmospheres: The Felt Meanings of Clinical Encounters*, "Journal of Psychopathology" 20, 351-357.

Costa, H., Ferro, G.d.S., Silva, T.F.B. (2021). *Olfactive Aesthetic Experience Within the Servicescape: The Olfactive Aesthetic Experience as Means to Provide a New Perception of the Servicescape*, "Projética, Londrina" 21(1), 67-87.

Curtin, D.W., Heldke, L.M. (1992) (eds). *Cooking, Eating, Thinking: Transformative Philosophies of Food*. Bloomington: Indiana University Press.

Daly, S. (2016). *Ennio Valentinelli: A Forgotten Futurist*, "Modern Language Notes" 131(1), 139-156.

Damian, P., Damian, K. (2006). *Environmental Fragrancing*. In J. Drobnick (ed.). *The Smell Culture Reader*. Oxford: Berg Publisher, 148-160.

Dante, A. (2006). *The Divine Comedy: Inferno, Purgatorio, Paradiso*. Translated and Edited by R. Kirkpatrick. London & New York: Penguin.

Darwin, C. (1871). *The Descent of Man, and Selection in Relation to Sex*, vol. I. London: John Murray.

Daudet, L. (1928). *Mélancholia. Courrier des Pays-Bas rédigé en exile*, vol. III. Paris: Grasset.

Dawkins, R. (2020). *Using Peirce (and Deleuze's Peirce) to Think About #Food-Porn and Other Instagram Signs*, "Angelaki: Journal of Theoretical Humanities" 25(5), 101-117.

de Beauvoir, S. (1956). *The Second Sex* (1949). Translated and Edited by H.M. Parshley. London: Jonathan Cape.

—— (1962). *The Prime of Life* (1960). Translated by P. Green. Cleveland & New York: The World Publishing Company.

de Borch, J.M. (1780). *Lettres sur les truffes du Piémont écrites par mr. le comte De Borch en 1780, á Milan: chez les freres Reycends libraires sous les arcades de Figini*. Milan: au monastère impérial de St. Ambroise.

De Carné, V. (2015). *Théâtre olfactif. Un itinéraire singulier*. In C. Jaquet (ed.). *L'Art olfactif contemporain*. Paris: Classiques Garnier, 255-270.

de Cupere, P. (2016). *Scent in Context: Olfactory Art*. Duffel: Stockmans.be.

De Matteis, F. (2021). *Affective Spaces: Architecture and the Living Body*. London & New York: Routledge.

—— (2022a). *Atmosphere in Architecture* (May 31, 2020), "International Lexicon of Aesthetics". Milano & Udine: Mimesis International, 81-85.

—— (2022b). *Dwelling* (May 31, 2020), "International Lexicon of Aesthetics". Milano & Udine: Mimesis International, 168-172.

—— (2022c). *The Climate of Spaces: On Architecture, Atmosphere and Time*, "Espes" 11(2), 28-37.

D'Errico, A. (2018). *The Nose Onstage: Olfactory Perceptions and Theatrical Dimension*. In V. Henshaw *et al.* (eds). *Designing with Smell: Practices, Techniques and Challenges*. London & New York: Routledge, 227-235.

Derrida, J. (2008). *The Animal That Therefore I Am* (2006). Edited by M.-L. Mallet, Translated by D. Wills. New York: Fordham University Press.

Detienne, M. (1972). *Les jardins d'Adonis. La mythologie des aromates en Gréce*. Paris: Gallimard.

de Vaan, M. (2016). *Etymological Dictionary of Latin: And the Other Italic Languages*. Leiden: Brill.

Dewey, J. (1980). *Art as Experience* (1934). New York: Perigee Books.

Diaconu, M. (2003). *Olfatto, identità, memoria. La costituzione del soggetto attraverso l'olfatto*, "La società degli individui" 2, 51-65.

—— (2005). *Tasten, Riechen, Schmecken. Eine Ästhetik der anästhesierten Sinne*. Würzburg: Königshausen & Neumann.

—— (2006a). *Patina – Atmosphere – Aroma: Towards an Aesthetics of Fine Differences*, "Analecta Husserliana" 92, 131-148.

—— (2006b). *Reflections on an Aesthetics of Touch, Smell and Taste*, "Contemporary Aesthetics" 4.

—— (2010). *La experiencia de la alteridad olfativa*, "Investigaciones Fenomenológicas" 2, 77-88.

—— (2021). *Der kontingente All-Faktor/The Contingent "All Factor"*. In Vv. Aa. *Smell it! Geruch in der Kunst/Scent in the Arts*. Köln: Wienand, 49-64.

—— (2022a). *Smell* (May 31, 2019), "International Lexicon of Aesthetics". Milano & Udine: Mimesis International, 405-410.

—— (2022b). *Being and Making the Olfactory Self: Lessons from Contemporary Artistic Practices*. In N. Di Stefano, M.T. Russo (eds). *Olfaction: An Interdisciplinary Perspective from Philosophy to Life Sciences*. Cham: Springer, 55-73.

—— (2022c). *The Stylistic of Olfactory Art as an Idiolect of the Atmosphere*, "Venti Journal" 2(2).

Dickens, C. (1992). *Oliver Twist* (1838). New York, London & Toronto: Alfred A. Knopf.

—— (2002). *Great Expectations* (1860-1861). London: Penguin.

Dickie, G. (1996). *The Century of Taste: The Philosophical Odyssey of Taste in the Eighteenth Century*. Oxford: Oxford University Press.

Diderot, D. (1916). *Letter on the Deaf and Dumb for the Use of those who Hear and Speak* (1751). In Id. *Diderot's Early Philosophical Works*. Translated by M. Jourdain. Chicago & London: The Open Court Publishing Company, 158-225.

Di Stefano, N., Murari, M., Spence, C. (2022). *Crossmodal Correspondences in Art and Science: Odours, Poetry, and Music*. In N. Di Stefano, M.T. Russo (eds). *Olfaction: An Interdisciplinary Perspective from Philosophy to Life Sciences*. Cham: Springer, 155-189.

Di Stefano, N., Russo, M.T. (2022) (eds). *Olfaction: An Interdisciplinary Perspective from Philosophy to Life Sciences*. Cham: Springer.

Dostoyevsky, F. (1950). *The Brothers Karamazov* (1879-1880). Translated by C. Garnett. New York: The Modern Library.

Doty, R.L., Tekeli, H. (2012). *Olfactory Function in Parkinson's Disease*. In G.M. Zucco, R.S. Herz, B. Schaal (eds). *Olfactory Cognition: From Perception and Memory to Environmental Odours and Neuroscience*, Advances in Consciousness Research, 85. Amsterdam & Philadelphia: John Benjamins Publishing Company, 155-177.

Dougan, H. (2015). *Seeing Smell*. In S. Smith, J. Watson, A. Kenny (eds). *The Senses in Early Modern England, 1558-1660*. Manchester: Manchester University Press.

Douglas, M. (2003). *Mary Douglas: Collected Works*, vol. II: *Purity and Danger: An Analysis of Concepts of Pollution and Taboo* (1966). London & New York: Routledge.

Drobnick, J. (2005). *Volatile Effects: Olfactory Dimensions of Art and Architecture*. In D. Howes (ed.). *Empire of the Senses*. Oxford: Berg, 265-280.

—— (2006a). *Eating Nothing: Cooking Aromas in Art and Culture*. In Id. (ed.). *The Smell Culture Reader*. Oxford: Berg, 342-356.

—— (2006b) *Volatile Architectures* (2002). In M. Taylor, J. Preston (eds). *Intimus: Interior Design Theory Reader*. Hoboken: John Wiley & Sons, 89-95.

—— (2014). *The Museum as Smellscape*. In N. Levent, A. Pascual-Leone (eds). *The Multisensory Museum: Cross-Disciplinary Perspectives on Touch, Sounds, Smell, Memory, and Space*. Lanham: Rowman & Littlefield, 177-196.

—— (2015). *Smell: The Hybrid Art*. In C. Jaquet (ed.). *L'Art olfactif contemporain*. Paris: Classiques Garnier, 173-189.

Dubois, D. (2022). *Towards a Situated Cognitive Approach of Olfactory Experiences and Languages*. In N. Di Stefano, M.T. Russo (eds). *Olfaction: An Interdisciplinary Perspective from Philosophy to Life Sciences*. Cham: Springer, 117-139.

Dulau, R., Pitte, J.-R. (1998) (eds). *Géographie des odeurs*. Paris: L'Harmattan.

Dumas, A. (1873). *Grand dictionnaire de cuisine*. Paris: Alphonse Lemerre.

Duranti, M., Pesola, A. (1996) (eds.). *Atelier Balla. Pittura, arredo, moda. Emanuel Zoo: suggestioni futuriste*. Bologna: Marescalchi Cortina.

Edwards, D. (2008a). *Artscience: Creativity in the post-Google Generation*. Cambridge & London: Harvard University Press.

—— (2008b). *Whiff: A Novel by Séguier, with Manga Art by Junko Murata*. Paris: Éditions Le Laboratoir.

—— (2018). *Creating Things that Matter: The Art and Science of Innovations that Last*. New York: Henry Holt.

Ekuan, K. (1998). *The Aesthetics of the Japanese Lunchbox* (1980). Edited by D.B. Stewart, Translated by D. Kenny. Cambridge & London: MIT Press.

Ellena, J.-C. (1994). *Creative Perfumery: Composition Techniques*. In P.M. Müller, D. Lamparsky (eds). *Perfumes: Art, Science and Technology* (1991). Berlin: Springer, 333-345.

—— (2013). *The Diary of a Nose* (2011). Translated by A. Hunter. New York: Rizzoli.

—— (2015). *Le parfum, un acte poétique*. In C. Jaquet (ed.). *L'Art olfactif contemporain*. Paris: Classiques Garnier, 139-153.

Ellison, R. (2014). *Invisible Man* (1952). London: Penguin.

Engen, T. (1991). *Odor Sensation and Memory*. New York: Praeger Press.

Fabbian, C. (2012). *Naso d'autore. L'odorato nella cultura e nella storia letteraria italiana*. Ravenna: Longo Editore.

Fabro, L. (1978). *Attaccapanni*. Torino: Einaudi.

Federici, S. (2004). *Caliban and the Witch: Women, the Body and Primitive Accumulation*. New York: Autonomedia.

—— (2012). *Revolution at Point Zero: Housework, Reproduction, and Feminist Struggle*. Oakland: PM Press.

Feloj, S. (2016). *Estetica del disgusto. Mendelssohn, Kant e i limiti della rappresentazione*. Roma: Carocci.

Ferris, M.C. (2018). *Dining in the Dixie Diaspora: A Meeting of Region and Religion*. In H.R. Diner, S. Cinotto (eds.). *Global Jewish Foodways: A History*. Lincoln & London: University of Nebraska Press, 291-322.

Fiala, J. (2022). *Sensing the Virtual: Atmosphere and Somaesthetics in Virtual Reality*, "The Journal of Somaesthetics" 8(2), 57-77.

Fischler, C. (1988). *Food, Self and Identity*, "Social Science Information" 27(2), 275-292.

Fitzgerald, F.S. (2001). *The Great Gatsby* (1925). Ware: Wordsworth Editions.

Fjellestad, D. (2001). *Towards an Aesthetics of Smell: Or, The Foul and the Fragrant in Contemporary Literature*, "Cauce. Revista de Filología y su Didáctica" 24, 637-651.

Flandrin, J.-L., Montanari, M. (2000) (eds). *Food: A Culinary History from Antiquity to the Present* (1996). Edited by A. Sonnenfeld, Translated by C. Botsford *et al.* London: Penguin.

Flaubert, G. (1910). *The Temptation of St. Antony* (1874). Translated by L. Hearn. New York: Alice Harriman Company.

Flavián, C., Ibáñez-Sánchez, S., Orús, C. (2021). *The Influence of Scent on Virtual Reality Experiences: The Role of Aroma-Content Congruence*, "Journal of Business Research" 123, 289-301.

Flikke, R. (2016). *South African Eucalypts: Health, Trees, and Atmospheres in the Colonial Contact Zone*, "Geoforum" 76, 20-27.

—— (2018). *Domestication of Air, Scents and Disease*. In H.A. Swanson, M.E. Lien, G.B. Ween (eds). *Domestication Gone Wild: Politics and Practices of Multispecies Relations*. Durham & London: Duke University Press, 176-195.

Fontaine, M. (2010). *Funny Words in Plautine Comedy*. Oxford: Oxford University Press.

Fontanille, J. (2004). *Soma et séma. Figures du corps*. Paris: Maisonneuve et Larose.

Forget, C.-P. (1832). *Médecine navale ou nouveaux éléments d'hygiène, de pathologie et de thérapeutique médico-chirurgicales, á l'usage des officiers de santé de la marine de l'Etat et du commerce*. Paris: J.-B. Baillière.

Foucault, M. (1995). *Discipline and Punish: The Birth of the Prison* (1975). Translated by A. Sheridan. New York: Vintage.

Fraigneau, V. (2019). *La sensorialité olfactive du paysage, médiatrice d'une reliance sensible*, "VertigO — La revue électronique en sciences de l'environnement" 19(3), 1-16.

Francesetti, G., Griffero, T. (2019) (eds). *Psychopathology* and *Atmospheres: Neither Inside nor Outside*. Newcastle upon Tyne: Cambridge Scholars Publishing.

Frank, A. (1997). *The Diary of a Young Girl* (1947). Edited by O.H. Frank, M. Pressler. New York: Knopf Doubleday.

Freud, S. (1962). *Civilization and its Discontents* (1930). Translated by J. Strachey. New York: W.W. Norton.

Frier, D. (2001). *Righting Wrongs, Re-Writing Meaning and Reclaiming the City in Saramago's* Blindness *and* All the Names. In Vv. Aa. *On Saramago*. Dartmouth: University of Massachusetts Dartmouth, 97-122.

Frisk, H. (1960). *Griechisches Etymologisches Wörterbuch*. Heidelberg: Carl Winter Universitätsverlag.

Gadda, C.E. (2017). *The Experience of Pain* (1963). Translated by R. Dixon. London: Penguin.

Gambaro, G. (2022). *Ecological Aesthetics* (May 31, 2020), "International Lexicon of Aesthetics". Milano & Udine: Mimesis International, 172-175.

Gandy, M. (2017). *Urban Atmospheres*, "Cultural Geographies" 24(3), 353-374.

Garay-Barayazarra, G., Puri, R.K. (2011). *Smelling the Monsoon: Senses and Traditional Weather Forecasting Knowledge among Kenyah Badeng Farmers of Sarawak, Malaysia*, "Indian Journal of Traditional Knowledge" 10(1), 21-30.

García Márquez, G. (1970). *One Hundred Years of Solitude* (1967). Translated by G. Rabassa. New York: Harper & Row.

—— (1989). *Love in the Time of Cholera* (1985). Translated by E. Grossman. London & New York: Penguin.

Gasquet, J. (1990). *Cézanne: A Memoir with Conversations* (1921). Translated by C. Pemberton. London: Thames & Hudson.

Geiling, N. (2013). *Why Do We Eat Popcorn at the Movies?*, "Smithsonian" (October 3).

Geiregat, S. (2022). *Trade Mark Protection for Smells, Tastes and Feels – Critical Analysis of Three Non-Visual Signs in the EU*, "IIC — International Review of Intellectual Property and Competition Law" 53(2), 219-245.

Geller, J. (1997). *The Aromatics of Jewish Difference: Or, Benjamin's Allegory of Aura*. In J. Boyarin, D. Boyarin (eds). *Jews and Other Differences: The New Jewish Cultural Studies*. Minneapolis & London: University of Minnesota Press, 203-256.

Gentilcore, D. (2016). *Food and Health in Early Modern Europe: Diet, Medicine and Society, 1450-1800*. London & New York: Bloomsbury.

Georgsdorf, W. (2021). *Osmodrama: Theatre for the Nose*, "Rivista di Estetica" 61(78), 3, 112-130.

Gibellini, P. (2017). *Gabriele D'Annunzio's "voluptuous nose": Extracts from the Letters to his Perfumer*. In D. Ciani Forza, S. Francescato (eds). *Perfume and Literature: The Persistence of the Ephemeral*. Padova: Linea, 215-256.

Gibson, J.J. (1969). *The Senses Considered as Perceptual Systems* (1966). London: George Allen & Unwin.

—— (1986). *The Ecological Approach to Visual Perception* (1979). Hove & New York: Psychology Press.

Goeltzenleuchter, B. (2018). *Scenting the Antiseptic Institution*. In V. Henshaw et al. (eds). *Designing with Smell: Practices, Techniques and Challenges*. London & New York: Routledge, 248-258.

—— (2021). *The Olfactory Counter-Monument: Active Smelling and the Politics of Wonder in the Contemporary Museum*. In G.-A. Lynn, D.R. Parr (eds). *Olfactory Art and the Political in an Age of Resistance*. London & New York: Routledge, 182-194.

Gottfried, J.A. (2005). *A Truffle in the Mouth Is Worth Two in the Bush: Odor Localization in the Human Brain*, "Neuron" 47(4), 473-476.

Graham, M. (2006). *Queer Smells: Fragrances of Late Capitalism or Scents of Subversion?*. In J. Drobnick (ed.). *The Smell Culture Reader*. Oxford & New York: Berg, 305-319.

—— (2014). *Anthropological Explorations in Queer Theory*. Farnham & Burlington: Ashgate Publishing.

Grammer, K., Fink, B., Neave, N. (2005). *Human Pheromones and Sexual Attraction*, "European Journal of Obstetrics & Gynecology & Reproductive Biology" 118(2), 135-42.

Gramsci, A. (1917). *Demagogia*, "Sotto la Mole" (October 10).

Grand-Clément, A., Ribeyrol, C. (2022). *Introduction. The Fragrant and the Foul: What Did Antiquity Smell Like?*. In Id. (eds). *The Smells and Senses of Antiquity in the Modern Imagination*. London & New York: Bloomsbury, 1-23.

Grant, C. (2017). *A Smell of Burning: A Memoir of Epilepsy*. London: Jonathan Cape.

Green, J.D., Reid, C.A., Kneuer, M.A., Hedgebeth, M.V. (2023). *The Proust Effect: Scents, Food, and Nostalgia*, "Current Opinion in Psychology" 50, 1-6.

Greimas, A.J., Fontanille, J. (1991). *Sémiotique des passions. Des états de choses aux états d'âme*. Paris: Éditions du Seuil.

Grieco, A.J. (2019). *Food, Social Politics and the Order of Nature in Renaissance Italy*. Milano: Officina Libraria.

Griffero, T. (2008). *Quasi-cose. Dalla situazione affettiva alle atmosfere*, "Trópos" 1, 75-92.

—— (2010). *Dal bello all'atmosferico. Un'estetica "dal punto di vista pragmatico"*. Introduction to G. Böhme. *Atmosfere, estasi, messe in scena. L'estetica come teoria generale della percezione* (2001). Edited by T. Griffero. Milano: Christian Marinotti Edizioni, 5-33.

—— (2014). *Atmospheres: Aesthetics of Emotional Spaces* (2010). Translated by S. De Sanctis. Farnham & Burlington: Ashgate.

—— (2017a). *Il pensiero dei sensi. Atmosfere ed estetica patica*. Milano: Guerini.

—— (2017b). *Felt-Bodily Communication: A Neophenomenological Approach to Embodied Affects*, "Studi di Estetica" 45(4), 2, 71-86.

—— (2019). *Is There Such a Thing as an 'Atmospheric Turn'? Instead of an Introduction*. In T. Griffero, M. Tedeschini (eds). *Atmosphere and Aesthetics: A Plural Perspective*. London: Palgrave Macmillan, 11-62.

—— (2020a). *Places, Affordances, Atmospheres: A Pathic Aesthetics*. London & New York: Routledge.

—— (2020b). *Better to Be in Tune: Between Resonance and Responsivity*, "Studi di Estetica" 48(4), 2, 93-118.

—— (2021a). *The Atmospheric "We": Moods and Collective Feeling*. Milano & Udine: Mimesis International.

—— (2021b). *Corporeal Landscapes: Can Somaesthetics and New Phenomenology Come Together?*, "The Journal of Somaesthetics" 7(1), 15-28.

—— (2022a). *Sniffing Atmospheres: Observations on Olfactory Being-In-The-World*. In N. Di Stefano, M.T. Russo (eds). *Olfaction: An Interdisciplinary Perspective from Philosophy to Life Sciences*. Cham: Springer, 75-90.

—— (2022b). *Atmosphere* (March 31, 2018), "International Lexicon of Aesthetics". Milano & Udine: Mimesis International, 77-80.

—— (2022c). *Dwelling Means Cultivating Atmospheres*, "Espes" 11(2), 8-19.

Griffero, T., Moretti, G. (2018) (eds). *Atmosphere/Atmospheres: Testing a New Paradigm*. Milano & Udine: Mimesis International.

Gumbrecht, H.U. (2012). *Atmosphere, Mood, Stimmung: On a Hidden Potential of Literature* (2011). Translated by E. Butler. Stanford: Stanford University Press.

Hall, E.T. (1966). *The Hidden Dimension*. New York: Doubleday.

Hall, I.R., Brown, G.T., Zambonelli, A. (2007). *Taming the Truffle: The History, Lore, and Science of the Ultimate Mushroom*. Portland: Timber Press.

Halliday, S. (2001). *Death and Miasma in Victorian London: An Obstinate Belief*, "BMJ Clinical Research" 323(7327), 1469-1471.

Han, B.-C. (2015). *The Burnout Society* (2010). Translated by E. Butler. Stanford: Stanford University Press.

—— (2017a). *The Scent of Time: A Philosophical Essay on the Art of Lingering* (2009). Translated by D. Steuer. Cambridge: Polity Press.

—— (2017b). *Saving Beauty* (2015). Translated by D. Steuer. Cambridge: Polity Press.

Harris, J. (1979). *Oral and Olfactory Arts*, "The Journal of Aesthetic Education" 13(4), 5-15.

Hartmann, S. (1913). *Perfume Land*, "The Forum" 50, 217-228.

Hassine, J.B., Candau, J., Perez, S., Sompairac, L., Adrian-Scotto, M., Gondolfo, G. (2021). *Espaces odorants et espaces olfactifs*, "Journal of Interdisciplinary Methodologies and Issues in Science" 9, 1-15.

Hauskeller, M. (1995). *Atmosphäre erleben. Philosophische Untersuchungen zur Sinneswahrnehmung*. Berlin: Akademie.

Heaney, S. (1980). *Poems, 1965-1975*. New York: Farrar, Straus & Giroux.

—— (2001). *The Sensual Philosopher: Mr. Palomar* (1985). In H. Bloom (ed.). *Italo Calvino*. Philadelphia: Chelsea House, 77-80.

Hegel, G.W.F. (1975). *Aesthetics: Lectures on Fine Art* (1835). Translated by T.M. Knox. Oxford: Oxford University Press.

Heldke, L. (2005). *But is it Authentic? Culinary Travel and the Search for the "Genuine Article"*. In C. Korsmeyer (ed.). *The Taste Culture Reader: Experiencing Food and Drink*. Oxford & New York: Berg, 385-394.

—— (2018). *It's Chomping All the Way Down: Toward an Ontology of the Human Individual*, "The Monist" 101(3): 247-260.

Helstosky, C. (2017). *Time Changes Everything: Futurist/Modernist Cooking*. In S. Bottinelli, M. d'Ayala Valva (eds). *The Taste of Art: Cooking, Food, and Counterculture in Contemporary Practices*. Fayetteville: University of Arkansas Press, 45-59.

Helttula, A. (1996). *Truffles in Ancient Greece and Rome*, "Arctos" 30, 33-47.

Henning, H. (1916). *Der Geruch*. Leipzig: Barth.

Henshaw, V. (2014). *Urban Smellscapes: Understanding and Designing City Smell Environments*. London & New York: Routledge.

Henshaw, V., McLean, K., Medway, D., Perkins, C., Warnaby, G. (2018) (eds). *Designing with Smell: Practices, Techniques and Challenges*. London & New York: Routledge.

Herz, R.S. (2008). *The Scent of Desire: Discovering Our Enigmatic Sense of Smell*. New York: Harper Perennial.

—— (2012). *Odor Memory and the Special Role of Associative Learning*. In G.M. Zucco, R.S. Herz, B. Schaal (eds). *Olfactory Cognition: From Perception and Memory to Environmental Odours and Neuroscience*, Advances in Consciousness Research, 85. Amsterdam & Philadelphia: John Benjamins Publishing Company, 95-114.

Herz, R.S., Schooler, J.W. (2002). *A Naturalistic Study of Autobiographical Memories Evoked by Olfactory and Visual Cues: Testing the Proustian Hypothesis*, "The American Journal of Psychology" 115(1), 21-32.

Hesse, H. (1969). *The Glass Bead Game (Magister Ludi)* (1943). Translated by R. Winston, C. Winston. New York, Chicago & San Francisco: Holt, Rinehart and Winston.

Higgins, H. (2002). *Fluxus Experience*. Berkeley, Los Angeles & London: University of California Press.

Hirsch, A.R. (1992). *Nostalgia: A Neuropsychiatric Understanding*. In J.F. Sherry, B. Sternthal (eds). *Advances in Consumer Research*. Provo: Association for Consumer Research, 19, 390-395.

Hoad, T.F. (1996) (ed.). *The Concise Oxford Dictionary of English Etymology* (1986). Oxford & New York: Oxford University Press.

Hobbes, T. (1969). *The Elements of Law: Natural and Politic* (1650). Edited by F. Tönnies (2nd edition). London: Frank Cass & Co.

Hoke, T. (1931). *Corner Saloon,* "American Mercury" 311-322.

Holley, A. (1999). *Éloge de l'odorat*. Paris: Odile Jacob.

—— (2006). *Le cerveau gourmand*. Paris: Odile Jacob.

Holmes, B. (2017). *Flavour: A User's Guide to Our Most Neglected Sense*. London: WH Allen.

Horkheimer, M., Adorno, T.W. (2002). *Dialectic of Enlightenment: Philosophical Fragments* (1947). Edited by G.S. Noerr, Translated by E. Jephcott. Stanford: Stanford University Press.

Horsley, M.N. (2022). *Sniff, Bite, Taste, Swallow: The Erotics of the Black Throat,* "Venti Journal" 2(2).

Howes, D. (2005). *Hyperesthesia, or, the Sensual Logic of Late Capitalism*. In Id. (ed.). *Empire of the Senses*. Oxford: Berg, 281-303.

—— (2008). *Olfaction and Transition: An Essay on the Ritual Uses of Smell,* "Canadian Review of Sociology" 24(3), 398-416.

Hsu, H.L. (2016). *Olfactory Art, Transcorporeality, and the Museum Environment,* "Resilience: A Journal of the Environmental Humanities" 4(1), 1-24.

—— (2019). *Atmospheric Literary Geography,* "Literary Geography" 5(1), 21-24.

—— (2020). *The Smell of Risk: Environmental Disparities and Olfactory Aesthetics*. New York: New York University Press.

—— (2022). *Colonial and Anti-Black Legacies of Fragrance and Deodorization,* "Venti Journal" 2(2).

Hulme, M. (2017). *Weathered: Cultures of Climate*. Newbury Park: SAGE Publications.

Hultén, B. (2020). *Sensory Marketing: An Introduction*. Newbury Park: SAGE Publications.

Hultén, B., Broweus, N., van Dijk, M. (2009). *Sensory Marketing*. London: Palgrave Macmillan.

Humboldt, A. von (1811). *Essai Politique sur la Royaume de la Nouvelle-Espagne*, vol. II. Paris: F. Schoell.

Hume, K. (1992). *Calvino's Fictions: Cogito and Cosmos*. Oxford: Oxford University Press.

Huxley, A. (2005). *Brave New World* (1932) — *Brave New World Revisited* (1958). New York, London, Toronto & Sidney: Harper Perennials.

Huysmans, J.-K. (1998). *Against Nature (À rebours)* (1884). Translated by M. Mauldon, Edited by N. White. Oxford: Oxford University Press.

Ibarretxe-Antuñano, I. (2021). *The Domain of Olfaction in Basque*. In Ł. Jędrzejowski, P. Staniewski (eds). *The Linguistics of Olfaction: Typological and Diachronic Approaches to Synchronic Diversity*. Amsterdam & Philadelphia: John Benjamins Publishing Company, 73-111.

Illich, I. (1985). *H2O and the Waters of Forgetfulness: Reflections on the Historicity of "Stuff"*. Dallas: The Dallas Institute of Humanities and Culture.

Inbar, Y., Pizarro, D., Iyer, R., Haidt, J. (2011). *Disgust Sensitivity, Political Conservatism, and Voting*, "Sage Journal" 3(5), 537-544.

Ingold, T. (2011). *Being Alive: Essays on Movement, Knowledge and Description*. London & New York: Routledge.

—— (2015). *The Life of Lines*. London & New York: Routledge.

—— (2020). *Correspondences*. Cambridge: Polity Press.

Iovino, S. (2014). *Storie dell'altro mondo. Calvino post-umano*, "Modern Language Notes" 129(1), 118-138.

Irigaray, L. (1999). *The Forgetting of Air in Martin Heidegger* (1983). London: The Athlone Press.

Ishii–Fôret, A. (2015). *Le voie de l'art olfactif chez Maki Ueda*. In C. Jaquet (ed.). *L'Art olfactif contemporain*. Paris: Classiques Garnier, 213-222.

Jacobs, L.F., Arter, J., Cook, A., Sulloway, F.J. (2015). *Olfactory Orientation and Navigation in Humans*, "Plos One" 10(6), 1-13.

James, W. (1884). *What is an Emotion?*, "Mind" 9(34), 188-205.

—— (1981). *The Principles of Psychology* (1890). Cambridge & London: Harvard University Press.

Jaquet, C. (2010). *Philosophie de l'odorat*. Paris: PUF.

—— (2015). *Introduction. Des objets à flairer à l'œuvre parfumée*. In Id. (ed.). *L'Art olfactif contemporain*. Paris: Classiques Garnier, 7-16.

—— (2018). *Philosophie du Kōdō. L'esthétique japonaise des fragrances*. Paris: PUF.

—— (2019). *La fragrance et la musique. Ou l'invention d'un art "sonolfactif"*, "Journal of Ancient Philosophy" 1, 433-450.

—— (2022). *Un art bien senti/Deeply sensed art*. In Vv. Aa. *Respirer l'art. Quand l'art contemporain sublime l'univers du parfum*. Milano: SilvanaEditoriale, 46-51.

Jenner (2000). *Civilization and Deodorization? Smell in Early Modern English Culture*. In P. Burke, B. Harrison, P. Slack (eds). *Civil Histories: Essays Presented to Sir Keith Thomas*. Oxford: Oxford University Press, 127-144.

Jerome, J.K. (1960). *Three Men in a Boat: To Say Nothing of the Dog* (1889). London & Glasgow: Collins.

Johnstone, M.A. (2012). *Aristotle On Odour and Smell*, "Oxford Studies in Ancient Philosophy" 43, 142-183.

Jonas, H. (2001). *The Phenomenon of Life: Toward a Philosophical Biology* (1966). Evanston: Northwestern University Press.

Jones, B.C. (1975). *Prohibition and Prosperity, 1920-1930*, "Social Science" 50(2), 78-86.

Jones, M.O. (2017). *Eating behind Bars: On Punishment, Resistance, Policy, and Applied Folkloristics*, "The Journal of American Folklore" 130(515), 72-108.

Jönsson, F., Stevenson, R. (2014). *Odor Knowledge, Odor Naming, and the "Tip-of-the-Nose" Experience*. In B. Schwarts, A. Brown (eds). *Tip-of-the-Tongue States and Related Phenomena*. Cambridge: Cambridge University Press, 305-326.

Julmi, C. (2017). *Situations and Atmospheres in Organizations: A (New) Phenomenology of Being-in-the-Organization*. Milano & Udine: Mimesis International.

Kaimal, G., Carroll-Haskins, K., Topoglu, Y., Ramakrishnan, A., Arslanbek, A., Ayaz, H. (2021). *Exploratory fNIRS Assessment of Differences in Activation in Virtual Reality Visual Self-Expression Including with a Fragrance Stimulus*, "Art Therapy: Journal of the American Art Therapy Association" 39(56), 1-10.

Kaiser, J. (2022). *Martial's Materials: Materiality in the Literary Epigram*, PhD Dissertation in Classical Studies, University of Pennsylvania.

Kalita, S.M. (2003). *Suburban Sahibs: Three Immigrant Families and Their Passage from India to America*. New Brunswick & London: Rutgers University Press.

Kant, I. (2006). *Anthropology from a Pragmatic Point of View* (1798). Edited by R.B. Louden. Cambridge: Cambridge University Press.

—— (2007). *Critique of Judgment* (1790). Translated by J.C. Meredith, Edited by N. Walker. Oxford: Oxford University Press.

Kaplan, D.M. (2012) (ed.). *The Philosophy of Food*. Berkeley, Los Angeles & London: University of California Press.

—— (2020). *Food Philosophy: An Introduction*. New York: Columbia University Press.

Kapoor, S. (2022a). *The Smells of Caste: Body, Self and Politics*. In N. Di Stefano, M.T. Russo (eds). *Olfaction: An Interdisciplinary Perspective from Philosophy to Life Sciences*. Cham: Springer, 21-34.

—— (2022b). *"The Air Smells Rotten": Caste and Senses in and around a Tannery*, "Venti Journal" 2(2).

Kappe, T. (1997). *Anmerkungen zu einer Biologie der Grenze*. In M. Bauer, T. Rahn (eds). *Die Grenze. Begriff und Inszenierung*. Berlin: Akademie Verlag, 133-146.

Keller, A. (2011). *Attention and Olfactory Consciousness*, "Frontiers in Psychology" 2(380), 1-13.

—— (2016). *Philosophy of Olfactory Perception*. London: Palgrave Macmillan.

Keller, A., Young, B.D. (2023) (eds). *Theoretical Perspectives on Smell*. London & New York: Routledge.

Keller, H. (1908). *Sense and Sensibility*, "The Century Magazine" 75, 34-55.

—— (2003). *The Story of my Life* (1903). New York: Modern Library.

Kettler, A. (2020). *The Smell of Slavery: Olfactory Racism and the Atlantic World*. Cambridge: Cambridge University Press.

—— (2022). *The Miasmatic Theft of Modernity: Sulfuric Aromata and Early Modern Empires*, "Venti Journal" 2(2).

Kierkegaard, S. (1946). *Repetition: An Essay in Experimental Psychology* (1843). Translated by W. Lowrie. Princeton: Princeton University Press.

Kinne, M.-L. (2021). *Mit den Augen riechen. Geruchsbilder seit der Reinaissance/To Smell with the Eyes: Images of Scents since the Reinassance.* In Vv. Aa. *Smell it! Geruch in der Kunst/Scent in the Arts.* Köln: Wienand, 81-97.

Kjellmer, V. (2021a). *Scented Bodies: Perfuming as Resistance and a Subversive Identity Statement.* In G.-A. Lynn, D.R. Parr (eds). *Olfactory Art and the Political in an Age of Resistance.* London & New York: Routledge, 146-156.

—— (2021b). *Scented Scenographics and Olfactory Art: Making Sense of Scent in the Museum,* "Konsthistorisk tidskrift/Journal of Art History" 90(2), 72-87.

Klein, E. (1971). *A Comprehensive Etymological Dictionary of the English Language: Dealing with the Origin of Words and their Sense Development Thus Illustrating the History of Civilization and Culture.* Amsterdam: Elsevier.

Kluck, S. (2019). *Atmospheres and Memory: A Phenomenological Approach.* In T. Griffero, M. Tedeschini (eds). *Atmosphere and Aesthetics: A Plural Perspective.* London: Palgrave Macmillan, 191-208.

Koczanowicz, D. (2017). *Eating Abroad: In Search for Culinary Experiences,* "Pragmatism Today" 8(2), 59-67.

—— (2023). *The Aesthetics of Taste: Eating within the Realm of Art.* Leiden & Boston: Brill.

Kohl, J.V. (2012). *Human Pheromones and Food Odors: Epigenetic Influences on the Socioaffective Nature of Evolved Behaviours,* "Socioaffective Neuroscience & Psychology" 2, 1-10.

Kolnai, A. (2004). *On Disgust* (1929). Edited and Translated by B. Smith, C. Korsmeyer. Chicago & La Salle: Open Court.

Koloji-Ostrow, A.O. (2015). *Roman Urban Smells: The Archaeological Evidence.* In M. Bradley (ed.). *Smell and the Ancient Senses.* London & New York: Routledge, 90-109.

Korsmeyer, C. (1999). *Making Sense of Taste: Food and Philosophy.* Ithaca: Cornell University Press.

—— (2004). *Gender and Aesthetics: An Introduction.* London & New York: Routledge.

Köster, E.G., Møller, P., Mojet, J. (2014). *A "Misfit" Theory of Spontaneous Conscious Odor Perception (MITSCOP): Reflections on the role and function of odor memory in everyday life,* "Frontiers in Psychology" 5(64), 1-12.

Kotler, P. (1974). *Atmospherics as a Marketing Tool,* "Journal of Retailing" 49(4), 48-64.

Krafft-Ebing, R. von (1933). *Psychopathia Sexualis, With Special Reference to the Antipathic Sexual Instinct: A Medico-Forensic Study* (1886). Translated by J. Rebman (12th German edition). Brooklyn: Physicians and Surgeons Book Company.

Krause, F. (2013). *Seasons as Rhythms on the Kemi River in Finnish Lapland,* "Ethnos: Journal of Anthropology" 78(1), 23-46.

Krishna, A. (2010) (ed.). *Sensory Marketing: Research on the Sensuality of Products.* London & New York: Routledge.

Krishna, A., Elder, R.S., Caldara, C. (2010). *Feminine to Smell but Masculine to Touch? Multisensory Congruence and its Effect on Aesthetic Experience,* "Journal of Consumer Psychology" 20, 410-418.

Kuruvilla, G., Mubiayi, I., Scego, I., Wadia, L. (2005). *Pecore nere: Racconti*. Edited by F. Capitani, E. Coen. Roma & Bari: Laterza.

Lähnemann, I. (2021). *Geruch gleich Gegenwart/Olfactor: Scent Is Present*. In Vv. Aa. *Smell it! Geruch in der Kunst/Scent in the Arts*. Köln: Wienand, 13-48.

Laporte, D. (2000). *History of Shit* (1978). Translated by N. Benabid, R. el-Khoury. Cambridge & London: MIT Press.

Latour, B. (2004). *How to Talk About the Body? The Normative Dimension of Science Studies*, "Body & Society" 10(2/3), 205-229.

Law, L. (2001). *Home Cooking: Filipino Women and Geographies of the Senses in Hong Kong*, "Cultural Geographies" 8(3), 264-283.

Lawless, H., Engen, T. (1977). *Associations to odors: Interference, Mnemonics, and Verbal Labeling*, "Journal of Experimental Psychology: Human Learning and Memory" 3(1), 52-59.

Lawrence D.H. (1955). *The Complete Short Stories*, vol. I. Melbourne, London & Toronto: William Heinemann.

—— (1977). *The Complete Poems of D.H. Lawrence*. Edited by V. De Sola Pinto, F.W. Roberts. London: Penguin.

Le Breton, D. (2017). *Sensing the World: An Anthropology of the Senses* (2006). Translated by C. Ruschiensky. London & New York: Routledge.

—— (2022). *Smell as a Way of Thinking About the World: An Anthropology*. In N. Di Stefano, M.T. Russo (eds). *Olfaction: An Interdisciplinary Perspective from Philosophy to Life Sciences*. Cham: Springer, 3-20.

Lee, J. (2017). *Odor and Order: How Caste Is Inscribed in Space and Sensoria*, "Comparative Studies of South Asia, Africa and the Middle East" 37(3), 470-490.

Lefebvre, H. (2004). *Rhythmanalysis: Space, Time and Everyday Life* (1992). Translated by S. Elden, G. Moore. London & New York: Continuum.

Le Guérer, A. (1994). *Scent: The Mysterious and Essential Powers of Smell* (1988). Translated by R. Miller. New York, Tokyo & London: Kodansha International.

—— (2015). *La reconnaisance artistique du parfum*. In C. Jaquet (ed.). *L'Art olfactif contemporain*. Paris: Classiques Garnier, 39-53.

Lehrer, J. (2007). *Proust Was a Neuroscientist*. Boston & New York: Houghton Mifflin.

Leimgruber, P. (2010). *Scent Marketing: The Effectiveness of Complex vs. Simple Scents*. Saarbrücken: VDM Verlag Dr. Müller.

Leopardi, G. (2013). *Zibaldone* (1798-1837). Edited by M. Caesar, F. D'Intino, Translated by K. Baldwin *et al*. New York: Farrar, Straus & Giroux.

Lerner, M.A. (2007). *Dry Manhattan: Prohibition in New York City*. Cambridge & London: Harvard University Press.

Leroi-Gourhan, A. (1993). *Gesture and Speech* (1964). Translated by A.B. Berger. Cambridge & London: MIT Press.

Leucadi, G. (2001). *Il naso e l'anima* (2000), "The Edinburgh Journal of Gadda Studies" 1.

Levent, N., Pascual-Leone, A. (2014) (eds). *The Multisensory Museum: Cross-Disciplinary Perspectives on Touch, Sounds, Smell, Memory, and Space*. Lanham: Rowman & Littlefield.

Levi, P. (1959). *If This is a Man* (1947). Translated by S. Woolf. New York: Orion Press.

—— (1990). *The Mnemogogues*. In Id. *The Sixth Day and Other Tales* (1966). Translated by R. Rosenthal. New York: Summit Books, 11-18.

Lévi-Strauss, C. (1964). *Mythologiques. Le cru et le cuit*. Paris: Plon.

Lindstrøm, M. (2005). *Brand Sense: Sensory Secrets Behind the Stuff We Buy*. New York: Free Press.

—— (2008). *Buyology: Truth and Lies About Why We Buy*. New York: Random House.

Lipovetsky, G., Serroy, J. (2013). *L'esthétisation du monde*. Paris: Gallimard.

Lipton, S. (2014). *Dark Mirror: The Medieval Origins of Anti-Jewish Iconography*. New York: Metropolitan Books.

Liuzza, M.T. (2020). *The Smell of Prejudice: Disgust, Sense of Smell and Social Attitude: An Evolutionary Perspective*, "Lebenswelt" 17, 42-58.

Liuzza, M.T., Lindholm, T., Hawley, C.B., Sendén, M.G., Ekström, I., Olsson, M.J., Olofsson, J.K. (2018). *Body Odor Disgust Sensitivity Predicts Authoritarian Attitudes*, "Royal Society Open Science" 5(2), 1-17.

Locke, J. (1997). *An Essay Concerning Human Understanding* (1689). Edited by R. Woolhouse. London: Penguin.

Locke, P.M. (2007). *The Liminal World of the Northwest Coast*. In S.L. Cataldi, W.S. Hamrick (eds). *Merleau-Ponty and Environmental Philosophy: Dwelling on the Landscapes of Thought*. New York: State University of New York Press, 51-66.

London, J. (1989). *John Barleycorn: Alcoholic Memoirs* (1913). Oxford: Oxford University Press.

Lovelock, J. (1979). *Gaia: A New Look at Life on Earth*. Oxford: Oxford University Press.

Lucretius (2007). *The Nature of Things*. Translated and with Notes by A.E. Stallings. London: Penguin.

Lynn, G.-A., Parr, D.R. (2021) (eds). *Olfactory Art and the Political in an Age of Resistance*. London & New York: Routledge.

MacLean, P.D. (1990). *The Triune Brain in Evolution: Role in Paleocerebral Functions*. New York & London: Plenum Press.

Majid, A., Burenhult, N. (2014). *Odors are Expressible in Language, as Long as you Speak the Right Language*, "Cognition" 130(2), 266-270.

Majid, A., Burenhult, N., Stensmyr, M., de Valk, J., Hansson, B.S. (2018). *Olfactory Language and Abstraction Across Cultures*, "Philosophical Transactions of the Royal Society of London" 373(1752), 1-8.

Manalansan IV, M.F. (2006). *Immigrant Lives and the Politics of Olfaction in the Global City*. In J. Drobnick (ed.), *The Smell Culture Reader*. Oxford & New York: Berg, 41-52.

Mancioppi, E. (2019). *Cibo, atmosfere ed estetizzazioni olfattive*, "E|C: Rivista dell'Associazione Italiana Studi Semiotici" 27, 1-9.

—— (2021a). *L'olfatto come senso estetico-politico*. In M. Montanari (ed.). *Cucina politica. Il linguaggio del cibo fra pratiche sociali e rappresentazioni ideologiche*. Roma & Bari: Laterza, 284-298.

—— (2021b). *Towards a sociopolitical aesthetics of smell*, "Rivista di Estetica" 61(78), 3, 131-151.

—— (2022a). *L'olfattivo. Per un'estetica sociale dell'odorato*. Pisa: Edizioni ETS.

—— (2022b). *Osmospheric Dwelling: Smell, Food, Gender and Atmospheres*, "Espes: The Slovak Journal of Aesthetics" 11(2), 38-53.

Mancioppi, E. Perullo, N. (2020). *Estetica aromatica. Odore, politiche dell'atmosfera e impegno percettivo*, "Rivista di Estetica" 60(73), 1, 118-135.

Mandic, D., Nirta, C., Pavoni, A., Philippopoulos-Mihalopoulos, A. (2018). *Introduction: Law and Smell*. In Id. (eds). *Smell: Law and the Senses Series*. London: University of Westminster Press, 3-9.

Mandoki, K. (2007). *Everyday Aesthetics: Prosaics, the Play of Culture and Social Identities*. Aldershot: Ashgate.

Manera, L. (2022a). *Elementi per un'estetica digitale. Media interattivi e nuove forme di educazione estetica*. Milano & Udine: Mimesis.

—— (2022b). *Contemporary Aesthetics Perspectives on Imagination and Reality Media*, "Aesthetics Preprint" 120, 93-105.

Marinetti, F.T. (1973). *The Founding and Manifesto of Futurism* (1909). In U. Apollonio (ed.). *Futurist Manifestos*. Translated by R. Brain, R.W. Flint, J.C. Higgitt, C. Tisdal. Boston: MFA Publications, 19-24.

—— (1977). *Collaudi futuristi*. Edited by G. Viazzi. Napoli: Guida Editori.

—— (2005). *Supplemento al Manifesto tecnico della Letteratura futurista* (1912). In W. Bohn (ed.). *Italian Futurist Poetry*. Toronto: University of Toronto Press, 12-13.

—— (2014). *The Futurist Cookbook* (1932). Translated by S. Brill, Edited by L. Chamberlain. London & New York: Penguin.

Marinucci, L. (2019). *Japanese Atmospheres: Of Sky, Wind and Breathing*. In T. Griffero, M. Tedeschini (eds). *Atmosphere and Aesthetics: A Plural Perspective*. London: Palgrave Macmillan, 93-118.

Markey, M. (1926). *"One More Story" Reporter at Large*, "The New Yorker", January 16, 13-14.

Marrone, G. (2014). *Gastromania*. Milano: Bompiani.

Martial (1919). *Epigrams*, vol. II. Translated by W.C.A. Ker. London & New York: William Heinemann & G.P. Putnam's Sons.

Martin, C. (2015). *The Invention of Atmosphere*, "Studies in History and Philosophy of Science" 52, 44-54.

Martina, G. (2021). *Objective Smells and Partial Perspectives*, "Rivista di Estetica" 61(78), 3, 27-46.

Marusek, S. (2018). *Reasonable or Offensive? Smell, Jurisdiction, and Public Right*. In D. Mandic, C. Nirta, A. Pavoni, A. Philippopoulos-Mihalopoulos (eds). *Smell: Law and the Senses Series*. London: University of Westminster Press, 32-41.

Mawani, R. (2000). *In Between and Out of Place: Racial Hybridity, Liquor and the Law in Late 19th and Early 20th Century British Columbia*, "Canadian Journal of Law and Society" 15(2), 9-38.

Mazzeo, M. (2013). *Introduzione. Fine di un naufragio. Aromi, atmosfere, parole*. Introduction to H. Tellenbach, *L'aroma del mondo. Gusto, olfatto e atmosfere* (1968). Edited and Translated by M. Mazzeo. Milano: Christian Marinotti Edizioni, 5-12.

—— (2022). *Il naso di Afrodite. Archeologia della bellezza olfattiva*, "Rivista Italiana di Filosofia del Linguaggio" 16(2), 40-52.

McCartney, W. (1968). *Olfaction and Odours: An Osphrésiological Essay*. Berlin, Heidelberg & New York: Springer.

McCormack, D.P. (2008). *Engineering Affective Atmospheres on the Moving Geographies of the 1897 Andrée Expedition*, "Cultural Geographies" 15(4), 413-430.

—— (2018). *Atmospheric Things: On the Allure of Elemental Envelopment*. Durham: Duke University Press.

McGann, J.P. (2017). *Poor Human Olfaction is a 19th-century Myth*, "Science" 356(6338), 1-7.

McGinley, M., McGinley, C. (2018). *Olfactory Design Elements in Theatre: The Practical Considerations*. In V. Henshaw, K. McLean, D. Medway, C. Perkins, G. Warnaby (eds). *Designing with Smell: Practices, Techniques and Challenges*. London & New York: Routledge, 219-226.

McGinn, C. (2011). *The Meaning of Disgust*. Oxford: Oxford University Press.

McGirr, L. (2016). *The War on Alcohol: Prohibition and the Rise of the American State*. New York & London: W.W. Norton & Company.

McHugh, J. (2012). *Sandalwood and Carrion: Smell in Indian Religion and Culture*. Oxford: Oxford University Press.

McLuhan, M. (1964). *Understanding Media: The Extensions of Man*. New York, Toronto & London: McGraw-Hill.

McPhee, M. (2020). *Miasmas in the Theatre: Encountering Carceral Atmospherics in Pests (2014)*, "Ambiances" 6, 1-18.

McQueen, D. (1993). *Aquinas on the Aesthetic Relevance of Tastes and Smells*, "The British Journal of Aesthetics" 33(4), 346-356.

McWilliams M.P., Coelho, D.H., Reiter, E.R., Costanzo, R.M. (2022). *Recovery from Covid-19 Smell Loss: Two-Years of Follow Up*, "American Journal of Otolaryngology-Head and Neck Medicine and Surgery" 43(103607), 1-4.

Medway, D., Warnaby, G. (2018). *Designing Smell into the Consumer Experience*. In V. Henshaw, K. McLean, D. Medway, C. Perkins, G. Warnaby (eds). *Designing with Smell: Practices, Techniques and Challenges*. London & New York: Routledge, 123-131.

Meier, A. (2017). *In 1902, Audiences Turned Up Their Noses at the First Perfume Concert*, "Hyperallergic" (June, 30).

Meigs, A. (1988). *Food as a Cultural Construction*, "Food and Foodways" 2, 341-357.

Merleau-Ponty, M. (2012). *Phenomenology of Perception* (1945). Translated by D.A. Landes. London & New York: Routledge.

Meyer, J.P. (2013). *When Pot Smells in Denver, the Nasal Ranger Goes in to Investigate*, "The Denver Post" (November 10, Updated April 28, 2016).

Millar, B. (2019). *Smelling Objects*, "Synthese" 196, 4279-4303.

Millay, E. St. V. (1956). *Collected Poems*. Edited by N. Millay. New York: Harper & Row.

Miller, W.I. (1997). *The Anatomy of Disgust*. Cambridge & London: Harvard University Press.

Milosz, O.V. de L. (1959) *O.V. de L. Milosz* (1877-1939). Paris: André Silvaire.

—— (1960). *Œuvres complètes. Poésies*, vol. I. Paris: André Silvaire.

Minkowski, E. (1927). *De la rêverie morbide au délire d'influence*, "Évolution Psychiatrique" 2, 130-184.

—— (1932). *Le problème des hallucinations et le problème de l'espace*, "Évolution Psychiatrique" 2(3), 57-76.

—— (1999). *Vers une cosmologie. Fragments philosophiques* (1936). Paris: Éditions Payot & Rivages.

Mol, A. (2008). *I Eat an Apple: On Theorizing Subjectivities*, "Subjectivity" 22, 28-37.

Montaigne, M. de (1948). *The Complete Works of Montaigne: Essays, Travel Journal, Letters*. Translated by D.M. Frame. Stanford: Stanford University Press.

Montale, E. (2012). *The Collected Poems of Eugenio Montale, 1925-1977*. Translated by W. Arrowsmith, Edited by R. Warren. New York & London: W.W. Norton & Company.

Montanari, M. (2006). *Food is Culture* (2004). Translated by A. Sonnenfeld. New York: Columbia University Press.

—— (2010). *Cheese, Pears, and History in a Proverb* (2008). Translated by B. Archer Brombert. New York: Columbia University Press.

Monteiro, G. (2001). *Presentation of José Saramago, Ceremony to Confer Doctor if Human Letters*, Honoris Causa *Upon José Saramago, October 22, 1999, University of Massachusetts Dartmouth*. In Vv Aa. *On Saramago*. Dartmouth: University of Massachusetts Dartmouth, xxiii-xxv.

Morante, E. (1979). *History: A Novel* (1974). Translated by W. Weaver. New York: Avon.

Morton, T. (2000). *The Poetics of Spice: Romantic Consumerism and the Exotic*. Cambridge: Cambridge University Press.

—— (2007). *Ecology Without Nature: Rethinking Environmental Aesthetics*. Cambridge & London: Harvard University Press.

—— (2010). *The Ecological Thought*. Cambridge & London: Harvard University Press.

—— (2016). *Dark Ecology: For a Logic of Future Coexistence*. New York: Columbia University Press.

—— (2019). *Being Ecological*. Cambridge & London: MIT Press.

Mucignat-Caretta, C. (2014) (ed.). *Neurobiology of Chemical Communication*. Boca Raton, London & New York: CRC Press.

Munari, B. (1928). *Il film futurista: Rumori...odori...colori...*, "Cinemalia: Rassegna d'arte cinematografica" 2, 13-14.

Munier, B. (2003). *Le parfum à travers les siècles. Des dieux de l'Olimpe au cyber-parfum*. Paris: Éditions du Félin.

Murdock, C.G. (1998). *Domesticating Drink: Women, Men, and Alcohol in America, 1870-1940*. Baltimore: The Johns Hopkins University Press.

Murley, T., Chambers IV, E. (2019). *The Influence of Colorants, Flavorants and Product Identity on Perceptions of Naturalness*, "Foods" 8, 317, 1-15.

Muzzarelli M.G., Tarozzi, F. (2003). *Donne e cibo. Una relazione nella storia*. Milano: Mondadori.

Nancy, J.-L. (2008). *Corpus* (1992). Translated by R.A. Rand. New York: Fordham University Press.

Ngamcharoen, P. (2021). *Common Scents, a Social Sense of Smell: Orientation, Territory, and the Evidence of Being*. In G.-A. Lynn, D.R. Parr (eds). *Olfactory Art and the Political in an Age of Resistance*. London & New York: Routledge, 32-43.

Nicklaus-Maurer, C. (2021). *How Smell Spread in 20th-Century Art*. In Vv. Aa. *Smell it! Geruch in der Kunst/Scent in the Arts*. Köln: Wienand, 107-114.

Nicolay, X. (2006) (ed.). *Odor in the Food Industry*. Cham: Springer.

Niedenthal, S., Fredborg, W., Lundén, P., Ehrndal, M., Olofsson, J.K. (2023). *A graspable olfactory display for virtual reality*, "International Journal of Human-Computer Studies" 169, 1-12.

Nietzsche, F. (2007). *Ecce Homo* (1888). Translated by D. Large. Oxford: Oxford University Press.

Nievo, I. (2010). *Il conte Pecorajo. Storia del nostro secolo* (1857). Edited by S. Casini. Venezia: Marsilio.

Nissin, L. (2022). *Smellscape of a Pompeian Neighborhood*, "Journal of Roman Archaeology" 35(2), 621-653.

Noë, A. (2004). *Action in Perception*. Cambridge & London: MIT Press.

Nogué, J. (1936). *Essai d'une description du monde olfactive*, "Journal de psychologie normale et pathologique" 33(1), 230-275.

Nordenfalk, C. (1985). *The Five Senses in Late Medieval and Renaissance Art*, "Journal of the Warburg and Courtauld Institutes" 48, 1-22.

Nordin, S. (2012). *Olfaction Impairment in Normal Aging and Alzheimer's Disease*. In G.M. Zucco, R.S. Herz, B. Schaal (eds). *Olfactory Cognition: From Perception and Memory to Environmental Odours and Neuroscience*, Advances in Consciousness Research, 85. Amsterdam & Philadelphia: John Benjamins Publishing Company, 199-217.

Novero, C. (2017). *Artists and Friends: Daniel Spoerri's Eat Art Gallery*. In S. Bottinelli, M. d'Ayala Valva (eds). *The Taste of Art: Cooking, Food, and Counterculture in Contemporary Practices*. Fayetteville: University of Arkansas Press, 191-210.

Nowak, Z. (2015). *Truffle: A Global History*. London: Reaktion Books.

O'Doherty, B. (1976). *Inside the White Cube: The Ideology of the Gallery Space*. Santa Monica & San Francisco: The Lapis Press.

Ogawa, T. (2018). *Phenomenology of the Wind and the Possibility of Preventive Medicine: A Discussion of Ki (Wind) Following Kaibara Ekiken (1630-1713)*. In L. Škof, P. Berndtson (eds). *Atmospheres of Breathing*. New York: Suny Press, 141-149.

—— (2021). *Phenomenology of Wind and Atmosphere*. Edited and Translated by L. Marinucci. Milano & Udine: Mimesis International.

Ogien, R. (2015). *Human Kindness and the Smell of Warm Croissants: An Introduction to Ethics* (2011). Translated by M. Thom. New York: Columbia University Press.

Onions, C.T. (1966) (ed.). *The Oxford Dictionary of English Etymology*. With the Assistance of G.W.S. Friedrichsen, R.W. Burchfield. Oxford: Oxford University Press.

Orwell, G. (1965). *The Road to Wigan Pier* (1937). London: Secker and Warburg.

—— (1981). *"Such, Such Were the Joys..."* (1947). In Id. *A Collection of Essays*. San Diego, New York & London: Harcourt Brace, 1-47.

Osborne, H. (1977). *Odours and Appreciation*, "The British Journal of Aesthetics" 17(1), 37-48.

Pallasmaa, J. (2012). *The Eyes of the Skin: Architecture and the Senses* (1995). Hoboken: John Wiley & Sons.

—— (2014). *Space, Place, and Atmospheres: Peripheral Perception in Existential Experience*. In C. Borch (ed.). *Architectural Atmospheres: Experience and Politics of Architecture*. Basel: Birkhäuser, 18-41.

—— (2019). *The Atmospheric Sense: Peripheral Perception and the Experience of Space*. In T. Griffero, M. Tedeschini (eds). *Atmosphere and Aesthetics: A Plural Perspective*. London: Palgrave Macmillan, 121-131.

Paparoni, D. (2013). *Wang Guangyi: Works and Thoughts 1985-2012*. Milano: Skira.

Paquet, D. (2004). *La dimension olfactive dans le théâtre contemporain*. Paris: L'Harmattan.

Parasecoli, F. (2007). *Hungry Engrams: Food and Non-Representational Memory*. In F. Allhoff, D. Monroe (eds.). *Food & Philosophy: Eat, Think and Be Merry*. Hoboken: Blackwell Publishing, 102-114.

—— (2022). *Gastronativism: Food, Identity, Politics*. New York: Columbia University Press.

Parker, R. (1983). *Miasma: Pollution and Purification in Early Greek Religion*. Oxford: Clarendon Press.

Parker, J.K., Methven, L., Pellegrino, R., Smith, B.C., Gane, S., Kelly, C.E. (2022). *Emerging Pattern of Post-COVID-19 Parosmia and Its Effect on Food Perception*, "Food" 11(7), 967, 1-17.

Parr, D.R. (2021). *Perfumes, Shea Butter, and Black Soap*. In G.-A. Lynn, D.R. Parr (eds). *Olfactory Art and the Political in an Age of Resistance*. London & New York: Routledge, 22-31.

Pendolino, A.L., Lund, V.J., Nardello, E., Ottaviano, G. (2018). *The Nasal Cycle: A Comprehensive Review*, "Rhinology Online" 1, 67-76.

Persky, S., Dolwick, A.P. (2020). *Olfactory Perception and Presence in a Virtual Reality Food Environment*, "Frontiers in Virtual Reality" 1, 1-8.

Perullo, N. (2006). *Per un'estetica del cibo*. Palermo: Aesthetica Preprint.

—— (2013). *La cucina è arte? Filosofia della passione culinaria*. Roma: Carocci.

—— (2016). *Taste as Experience: The Philosophy and Aesthetics of Food* (2012). New York: Columbia University Press.

—— (2017). *Can Cuisine Be Art? A Philosophical (and Heterodox) Proposal.* In S. Bottinelli, M. D'Ayala Valva (eds). *The Taste of Art: Cooking, Food and Counterculture in Contemporary Practices.* Fayetteville: University of Arkansas Press, 23-44.

—— (2018). *Haptic Taste as a Task,* "The Monist" 101(3), 261-276.

—— (2019). *Food in Wang Guangyi's Art.* In T. Andina, E. Onnis (eds). *The Philosophy and Art of Wang Guangyi.* London & New York: Bloomsbury, 205-219.

—— (2020a). *Estetica Ecologica. Percepire saggio, vivere corrispondente.* Milano & Udine: Mimesis.

—— (2020b). *Epistenology: Wine as Experience.* New York: Columbia University Press.

—— (2022a). *Aesthetics Without Objects: Towards a Process-Oriented Aesthetic Perception.* "Philosophies" 7(1), 21, 1-19.

—— (2022b). *Haptic Experience* (May 31, 2021), "International Lexicon of Aesthetics". Milano & Udine: Mimesis International, 250-254.

Perullo, N., Tonatto, D. (2021). *Re-humanizing Smell: A Conversation,* "Rivista di Estetica" 61(78), 3, 63-73.

Pessoa, F. (2003). *The Book of Disquiet* (1998). Edited and Translated by R. Zenith. London & New York: Penguin.

Petronius (1997). *The Satyricon.* Translated by P.G. Walsh. Oxford: Oxford University Press.

Philippopoulos-Mihalopoulos, A. (2013). *Atmospheres of Law: Senses, Affects, Lawscapes,* "Emotion, Space and Society" 1(7), 35-44.

—— (2015). *Spatial Justice: Body, Lawscape, Atmosphere.* London & New York: Routledge.

—— (2019). *Atmospheric Aestheses: Law as Affect.* In T. Griffero, M. Tedeschini (eds). *Atmosphere and Aesthetics: A Plural Perspective.* London: Palgrave Macmillan, 159-174.

—— (2021). *Ontological Anosmia,* "Rivista di Estetica" 61(78), 3, 95-111.

Picoche, J. (2002). *Dictionnaire étymologique du français.* Paris: Le Robert.

Piesse, G.W.S. (1862). *The Art of Perfumery, and the Methods of Obtaining the Odours of Plants...* London: Longman Green, Longman, and Roberts.

Pitte, J.-R. (1991). *Gastronomie français. Histoire et géographie d'une passion.* Paris: Fayard.

Platina (1999). *Platina's on Right Pleasure and Good Health: A Critical Abridgement and Translation of* De Honesta Voluptate et Valetudine (1474). Translated by M.E. Milham. Asheville: Pegasus.

Plato (1971). *Phaedo.* In Id. *Euthyphro — Apologycrito — Phaedo — Phaedrus.* Translated by H.N. Fowler. Cambridge & London: Harvard University Press, 193-403.

—— (1975). *Philebus.* Translated by J.C.B. Gosling. Oxford: Clarendon Press.

—— (1982). *Hippias Major.* Translated by P. Woodruff. Oxford: Basil Blackwell.

—— (2000). *The Republic.* Edited by G.R.F. Ferrari, Translated by T. Griffith. Cambridge: Cambridge University Press.

—— (2008). *Timaeus*. In Id. *Timaeus and Critias*. Translated by R. Waterfield. Oxford: Oxford University Press, 1-99.

Plautus (1955). *The Haunted House (Mostellaria)*. Translated by F.O. Copley. Indianapolis & New York: The Liberal Arts Press.

Plessner, H. (1970). *Laughing and Crying: A Study of the Limits of Human Behavior* (1941). Translated by J.S. Churchill, M. Grene. Evanston: Northwestern University Press.

—— (1980). *Die Einheit der Sinne* (1923). In Id. *Gesammelte Schriften*, vol. III: *Anthropologie der Sinne*. Frankfurt am Main: Suhrkamp.

Pliner, P., Salvy, S.-J. (2006). *Food Neophobia in Humans*. In R. Shepherd, M. Raats (eds). *The Psychology of Food Choice*. Wallingford: Cabi, 75-92.

Pliny (the Elder) (1945). *Natural History*, vol. IV, libri XII-XVI. Translated by H. Rackham. London & Cambridge: Harvard University Press.

Plunkett, G. (2014). *Death by Mustard Gas: How Military Secrecy and Lost Weapons Kill*. Newport: Big Sky Publishing.

Pollan, M. (2013). *Cooked: A Natural History of Transformation*. London: Penguin.

Pollock, D.K. (1998). *Food and Sexual Identity among the Culina*. In C.M. Counihan, S.L. Kaplan (eds). *Food and Gender: Identity and Power*. London & New York: Routledge, 12-29.

Ponzo, J. (2021). *The Perfume and the Spirit: From Religion to Perfumery*, "Rivista di Estetica" 61(78), 3, 47-62.

Porteous, J.D. (1985). *Smellscape*, "Progress in Human Geography" 9(3), 356-378.

—— (1996). *Environmental Aesthetics: Ideas, Politics and Planning*. London & New York: Routledge.

Porter, J. Anand, T., Johnson, B., Khan, R.M., Sobel, N. (2005). *Brain Mechanisms for Extracting Spatial Information from Smell*, "Neuron" 47, 581-592.

Potter, D.S. (1999). *Odor and Power in the Roman Empire*. In J.I. Porter (ed.). *Constructions of the Classical Body*. Ann Arbor: The University of Michigan Press, 169-189.

—— (2015). *The Scent of Roman Dining*. In M. Bradley (ed.). *Smell and the Ancient Senses*. London & New York, 120-132.

Powers, M. (1998). *Faces along the Bar: Lore and Order in the Workingman's Saloon, 1870-1920*. Chicago: University of Chicago Press.

Proust, M. (1956). *Jean Santeuil* (1952). Translated by G. Hopkins. New York: Simon and Schuster.

—— (1998). *Swann's Way, In Search of Lost Time*, vol. I. Translated by C.K.S. Moncrieff, T. Kilmartin, Revised by D.J. Enright. New York: The Modern Library.

—— (2003). *The Prisoner* (1923). Translated by C. Clark. London: Penguin.

Quitard, P.-M. (1842). *Dictionnaire étymologique, historique et anecdotique des proverbes et des locutions proverbiales de la langue française en rapport avec des proverbes et des locutions proverbiales des autres langues*. Paris & Strasbourg: P. Bertrand & Vve Levrault.

Reinarz, J. (2014). *Past Scents: Historical Perspectives on Smell*. Urbana, Chicago & Springfield: University of Illinois Press.

—— (2021). *Dem Geruch Gestalt geben. Historische Impressionen von Geruchssinn und Kunst/Framing Scent: Historical Impressions of Smell and Art.* In Vv. Aa. *Smell it! Geruch in der Kunst/Scent in the Arts.* Köln: Wienand, 173-191.

Rempel, J.E. (2006). *Olfaktorische Reize in der Markenkommunikation. Theoretische Grundlagen und empirische Erkenntnis zum Einsatz von Düften.* Wiesbaden: Deutscher Universitäts-Verlag.

Rendell, J. (2000). *Introduction: "Gender, Space".* In J. Rendell, B. Penner, I. Borden (eds). *Gender Space Architecture: An Interdisciplinary Introduction.* London & New York: Routledge, 101-111.

Renders, R. (2016). *Fasten Your Nostrils: An Exploration of the Aesthetic Potential of Smell in the Work of Peter de Cupere.* In P. de Cupere, *Scent in Context: Olfactory Art.* Duffel: Stockmans.be, 49-57.

Renowden, G. (2005). *The Truffle Book.* Amberley: Limestone Hills.

Ricci, F. (2001). *Painting with Words, Writing with Pictures: Words and Image in the Work of Italo Calvino.* Toronto, Buffalo & London: Toronto University Press.

Riedel, F. (2019a). *Atmosphere.* In J. Slaby, C. von Scheve (eds). *Affective Societies: Key Concepts.* London & New York: Routledge, 85-95.

—— (2019b). *"The Atmospheres of Tones": Notions of Atmospheres in Music Scholarship Between 1840 and 1930.* In T. Griffero, M. Tedeschini (eds). *Atmosphere and Aesthetics: A Plural Perspective.* London: Palgrave Macmillan, 293-312.

Riera, C.E., Tsaousidou, E., Halloran, J., Follett, P., Hahn, O., Pereira, M.M.A., Engström Ruud, L., Alber, J., Tharp, K., Anderson, C.M., Brönneke, H., Hampel, B., de Magalhaes Filho, C.D., Stahl, A., Brüning, J.C., Dillin, A. (2017). *The Sense of Smell Impacts Metabolic Health and Obesity,* "Cell Metabolism" 26(1), 198-211.

Rindisbacher, H.J. (1993). *The Smell of Books: A Cultural-Historical Study of Olfactory Perception in Literature.* Ann Arbor: Michigan University Press.

Rittersma, R.C. (2010). *In vino veritas, in tuberi fraus. Essai sur la sémantique historique du vin et de la truffe,* "Petit Propos Culinaires" 31, 84-92.

—— (2011). *A Culinary Captatio Benevolentiae: The Use of the Truffle as a Promotional Gift by the Savoy Dynasty in the Eighteenth Century.* In D. de Vooght (ed.). *Royal Taste: Food, Power and Status at the European Courts after 1789.* Farnham: Ashgate, 31-55.

Roberts, T., Roiser, J.P. (2010). *In the Nose of the Beholder: Are Olfactory Influences on Human Mate Choice Driven by Variation in Immune System Genes or Sex Hormone Levels?,* "Experimental Biology and Medicine" 235(11), 1277-1281.

Robinson, K. (2020). *The Sense of Smell in the Middle Ages: A Source of Certainty.* London & New York: Routledge.

Robinson, S. (2021). *Architecture is a Verb.* New York & London: Routledge.

Roch, M. (2009). *L'intelligence d'un sens. Odeurs miraculeuses et odorat dans l'Occident du haut Moyen Âge (Ve-VIIIe siècles).* Turnhout: Brepols.

Roudnitska, E. (1977). *L'esthétique en question.* Paris: PUF.

Rousseau, J. (1979). *Emile, or On Education* (1762). Translated by A. Bloom. New York: Basic Books.

Rousseau, S. (2012). *Food Media: Celebrity Chefs and the Politics of Everyday Interference*. London & New York: Berg.

Rozin, P. (1982). *"Taste-smell Confusions" and the Duality of the Olfactory Sense*, "Perception and Psychophysics" 31(4), 397-401.

Runciman, J.F. (1915). *Noises, Smells and Colours*, "The Musical Quarterly" 1(2), 149-161.

Rybczynski, W. (1986). *Home: A Short History of an Idea*. New York: Viking Press.

Sacks, O. (1987). *The Man Who Mistook His Wife for a Hat, and Other Clinical Tales* (1985). New York: Harper & Row.

—— (1995). *Migraine* (Revised and Expanded Edition) (1970-1985). London & Oxford: Picador.

Saito, Y. (2007). *Everyday Aesthetics*. Oxford: Oxford University Press.

—— (2017a). *Aesthetics of the Familiar: Everyday Life and World-Making*. Oxford: Oxford University Press.

—— (2017b). *The Ethical Dimensions of Aesthetics Engagement*, "Espes" 6(2), 19-29.

—— (2022). *Aesthetics and Ethics of Relationality: Philosophies of Arnold Berleant and Watsui Tetsuro Compared*, "Popular Inquiry" 1, 170-184.

Salvatori, M. (1986). *Italo Calvino's* If on a Winter's Night a Traveler: *Writer's Authority, Reader's Autonomy*, "Contemporary Literature" 27(2), 182-212.

Saramago, J. (2011). *Small Memories* (2006). Translated by M.J. Costa. Boston & New York: Houghton Mifflin Harcourt.

—— (2017). *Blindness* (1995). Translated by G. Pontiero. London: Vintage.

Sartre, J.-P. (1950). *Baudelaire* (1947). Translated by M. Turnell. New York: New Directions.

—— (1956). *Being and Nothingness: An Essay on Phenomenological Ontology* (1943). Translated by H.E. Barnes. New York: Philosophical Library.

—— (1964). *Nausea* (1938). Translated by L. Alexander. New York: New Directions.

Savic, I., Berglund, H. (2004). *Passive Perception of Odors and Semantic Circuits*, "Human Brain Mapping" 21(4), 271-278.

Scappi, B. (2008). *The* Opera *of Bartolomeo Scappi: The Art and Craft of a Master Cook* (1570). Translated by T. Scully. Toronto, Buffalo & London: University of Toronto Press.

Scassillo, F. (2020) (ed.). *Resounding Spaces: Approaching Musical Atmospheres*. Milano & Udine: Mimesis International.

Schlosser, E. (2001). *Fast Food Nation: The Dark Side of the All-American Meal*. Boston & New York: Houghton Mifflin.

Schmitz, H. (2011). *Emotions Outside the Box: The New Phenomenology of Feeling and Corporeality* (2010, Translated by R.O. Müllan, with an Introduction by J. Slaby, R.O. Müllan), "Phenomenology and the Cognitive Sciences" 10(2), 241-259.

—— (2019a). *New Phenomenology: A Brief Introduction*. Translated by R.O. Müllan with Support from M. Bastert, and with an Introduction by T. Griffero. Milano & Udine: Mimesis International.

—— (2019b). *Atmospheric Spaces*. In T. Griffero, M. Tedeschini (eds). *Atmosphere and Aesthetics: A Plural Perspective*. London: Palgrave Macmillan, 63-76.

Schopenhauer, A. (2009). *The Two Fundamental Problems of Ethics* (1841). Translated and Edited by C. Janaway. Cambridge: Cambridge University Press.

Scruton, R. (1979). *The Aesthetics of Architecture*. Princeton: Princeton University Press.

Seixo, M.A. (2001). *The Edge of Darkness, or Why Saramago Never Wrote about the Colonial War in Africa*. In Vv. Aa. *On Saramago*. Dartmouth: University of Massachusetts Dartmouth, 205-219.

Senden, M. von (1960). *Space and Sight: The Perception of Space and Shape in the Congenitally Blind Before and After Operation* (1932). Translated by P. Heath. Glencoe: Free Press.

Seremetakis, N. (2019). *The Memory of the Senses, Part II: Still Acts*. In Id. (ed.). *The Senses Still: Perception and Memory as Material Culture in Modernity* (1994). London & New York: Routledge, 23-43.

Sermolino, M. (1952). *Papa's Table d'Hôte*. Philadelphia: J.B. Lippincott & Co.

Serra, C. (2019). *Tre immagini per suoni e profumi*. In V. Bochicchio, M. Mazzeo, G. Squillace (eds). *A lume di naso. Olfatto, profumo, aromi tra mondo antico e contemporaneo*. Macerata: Quodlibet, 147-160.

Serres, M. (2008). *The Five Senses: A Philosophy of Mingled Bodies* (1985). Translated by M. Sankey, P. Cowley. London & New York: Continuum.

—— (2014). *Le gaucher boiteux. Puissance de la pensée*. Paris: Pommier.

Shapiro, L. (2001). *Perfection Salad: Women and Cooking at the Turn of the Century* (1986). Berkeley, Los Angeles & London: University of California Press.

Sharp, J. (1983). *Sounds, Noises, and Smells: Sensory Experience in Futurist Art*. In A. Coffin Hanson (ed.). *The Futurist Imagination: Word + Image in Italian Futurist Painting, Drawing, Collage and Free-Word Poetry*. New Haven: Yale University Art Gallery, 16-29.

Sheldrake, M. (2020). *Entangled Life: How Fungi Make Our Worlds, Change Our Minds, and Shapes Our Futures*. New York: Random House.

Shell, E.R. (1986). *Chemists Whip Up a Tasty Mess of Artificial Flavors*, "The Smithsonian" 17(1), 79-88.

Shepherd, G.M. (2004). *The Human Sense of Smell: Are We Better Than We Think?*, "Plos Biology" 2(5), 1-4.

Shepherd, R., Raats, M. (2006) (eds). *The Psychology of Food Choice*. Wallington & Cambridge: Cabi.

Shiner, L. (2020). *Art Scents: Exploring the Aesthetics of Smell and the Olfactory Arts*. Oxford: Oxford University Press.

—— (2021). *Opening the Way for an Olfactory Aesthetics: Smell's Cognitive Powers*, "Rivista di Estetica" 61(78), 3, 8-26.

Shiner, L., Kriskovets, Y. (2007). *The Aesthetics of Smelly Art*, "The Journal of Aesthetics and Art Criticism" 65(3), 273-286.

Shusterman, R. (2008). *Body Consciousness: A Philosophy of Mindfulness and Somaesthetics*. Cambridge: Cambridge University Press.

—— (2011a). *Somatic Style*, "The Journal of Aesthetics and Art Criticism" 69(2), 147-159.

—— (2011b). *Soma, Self, and Society: Somaesthetics as Pragmatist Meliorism*, "Metaphilosophy" 42(3), 314-327.

—— (2012). *Thinking Through the Body: Essays in Somaesthetics*. Cambridge: Cambridge University Press.

—— (2015). *Transactional Experiential Inquiry: From Pragmatism to Somaesthetics*, "Contemporary Pragmatism" 12, 180-195.

—— (2016). *Somaesthetics and the Fine Art of Eating*. In S. Irvin (ed.). *Body Aesthetics*. Oxford: Oxford University Press, 261-280.

—— (2021). *Ars Erotica: Sex and Somaesthetics in the Classical Arts of Love*, Cambridge: Cambridge University Press.

Sibley, F.N. (1965). *Aesthetic and Non-aesthetic*, "The Philosophical Review" 74, 134-159.

—— (2006). *Smells, Tastes and Aesthetics*. In Id. *Approaches to Aesthetics: Collected Papers on Philosophical Aesthetics*. Edited by J. Benson, B. Redfern, J. Roxbee Cox. Oxford: Oxford University Press, 207-255.

Sidonius (1956). *Poems and Letters*, vol. I. Translated by W.B. Anderson. Cambridge & London: Harvard University Press.

Simmel, G. (1950). *The Metropolis and Mental Life* (1903). In Id. *The Sociology of Georg Simmel*. Translated and Edited by K.H. Wolff. Glencoe: The Free Press, 409-242.

—— (2009). *Sociology: Inquiries into the Construction of Social Forms* (1908). Translated and Edited by A.J. Blasi, A.K. Jacobs, M. Kanjirathinkal. Leiden: Brill.

Skinner-Petit, S. (1976). *Nauru ou la civilization de l'odorat*, "Objets et Mondes" 16(3), 125-128.

Škof, L., Berndtson, P. (2018) (eds). *Atmospheres of Breathing*. New York: Suny Press.

Slaby, J., Scheve, C. von (2019) (eds). *Affective Societies: Key Concepts*. London & New York: Routledge.

Sloterdijk, P. (2002). *Terror from the Air*. Translated by A. Patton, S. Corcoran. Los Angeles: Semiotext(e).

—— (2011). *Spheres I: Bubbles. Microspherology* (1998). Translated by W. Hoban. Los Angeles: Semiotext(e).

—— (2014). *Spheres II: Globes. Macrospherology* (1999). Translated by W. Hoban. Los Angeles: Semiotext(e).

—— (2016*). Spheres III: Foams. Plural Spherology* (2004). Translated by W. Hoban. Los Angeles: Semiotext(e).

Smith, A.F. (1999). *Popped Culture: A Social History of Popcorn in America*. Columbia: University of South Carolina Press.

Smith, B.C. (2015). *The Chemical Senses*. In M. Matthen (ed.). *The Oxford Handbook of Philosophy of Perception*. Oxford & New York: Oxford University Press, 314-352.

Smith, M.M. (2006). *How Race is Made: Slavery, Segregation, and the Senses*. Chapel Hill: The University of North Carolina Press.

Soble, L., Stroud, K., Weinstein, M. (2020). *Eating Behind Bars: Ending the Hidden Punishment of Food in Prison*. Oakland: Impact Justice.

Sompairac, L. (2021). *De la perception des odeurs quotidiennes à l'olf-action. Études de cas à Pékin, Bombay, Rio de Janeiro, São Paulo et Nice*, PhD Dissertation in Sociology, Université Côte d'Azur.

Songster, M. (2018). *The* GhostFood *Project: Enhancing Flavor through Personalized Smellscapes*. In V. Henshaw, K. McLean, D. Medway, C. Perkins, G. Warnaby (eds). *Designing with Smell: Practices, Techniques and Challenges*. London & New York: Routledge, 43-56.

Souriau, E. (1947). *La correspondance des arts. Éléments d'esthétique comparée*. Paris: Flammarion.

Spaid, S. (2021). *Value Disgust: Appreciating Stench's Role in Attention, Retention, and Deception*, "Rivista di Estetica" 61(78), 3, 74-94.

Spain, D. (1992). *Gendered Spaces*. Chapel Hill & London: The University of North Carolina Press.

Spangenberg, E.R., Grohmann, B., Sprott, D.E. (2005). *It's Beginning to Smell (and Sound) a Lot Like Christmas: The Interactive Effects of Ambient Scent and Music in a Retail Setting*, "Journal of Business Research" 58(11), 1583-1589.

Speed, L.J., Iravani, B., Lundström, J.N., Majid, A. (2022). *Losing the Sense of Smell Does not Disrupt Processing of Odor Words*, "Brain and Language" 235, 1-10.

Spence, C. (2017). *Gastrophysics: The New Science of Eating*. New York: Penguin Random House LLC.

—— (2020). *Scenting the Anosmic Cube: On the Use of Ambient Scent in the Context of the Art Gallery or Museum*, "i-Perception" 11(6), 1-26.

Spoerri, D. (1966). *An Anecdoted Topography of Chance (Re-Anecdoted Version)* (1962). Translated by E. Williams. New York, Cologne & Paris: Something Else Press.

—— (1970). *The Mythological Travels of a Modern Sir John Manderville, Being an Account of the Magic, Meatballs and Other Monkey Business Peculiar to the Sojourn of Daniel Spoerri upon the Isle of Symi, Together with Divers Speculations Thereon*. Translated by E. Williams. New York: Something Else Press.

Squillace, G. (2012). *I profumi nel* De odoribus *di Teofrasto*. In A. Carannante, M. D'Acunto (eds.). *I profumi nelle società antiche*. Paestum: Pandemos, 247-263.

—— (2014). *I giardini di Saffo. Profumi e aromi nella Grecia antica*. Roma: Carocci.

Stamelman, R.H. (2006). *The Eros — and Thanatos — of Scents* (2002). In J. Drobnick (ed.). *The Smell Culture Reader*. Oxford & New York: Berg, 262-276.

Steffen, P.R., Hedges, D., Matheson, R. (2022*). The Brain is Adaptive not Triune: How the Brain Responds to Threat, Challenge, and Change*, "Frontiers in Psychiatry" 13, 1-10.

Stenslund, A. (2015). *A Whiff of Nothing: The Atmospheric Absence of Smell*, "The Senses and Society" 10(3), 341-360.

—— (2017). *The Harsh Smell of Scentless Art: On the Synaesthetic Gesture of Hospital Atmosphere*. In S.A. Schroer, S.B. Schmitt (eds). *Exploring Atmospheres Ethnographically*. London & New York: Routledge, 153-171.

Stevens, J. (1927). *Saloon Days*, "American Mercury" 11(43), 264-275.

Stöhr, A. (1998). *Air-Design als Erfolgsfaktor im Handel. Modellgestützte Erfolgsbeurteilung und strategische Empfehlungen*. Wiesbaden: Deutscher Universitätsverlag.

Straus, E.W. (1952). *The Upright Posture*, "The Psychiatric Quarterly" 26(4), 529-561.

Strik Lievers, F. (2021). *Smelling over Time: The Lexicon of Olfaction from Latin to Italian*. In Ł. Jędrzejowski, P. Staniewski (eds). *The Linguistics of Olfaction: Typological and Diachronic Approaches to Synchronic Diversity*. Amsterdam & Philadelphia: John Benjamins Publishing Company, 369-420.

Strojnik, L., Grebenc, T., Ogrinc, N. (2020). *Species and Geographic Variability in Truffle Aromas*, "Food and Chemical Toxicology" 142, 1-11.

Studio Ólafur Elíasson (2016). *Unspoken Spaces*. London: Thames & Hudson.

Süskind, P. (1986). *Perfume: The Story of a Murdered* (1985). Translated by J.E. Woods. London: Penguin.

Sutherland, J. (2017). *Orwell's Nose: A Pathological Biography*. London: Reaktion Books.

Sutton, D.E. (2001). *Remembrance of Repasts: An Anthropology of Food and Memory*. Oxford & New York: Berg.

Tafalla, M. (2013a). *Anosmic Aesthetics*, "Estetika: The Central European Journal of Aesthetics" 56(1), 53-80.

—— (2013b). *A World Without the Olfactory Dimension*, "Anatomical Record" 2, 1287-1296.

—— (2014). *Smell and Anosmia in the Aesthetic Appreciation of Gardens*, "Contemporary Aesthetics" 12.

Talou, T., Gaset, A., Delmas, M., Kulifaj, M., Montant, C. (1990). *Dimethyl Sulphide: The Secret for Black Truffle Hunting by Animals?*, "Mycological Research" 94(2), 277-278.

Tanizaki, J. (1977). *In Praise of Shadows* (1933). Translated by T.J. Harper, E.G. Seidensticker. Sedgwich: Leete's Island Books.

Tardieu, A. (1878). *Étude médico-légale sur les attentats aux mœurs* (7th edition). Paris: J.-B. Baillière et Fils.

Tedeschini, M. (2019). *Atmosphere and Taste, Individual and Environment*. In T. Griffero, M. Tedeschini (eds). *Atmosphere and Aesthetics: A Plural Perspective*. London: Palgrave Macmillan, 265-285.

Telfer, E. (1996). *Food for Thought: Philosophy and Food*. London & New York: Routledge.

Tellenbach, H. (1968). *Geschmack und Atmosphäre. Medien menschlichen Elementarkontaktes*. Salzburg: Otto Müller.

—— (1981). *Tasting and Smelling – Taste and Atmosphere – Atmosphere and Trust*, "Journal of Phenomenological Psychology" 12(2), 221-230.

Tetsuro, W. (1961). *A Climate: A Philosophical Study* (1935). Translated by G. Bownas. Japan: Printing Bureau, Japanese Government.

Theophrastus (1916). *Concerning Odours*. In Id. *Enquiry into Plants: and Minor Works on Odours and Weather Signs*, vol. II. Translated by A. Hort. London: W. Heinemann; New York: G.P. Putnam's Sons.

Thibaud, J.-P. (2019). *The Lesser Existence of Ambiance*. In T. Griffero, M. Tedeschini (eds). *Atmosphere and Aesthetics: A Plural Perspective*. London: Palgrave Macmillan, 175-187.

Thiebaud, N., Johnson, M.C., Butler, J.L., Bell, G.A., Ferguson, K.L., Fadool, A.R., Fadool, J.C., Gale, A.M., Gale, D.S., Fadool, D.A. (2014). *Hyperlipidemic Diet Causes Loss of Olfactory Sensory Neurons, Reduces Olfactory Discrimination, and Disrupts Odor-Reversal Learning*, "Journal of Neuroscience" 34 (20), 6970-6984.

Thomas Aquinas (Saint) (1955). *On the Truth of the Catholic Faith: Summa Contra Gentiles*, vol. I. Translated by A.C. Pegis. New York: Doubleday.

Thomas, P. (1967). *Down These Mean Streets*. New York: Alfred A. Knopf.

Thompson, S., Hogget, P. (2012) (eds). *Politics and Emotions: The Affective Turn in Contemporary Political Studies*. London & New York: Continuum.

Timberlake, J.H. (2014). *Prohibition and the Progressive Movement, 1900-1920*. Cambridge: Harvard University Press.

Tizard, I., Skow, L. (2021). *The Olfactory System: The Remote-sensing Arm of the Immune System*, "Animal Health Research Reviews" 22, 14-25.

Tomasi di Lampedusa, G. (1960). *The Leopard* (1958). Translated by A. Colquhoun. New York: Pantheon Books.

Toner, J. (2016) (ed.). *A Cultural History of the Senses in Antiquity*. London: Bloomsbury.

Trachtenberg, J. (1943). *The Devil and the Jews: The Medieval Conception of the Jew and its Relation to Modern Antisemitism*. New Heaven & London: Yale University Press & Oxford University Press.

Tsing, A.L. (2015). *The Mushroom at the End of the World: On the Possibility of Life in Capitalistic Ruin*. Princeton: Princeton University Press.

Tuan, Y.-F. (1974). *Topophilia: A Study of Environmental Perception, Attitudes, and Values*. Englewood Cliffs: Prentice-Hall.

—— (1977). *Space and Place: The Perspective of Experience*. Minneapolis & London: University of Minnesota Press.

—— (1995). *Passing Strange and Wonderful: Aesthetics, Nature, and Culture* (1993). New York & Tokyo: Kodansha.

—— (2013). *Romantic Geography: In Search of the Sublime Landscape*. Madison: The University of Wisconsin Press.

Tullett, W. (2014). *The Macaroni's "Ambrosial Essences": Perfume, Identity and Public Space in Eighteenth-Century England*, "Journal for Eighteenth-Century Studies" 38(2), 163-180.

Turin, L. (2006). *The Secret of Scent: Adventures in Perfume and the Science of Smell*. New York: HarperCollins.

Tuzin, D. (2006). *Base Notes: Odor, Breath and Moral Contagion in Ilahita*. In J. Drobnick (ed.). *The Smell Culture Reader*. Oxford: Berg, 59-67.

Ustun, B., Reissland, N., Covey, J., Schaal, B., Blissett, J. (2022). *Flavor Sensing in Utero and Emerging Discriminative Behaviors in the Human Fetus*, "Psychological Science" 33(10), 1651-1663.

Valentinelli, E. (1996). *L'arte degli odori. Manifesto futurista* (1916). In M. Duranti, A. Pesola (eds.). *Atelier Balla. Pittura, arredo, moda. Emanuel Zoo: suggestioni futuriste.* Bologna: Marescalchi Cortina, 133-134.

van Bibber III (1925). *The Talk of the Town,* "The New Yorker", February 28, 1-3.

van Campen, C. (2014). *The Proust Effect: The Senses as Doorways to Lost Memories.* Translated by J. Ross. Oxford: Oxford University Press.

Vannini, P. (2020). *COVID-19 as Atmospheric Dis-Ease: Attuning into Ordinary Effects of Collective Quarantine and Isolation,* "Space and Culture" 23(3), 269-273.

Varney, W. (1996). *The Briar Around the Strawberry Patch: Toys, Women, and Food,* "Women's Studies International Forum" 19(3), 267-276.

Verbeek, C. (2016). *Surreal Aroma's: (Re)constructing the Volatile Heritage of Marcel Duchamp,* "Relief" 10(1), 133-142.

—— (2018). *Inhaling Futurism: On the Use of Olfaction in Futurism and Olfactory (Re)constructions.* In V. Henshaw, K. McLean, D. Medway, C. Perkins, G. Warnaby (eds). *Designing with Smell: Practices, Techniques and Challenges.* London & New York: Routledge, 201-210.

—— (2020). *In Search of Lost Scents: The Olfactory Dimension of Italian Futurism.* In G. Berghaus (ed.). *International Yearbook of Futurism Studies,* vol. X. Berlin: De Gruyter, 247-275.

—— (2021). *On the "Odoresque" and "Aero-Perfumes": Smell Related Neologisms in Avant-garde and Contemporary Art and Scholarship,* "Amfiteater" 9(2), 122-134.

Verbeek, C., van Campen, C. (2013). *Inhaling Memories: Smell and Taste Memories in Art, Science, and Practice,* "The Senses and Society" 8(2), 133-148.

Verbeek, C., Leemans, I., Fleming, B. (2022). *How Can Scents Enhance the Impact of Guided Museum Tours? Towards an Impact Approach for Olfactory Museology,* "The Senses and Society" 17(3), 315-342.

Viberg, Å. (2021). *Why Is Smell Special? A Case Study of a European Language: Swedish.* In Ł. Jędrzejowski, P. Staniewski (eds). *The Linguistics of Olfaction: Typological and Diachronic Approaches to Synchronic Diversity.* Amsterdam & Philadelphia: John Benjamins Publishing Company, 35-72.

Vischer, T., Walter, B. (2003). *Roth Time: A Dieter Roth Retrospective.* New York: The Museum of Modern Art; Baden: Lars Müller Publishers.

Vonnegut, K. (1979). *Jailbird: A Novel.* New York: Delacorte Press/Seymour Lawrence.

Vv. Aa. (2022). *Respirer l'art. Quand l'art contemporain sublime l'univers du parfum.* Milano: SilvanaEditoriale.

Warhol, A. (1975). *The Philosophy of Andy Warhol (From A to B and Back Again).* New York & London: Harcourt Brace Jovanovich.

Waskul, D.D., Vannini, P. (2008). *Smell, Odor, and Somatic Work: Sense-Making and Sensory Management,* "Social Psychology Quarterly" 71(1), 53-71.

Watsuji, T. (1961). *A Climate: A Philosophical Study* (1935). Translated by G. Bownas. West Port: Greenwood Press.

Weber. M. (1924). *Gesammelte Aufsätze zur Soziologie und Sozialpolitik.* Tübingen: Mohr.

—— (1930). *The Protestant Ethic and the Spirit of Capitalism* (1904-1905). Translated by T. Parsons. London: George Allen & Unwin Ltd.

Weizsäcker, V. von (1940). *Der Gestaltkreis. Theorie der Einheit von Wahrnehmen und Bewegen.* Leipzig: Thieme.

White, C. (1998) (ed.). *Early Christian Lives.* London: Penguin.

Wicky, E. (2018). *L'art olfactif contemporain, ses médias et leurs inventions fin-de-siècle,* "Sens public" 1-18.

—— (2022). *Navigating by Smell: On Scent, the Sea and Distance,* "Venti Journal", 2(2).

Willander, J., Larsson, M. (2007). *Olfaction and Emotion: The Case of Autobiographical Odor Memory,* "Memory & Cognition" 35, 1659-1663.

Wilson, S. (2010). *O Corpo do Brasil: The Role of the Brazilian Body in the Art of Ernesto Neto,* Master's Degree Dissertation in Art History and Archaeology, Washington University in St. Louis.

Winterbourne, A.T. (1981). *Is Oral and Olfactory Art Possible?,* "The Journal of Aesthetic Education" 15(2), 95-102.

Wiseman, M.B. (2019). *Food, Art, a Hymn to Nature.* In T. Andina, E. Onnis (eds). *The Philosophy and Art of Wang Guangyi.* London & New York: Bloomsbury, 191-203.

Wood, S. (1994). *The Reflections of Mr. Palomar and Mr. Cogito: Italo Calvino and Zbigniew Herbert,* "Modern Language Notes" 109, 128-141.

Woolf, V. (1977). *The Letters of Virginia Woolf. Volume III: 1923-1928.* Edited by N. Nicolson, J. Trautmann Banks. New York & London: Harcourt Brace Jovanovich.

—— (1978). *The Diary of Virginia Woolf. Volume II: 1920-1924.* Edited by A.O. Bell, Assisted by A. McNeillie. San Diego, New York & London: Harcourt Brace Jovanovich.

—— (2003). *Congenial Spirits: The Selected Letters of Virginia Woolf.* Edited by J. Trautmann. London: Pimlico.

—— (2012). *On Being Ill* (1930). Ashfield: Paris Press.

Wu, D., Wang, V.Y., Chen, Y.-H., Ku, C.-H., Wang, P.-C. (2022). *The Prevalence of Olfactory and Gustatory Dysfunction in Covid-19: A Systematic Review,* "Auris Nasus Larynx" 49(2), 165-175.

Wu, Y., Chen, K., Ye, Y., Zhang, T., Zhou, W. (2020). *Humans Navigate with Stereo Olfaction,* "PNAS" 117(27), 16065-16071.

Yi, A. (2017). *How I Solved It: Transforming Ideas into Smells,* "The New Yorker" May 9.

Yom-Tom, E., Lekkas, D., Jacobson, N.C. (2021). *Association of COVID 19 Induced Anosmia and Ageusia with Depression and Suicidal Ideation,* "Journal of Affective Disorder" 5, 1-4.

Young, B.D. (2016). *Smelling Matter,* "Philosophical Psychology" 29(4), 520-534.

Zambonelli, A., Iotti, M., Murat, C. (2016) (eds). *True Truffle (Tuber spp.) in the World: Soil Ecology, Systematics and Biochemistry.* Cham: Springer.

Zarychta, E. (2022). *How Smells and Human Rights Intersect*, "BC Human Rights Clinic", May 10.

Zhou, J. (2022). *The Preliminary Study on Smellscape Theory*, Master's Degree Dissertation in Architecture, Building-Architecture Engineering, Politecnico di Torino.

Zola, É. (2009). *The Belly of Paris* (1873). Translated by B. Nelson. Oxford: Oxford University Press.

ATMOSPHERIC SPACES
book series directed by Tonino Griffero

MIMESIS GROUP
www.mimesis-group.com

MIMESIS INTERNATIONAL
www.mimesisinternational.com
info@mimesisinternational.com

MIMESIS EDIZIONI
www.mimesisedizioni.it
mimesis@mimesisedizioni.it

ÉDITIONS MIMÉSIS
www.editionsmimesis.fr
info@editionsmimesis.fr

MIMESIS COMMUNICATION
www.mim-c.net

MIMESIS EU
www.mim-eu.com

Printed by
Rotomail Italia S.p.A.
October 2023

www.ingramcontent.com/pod-product-compliance
Lightning Source LLC
Chambersburg PA
CBHW010114270326
41928CB00021B/3251